Eat to Live

eat to live

A PHYTOESTROGEN PROTECTION PLAN FOR LIFE

Sue Radd and Dr Kenneth Setchell

Newleaf

To my parents Angela and Joe, for their endless support and encouragement in my mission to inspire healthy eating—Sue

To my parents Janet and Kenneth: their self-sacrificing spirit helped nurture my appetite for discovery—Ken

First published in Ireland 2003 by
Newleaf
an imprint of
Gill & Macmillan Ltd
Hume Avenue, Park West, Dublin 12
with associated companies throughout the world
www.gillmacmillan.ie

Copyright © 2002 Sue Radd and Dr Kenneth Setchell
First published in Australia in 2002 by Hodder Headline Australia Pty Limited. This Newleaf updated and revised edition is published by arrangement with Hodder Headline Australia Pty Limited.

0 7171 3544 6

Printed by ColourBooks Ltd, Dublin.

5 4 3 2 1

Table of Contents

PART III
Your phytoestrogen eating plan

Acknowledgments

To the past staff and colleagues at the Medical Research Council's Clinical Research Centre in Harrow, England, who were instrumental in providing technical and scientific support in the early and exciting phase of our serendipitous discovery of the first phytoestrogens in human and animal urine. In particular, thanks go to Elvira Conway (Research Assistant) who painstakingly performed the laboratory work that helped isolate the first lignans from some 45 litres of monkey urine. To the late Professor David Kirk, a world class steroid chemist at the then Westfield College of the University of London, for hours of stimulating discussion and who played a pivotal role in providing complementary analytical expertise during these exciting times of discovery. Acknowledgments are warranted to Linda Zimmer-Nechemias, Brian Wolfe and Wayne Brashear, staff at the Children's Hospital Medical Center in Cincinnati, who through their stellar technical work and dedication enabled us to sustain our early research momentum in phytoestrogens to further advance our understanding of the important role that phytoestrogens play in health and disease. We are particularly indebted to the collaborations, not to mention the hours of debate on the woes of English soccer, with our friend and colleague Dr Stephen Barnes at the University of Birmingham in Alabama. These were crucial in realising our early belief that phytoestrogens had powerful anticancer properties.

To our professional colleagues and peers—too many to mention individually—you have been a pleasure to interact with over the last 25 years of research on phytoestrogens. In particular, thanks go to Professor Jan Sjövall, a mentor extraordinaire, and to Dr Magnus Axelson, both at the Karolinska Institute in Stockholm, Sweden, and Professor Herman Adlercreutz at the University of Helsinki, Finland, who were astute enough to recognise the importance of our early discoveries and who contributed significantly to promote the wider interest in phytoestrogens among our peers.

We are particularly grateful to several of our colleagues who took the trouble to proofread either all, or part of this book for accuracy and for providing helpful suggestions about its content. Special thanks go to Dr Nadine Brown and Dr Frank Biro at Children's Hospital, Cincinnati; to Dr Edwin Lephart at Brigham Young University, Utah; to Dr Gisela Wilcox at Monash Medical Centre, Melbourne and Australian dietitians Deidre Coote, Barbara Eden, Roy Octavianus, Liz Ryan, Angela Saunders, Carol Zeuschner and Leanne Wagner—experts in clinical nutrition, public health and private practice. Sincere thanks also go to Dr Rosemary Stanton AOM—a pioneering force and role model to nutritionists in Australia (and elsewhere!) for her encouragement to develop all our own recipes and for her advice on publishing issues.

To close friends Kit and Tim Kemp of the Firmdale Group of Hotels, London, for providing us, on numerous occasions, with the most fantastic of venues in London to collaborate on the research and writing of this book. Their boutique hotels need to be seen to be believed and we are ever grateful for their support and interest in our mission to provide education on health and nutrition to the public.

Thanks also go to our 'foodie' friends Sylvia Vujkovic, Robert Kokolic and Valerie Gersbach for several recipe ideas and Sue's mother Angela Lazic for washing countless dishes and for her tireless support in recipe development. We really appreciate the efforts of our literary barometers—they ensured the text was readable and understandable by the intelligent public—Berit Hanly, Manuela James, Nada Schmidt and Tracey Wijeyesinghe. To Grenville and Carla Kent—the 'fattest of friends' (a most endearing term reserved for friendships with great width and breadth)—for their moral support since conception of the book and creative advice on copy editing. For excellent technical help in the preparation of diagrams we thank Jan Warren.

We thank also a number of industries for providing unconditional educational grants at the early stages in the preparation of this book. This enabled us to surmount the financial hurdles faced by trying to research and write from two different continents! We acknowledge support from Central Soya (Fort Wayne, Indiana, USA); Dr Chung's Food Company (Seoul, S. Korea); Infant Formula Council (Atlanta, Georgia, USA); Protein Technologies International (St Louis, Missouri, USA); Sanitarium Health Food Company (Berkeley Vale, Australia); Schouten (Minneapolis, Minnesota USA); Solbar Plant Extracts (Ashdod, Israel); and Wyeth-Ayerst International (St Davids,

Pennsylvania, USA). Furthermore, it would be remiss not to give mention to the Medical Research Council (MRC) and Ministry of Agriculture Fisheries and Food (MAFF), now the Food Standards Agency (FSA), both in the UK, and the American Cancer Society (ACS), American Institute of Cancer Research (AICR), and National Institutes of Health (NIH) in the USA that have collectively over the last 20 years provided more than 90 per cent of the funding for our research studies on phytoestrogens. Without this support obtaining the scientific data to support the writing of this book would not have been possible. Since publication of the original text in Australia we have revised, updated, and corrected typographical errors in this edition.

We are indebted to Dr Eva Lydeking-Olsen (Institute for Optimum Nutrition, Broenshoej, Denmark), Dr Paola Albertazzi (Hull Royal Infirmary, England), Dr Aedin Cassidy (Unilever Research, Colworth House, England), Professor David Jenkins (University of Toronto, Canada), Mrs Marie Moyes (Toronto, Canada) and Mr David Borkovic (Melbourne, Australia) for kindly sharing with us case histories illustrating what can be achieved with phytoestrogen-rich foods.

Finally, we thank Lisa Highton, Publishing Director at Hodder Headline Australia, and her supportive staff for having the foresight to recognise the importance of our message and for enabling it to reach your table!

Foreword

This book will show you a whole new way to look at food. While many nutrition books tell you what not to eat, *Eat to Live* is all about eating *more* of certain foods to help you stay well! Our advice is backed by more than 20 years of scientific research—including our own. This is no fad diet.

In this book we explain how a deficiency in the typical Western diet of protective plant compounds called phytoestrogens is a major reason for the high rates of most hormone-linked diseases. Such diseases include cardiovascular disease, our number one killer, and cancer, perhaps our greatest fear. Less obvious, but just as important, are osteoporosis, predicted to reach epidemic proportions in the next few decades, Alzheimer's disease, and the distressing symptoms that accompany menopause for many Western women.

Hardly a month goes by without the release of exciting new research on phytoestrogens, highlighting their many potential health benefits. Phytoestrogens are now a 'hot button' among nutrition scientists. In just about every university renowned for nutrition research you will find someone studying phyto-estrogens. More than 5000 medical and scientific papers have been published in the last five years, and there has been an escalation in the number of symposia dealing with this subject. Media interest is at an all-time high. The recent advice from professional medical authorities around the world cautioning against the widespread use of hormone replacement therapy (HRT) will only heighten interest in natural alternative therapies for many postmenopausal women.

Twenty years ago nobody had heard of phytoestrogens—nor were they interested. They made an infamous splash in the 1940s by being linked to infertility in sheep that grazed on a particular type of clover in Western Australia found to be super rich in phytoestrogens. Afterwards, the word 'phytoestrogen' all but disappeared from the scientific literature. What resurrected interest in these natural compounds was our chance discovery and identification of several unique and previously unknown phytoestrogens in people's urine, and later in blood. We all have small amounts of these 'hormone-like' compounds in our body because they come from our diet. What intrigued us in the late 1970s, however, was our discovery that if soy foods or linseeds are eaten the concentrations of phytoestrogens in the blood soar. We then went on to show that people who regularly eat these foods, like Asians and vegetarians, have huge levels of phytoestrogens in their body—and guess what? These people do not suffer the ravages of the common diseases that kill most Westerners. In two landmark scientific publications in 1980 and 1984, we proposed that phytoestrogens offered the clue to healthy living, initially suggesting they were nature's 'anticancer' agents. This pioneering work has since been recognised through awards and has featured as plenary lectures at many medical and nutrition conferences around the world.

Our key message in this book is that if your diet lacks phytoestrogens you are missing out on vital protection and in the long-run this will increase your risk of degenerative diseases. A high level of phytoestrogens in your body can simply be regarded as a sign of a healthy diet. Asians traditionally consume a diet that leads to high levels of phytoestrogens in the body. They have among the best health statistics in the world—vegetarians too. Yet everyone can benefit by simply including more phytofoods in their diet. *Eat to Live* is a global diet. The information we provide is relevant to the whole family—including men and children. Research shows that what we eat early in life governs our susceptibility to many diseases later in life. *Eat to Live* explains how the combination of early and life-long intake of phytoestrogens is probably the best formula for healthy living—and that it's never too late to start.

The food and pharmaceutical industries are keenly following these new findings. Functional foods and supplements enriched with phytoestrogens are now widespread in the marketplace in many countries. Phytoestrogens are so highly regarded that manufacturers are starting to declare the phytoestrogen content on product labels. Researchers have even isolated the gene from soybeans that is responsible for making isoflavones, one of the important families of phytoestrogens. Despite the fear many people currently have with the use of gene technology to produce foods, we predict that it will not be long before common plant foods become genetically modified to contain high levels of phytoestrogens. But you don't have to buy special products to obtain protective levels of phytoestrogens. These foods are available now from your supermarket and greengrocer.

The stimulus to write a book on this topic came from the huge interest we observed while speaking at international meetings, and answering frequent media and consumer questions. With our combined experience as a prominent nutritionist and a recognised pioneer in this field of research, we also wanted to sort out the misunderstandings and myths about phytoestrogens—as these 'smart' natural molecules are often mistaken for estrogens.

We have translated a large body of heavy science into everyday language. Whether this is the first time you are hearing about phytoestrogens or not, we believe you will find this book a comprehensive and easy-to-read guide. *Eat to Live* explains what phytoestrogens are, why they are so important to our health, and where to find them. We also show you just how easy it is to eat the phytoestrogen-rich way by providing meal plans, shopping lists and delicious recipes that you can make at home.

Eat to Live offers a compelling argument for using the inherent health benefits of the right foods as the key to a happier and healthier life. We hope you enjoy it and will share it with your family and friends.

part 1

Phytoestrogens: what they are and how they work

chapter 1

Phytoestrogen deficiency: a major cause of modern disease

The epidemic of degenerative diseases that plague people in Western countries is caused by a diet lacking in protective plant foods. In other words, it's not so much what we eat at the moment, but what we're not eating that's important to our health.

Natural compounds called phytoestrogens have been identified as a key deficiency in the Western diet and consequently they have become one of the hottest topics in medical research. In the 20 years since their importance was first recognised, a mountain of research has shown the potential health benefits of a phytoestrogen-rich diet, including reducing the risk of:

- breast cancer
- prostate and other cancers
- heart disease and stroke

- osteoporosis
- menopausal symptoms
- brain diseases linked with ageing
- inflammatory diseases such as rheumatoid arthritis

These are bold claims but they are supported by thousands of research papers in scientific and medical journals. They are not just anecdotal tales promoting yet another fad diet and ignoring the importance of other lifestyle factors such as exercise, stress and smoking.

In October 1999 the US Food and Drug Administration (FDA) approved a health claim allowing food labels to proclaim that soy protein reduces the risk of heart disease by lowering blood cholesterol. In the absence of EU legislation, the Joint Health Claims Initiative (JHCI) in the UK endorsed a similar health claim for soy protein and blood cholesterol in July 2002. Food manufacturers in the UK can make the following claim on food packaging and in advertising for products that meet certain criteria: 'The inclusion of at least 25 g of soy protein per day as part of a diet low in saturated fat can help reduce blood cholesterol.' Soy protein is one of our richest sources

WHAT ARE PHYTOESTROGENS?

Phyto means plant, and *estrogen* is a hormone vital to men and women. So phytoestrogens are estrogen-like substances that come from plants. But they are not identical to estrogens. They are natural plant protectants that also have a range of positive effects on the body and are probably one of the most important reasons why a plant-rich diet offers such protection against many diseases.

of phytoestrogens. A pivotal study of patients with high cholesterol at Wake Forest University School of Medicine in the US
showed that the more phytoestrogens present in the soy protein,
the greater the cholesterol reduction. In 1999, more than 300 new
soy foods were launched on the US market, many of which display this health claim and quote the phytoestrogen level. Purified
phytoestrogens are also available as over-the-counter pills and
supplements, and large food and agri-food companies world-wide
such as Archer Daniel Midland, Danon, Dupont, General Mills,
Haldane Foods, Heinz, Kellogg's, Nestlé, Nutricia, Parmalat and
Vander Moortle now see phytoestrogens as a marketing buzz word.
The interest is so high that even major dairy companies such as
Dean Foods in the US and National Foods Limited and Pauls
Parmalat in Australia, are investing in this area of nutrition.

There is overwhelming evidence from population-based
studies that people who consume the highest levels of phytoestrogens enjoy better health and live longer. Asians and
vegetarians are two groups who are often studied, as are people
who consume a traditional Mediterranean diet.

The Asian advantage

Japanese people have much lower rates of cancer and heart disease, the killer diseases of Western countries, and the traditional
Japanese diet offers 30 to 100 times more phytoestrogens than
the modern Western diet. You might wonder whether the
Japanese advantage comes from being lucky enough to have
healthier genes. While genes are important, this cannot be the
explanation because Japanese people who migrate to the US
tend to acquire similar rates of disease as Americans within
just a few generations as they adopt a more American diet.

Disease rates in Asia are dramatically rising as traditional phytoestrogen-rich foods such as tofu are being replaced with Western-style fast food diets. Statistics from Japan's Ministry of Agriculture, Forestry and Fisheries show that from 1955 to 1990, the average intake of meat increased sixfold from 5 kg to 29 kg per year while the intake of cereal grains fell from 118 kg to 104 kg. Despite this alarming trend, people in Asia still have much lower rates of the major diseases that kill people living in the European Union.

The benefits of phytoestrogens go beyond just the major killers. Middle-aged women in Asia report fewer symptoms of the menopause. Only five per cent of Japanese women complain of hot flushes, compared with 85 per cent for North American women. Asian women also have fewer hip fractures, and phytoestrogens from foods such as soy have been implicated because they help prevent bone loss.

Mediterranean magic

The darling of all diets—probably because of its rich flavours—the traditional Mediterranean diet also produces lower rates of heart disease and certain cancers. This diet is rich in plant foods such as vegetables, fruits, legumes, nuts, grains and olive oil. All of these foods are sources of phytoestrogens. Wine is usually drunk at meals and in moderation, while dairy products and red meat are limited.

Yet the modern Italian restaurant does not follow this diet. Portion sizes are large, and meat and cheese will feature prominently, while legumes and the large quantity of vegetables and salads typically consumed in the Mediterranean diet are usually lacking. Again, the Western influence has meant the inclusion of more animal products at the expense of plant foods with all their protective elements.

The vegetarian winner

Vegetarians have amazing health statistics—such as a 25 per cent lower risk of dying from heart disease—according to a review of five large international studies from the US, England and Germany. They also have a lower risk of many types of cancers based on numerous studies of Seventh-day Adventists, about half of whom are vegetarians. One impressive finding from Loma Linda University in the US was a 70 per cent reduction in prostate cancer risk among Californian Seventh-day Adventist men who drank soy milk more than once a day. Soy milk is rich in phytoestrogens.

The hazards of the Western lifestyle

Most people know that the typical Western diet contains too many calories and excessive amounts of animal fat and certain foods such as red meat that are all linked to increased risk of heart disease and cancer. What makes the Western diet a recipe for disaster, though, is that it lacks many protective elements, especially phytoestrogens. Estimates of the American and British diets put phytoestrogen intakes at less than 1 mg per day. This is because most Western diets lack plant foods that provide phytoestrogens and other important plant protectants, called phytoprotectants. These foods include wholegrains, nuts, vegetables and legumes such as soybeans, kidney beans, lentils and chickpeas. If you regularly eat a typical Western diet, you are missing out on the foods that prevent degenerative diseases.

The optimum diet

The common thread in all the protective diets, be they Asian, Mediterranean or vegetarian, is that they are rich in plant foods that provide us with a huge array of protectants (see Table 1.1 for examples), of which phytoestrogens are one of the most important families. There is more evidence supporting the health benefits of phytoestrogens than for any other family of plant constituents.

Traditional societies have long recognised the value of plants, not just as healthy foods, but for medicinal purposes. They may not have understood the science, but many have eaten phyto-estrogens naturally and safely for millennia—so the recent research can actually be regarded as a rediscovery of ancient knowledge. Many Westerners are unaware of the benefits of a phytoestrogen-rich diet, which is understandable because a diet deficient in these phytoprotectants does not cause obvious symp-toms immediately.

How to get phytoestrogens

Phytoestrogens are widely available in plant foods, but not in animal products such as meat or dairy. The highest amounts of phytoestrogens are found in linseeds and soybeans and prod-ucts made from them. Legumes also contain high levels. Other valuable sources include wholegrains, nuts, seeds, vegetables and fruits. The best way to get a regular dose is to choose cuisines based around these foods. Realistically, you are more likely to consume regular doses of phytoestrogens if they come

TABLE 1.1

IMPORTANT PHYTOPROTECTANTS FOUND IN PLANT FOODS

Phytoprotectant	Main sources
Allium compounds	Garlic, onions, leeks, chives
Carotenoids	Orange, dark-green and red-coloured fruits and vegetables
Catechins	Green and black tea
Coumestans*	Alfalfa and other sprouts
Curcumin	Turmeric
Flavonoids*	Most fruits and vegetables
Glyceritinic acid	Licorice
Inositol hexaphosphate	Legumes and cereals
Isoflavones*	Legumes, especially soybeans, soy protein, most soy products, alfalfa
Isothiocyanates, indoles	Cruciferous vegetables such as broccoli, cabbage, cauliflower
Lignans*	All plant foods, particularly linseeds, wholegrains and rye
Limonene	Citrus fruits
Phenols	Most fruits and vegetables
Phytosterols	Vegetable oils, legumes and seeds
Protease inhibitors	Legumes, especially soybeans and seeds
Saponins	Legumes
Terpenoids	Citrus fruits, cherries, caraway seeds

*These phytoprotectants belong to the phytoestrogen family

in a variety of great tastes, so to help we have included a selection of delicious recipes (see pages 189–280). This way you can choose the best elements of cuisine from around the world.

Phytoestrogen supplements may be helpful for some conditions but are not likely to have the full range of effects of phytoestrogen-rich whole foods. We strongly advocate choosing foods that have stood the test of time.

How does your diet rate?

Try the five-minute quiz on the following pages to rate your current diet and see if you are adequately phytoprotected.

What this book will tell you

This book is your guide to improving your health by overcoming a diet lacking in phytoestrogens.

- Part I explains how phytoestrogens work and why they don't have the bad side effects of estrogens and synthetic chemicals.
- Part II gives you detailed advice on avoiding major Western diseases.
- Part III is your DIY guide to enriching your diet with phytoestrogens. We cover food and supplement options. It is also the fun part—a feast of easy recipes for you and your family to enjoy.

Our goal is to bring to your attention why it is so important to eat foods that contain phytoestrogens. Not just for the short-term as a health kick but as a permanent addition to your lifestyle. This is the hottest subject in nutritional research worldwide and you will see why as you read on. This book is your key to a healthier, happier life. Enjoy reading and bon appetit!

QUIZ: ARE YOU PHYTOPROTECTED?	
1. Do you use soy milk in place of dairy milk each day or almost daily on cereals and in cooking?	5 points
2. Do you eat soybeans or foods made from soybeans such as tofu, soy burgers, soy hot dogs, soy based deli slices, soy nuts or green soybeans (Edamame) on average three times or more each week?	5 points
3. Do you eat other legumes or beans such as chickpeas, lentils, red kidney beans, navy beans or foods prepared from these such as hommus or dhal (lentil pureé) on average three times or more each week?	2 points
4. Do you eat linseeds or use linseed meal (ground linseeds), e.g. on cereal, mixed into yoghurt or in bread, at least three times each week?	5 points
5. Do you add sprouts such as alfalfa or soy sprouts to your salads or sandwiches once or more per week?	3 points
6. Do you, on average, eat two servings of fruit, mostly fresh, each day? (1 serving = 1 piece of medium-sized fruit = 3 pieces of smaller sized fruit such as apricots = 1 cup of berries or 1 cup diced or canned fruit = 4–6 larger pieces of dried fruit = 2 tablespoons of sultanas or raisins)	3 points

7. Do you, on average eat at least five servings of vegetables of a variety of colours each day? (1 serving = $\frac{1}{2}$ cup cooked vegetables = 1 cup salad)	3 points
8. Do you, on average, eat three or more servings of wholemeal or wholegrain foods each day? (1 serving = $\frac{3}{4}$ cup wholegrain breakfast cereal = 1 slice of wholegrain, wholemeal or dark rye bread = $\frac{1}{2}$ cup cooked brown rice or wholemeal pasta)	3 points
9. Do you, on average, eat nuts and seeds—including nut butters such as peanut butter—at least three times each week?	2 points
10. Do you mostly choose fruit juices, tomato or vegetable juices in preference to soft drinks, cordials, or fruit-flavoured drinks?	1 point
11. Do you drink green or black tea (with or without milk) or herbal tea most days?	1 point
12. Do you mostly use extra virgin olive oil in cooking or as a dip for bread in place of margarine or butter?	1 point
13. Do you eat 30 or more types of food each day? To check, count the number of different foods, including each single ingredient in recipes and dishes. Count each food or ingredient only once.	1 point

Now add up your score   _____

How did you do?   *Points*

Excellent protection. Your diet is high in phytoprotectants.   **26–35**

Good protection. A little room for improvement by
extending your range of phytoestrogen foods.   **16–25**

Some protection. A good start, but read on for easy
ways to improve your diet.   **6–15**

You are currently poorly phytoprotected. Read on and
take some immediate action to improve your diet.   **0–6**

chapter 2

Nature's designer estrogens

Human life is dependent on estrogen. Our bodies require a certain amount of estrogen to function normally and to ensure optimal health, especially as we age. Estrogen is essential in our younger years for the normal development of the male and female reproductive systems. It is also needed to sustain pregnancy. Importantly, men need estrogen as much as women do to protect their heart and blood vessels. And, in a lifetime, men actually make more estrogen than women!

Yet estrogens provide both positive and negative effects. Research studies confirm that imbalances in estrogen are strongly linked to many major Western diseases, including heart disease and cancers such as prostate and breast cancer.

Estrogen is powerful and can cause damage, so it tends to evoke tremendous fears, particularly among women. For example, excess estrogen can promote the growth of cancers of the breast and womb and has been linked to reproductive abnormalities. A major study found that women who take hormone replacement therapy (HRT) increase their risk of breast cancer, although it protects against colon cancer and hip fracture.

With too little estrogen the body also functions poorly and this heightens the risk of many diseases. For example, women's sudden loss of estrogen during menopause dramatically raises the risk of cardiovascular disease. Figures from the British Heart Foundation for the year 2000 reveal that heart disease and stroke combined killed more women than men in the United Kingdom. At the same time calcium is rapidly lost from bone, signalling the start of osteoporosis.

Men and women require balanced levels of estrogen, and researchers have long dreamed of a designer drug that can achieve the good effects without the bad. Yet nature has already done this for us in the form of phytoestrogens.

What are phytoestrogens?

Phytoestrogens are natural plant molecules, similar in shape and size to the human body's estrogen, but not identical. This slight difference means they don't have all the same effects as estrogens—luckily, since some of the effects of estrogen can be bad.

The food we eat contains three main families of phytoestrogens: isoflavones, lignans and coumestans. Soybeans provide the richest source of isoflavones, while linseeds are super-rich in lignans. Coumestans, which are less abundant in the diet, can be found in alfalfa and other sprouts. Plant foods in general will contain mixtures of these phytoestrogens in lower but nevertheless useful amounts. And, there are many other phytoestrogens yet to be discovered.

Balancing hormones

Phytoestrogens have become a buzz word in medical science because of evidence that while they are only 'weak estrogens', they are still able to provide relief from estrogen deficiency and reduce risk factors of major hormone-related diseases. In other words, they can act like estrogen substitutes.

Amazingly, phytoestrogens can also behave as anti-estrogens, blocking estrogen's harmful effects. They seem to have an inbuilt barometer, acting like estrogens or anti-estrogens depending upon the circumstances and on what the body needs. They can do this because they communicate their messages through specialised estrogen receptors found throughout the body. Let's look at this with some simple analogies.

Estrogen impersonators and blockers

Imagine a cargo ship travelling around the world and stopping at different ports to deliver its cargo. Estrogens travel around the body in the blood, going to different organs and docking at ports called estrogen receptors. From these ports they send strong signals for various things to happen. Some of these signals are good while others are bad. Phytoestrogens are similar ships that can dock at the same ports, but the signals they send out are weak.

Phytoestrogens are able to impersonate estrogens because of their similar molecular shape. However there are important differences in the way they work. Scientists have discovered that phytoestrogens are selective in their effects because they are fussier than estrogens about where and how they dock. There are two types of estrogen receptors (docks) in the body. These are called alpha and beta. While estrogens normally dock to both of these receptors equally, given the choice phytoestrogens prefer the beta receptors. This is desirable since beta receptors are found in large numbers in the bone, brain and blood vessels—places where estrogen is known to have positive effects.

In certain parts of the body such as the breast and womb where there aren't many beta receptors, phytoestrogens have to dock with the alpha receptors. In doing so this stops estrogens from docking and sending signals that could promote the growth of existing cancer. In this situation phytoestrogens work as anti-estrogens and have a protective effect. Preventing estrogen from docking is the strategy used to stop breast cancer from recurring. That's how the drug Tamoxifen works and it has been used for more than 30 years in about 80 per cent of women diagnosed with breast cancer.

Because they can act as both estrogen impersonators and blockers, depending on the need, phytoestrogens are like the new estrogen drugs called Selective Estrogen Receptor Modulators, or SERMs. Raloxifene, marketed under the trade name Evista, was the first of a new generation of SERMs to be approved in several countries because it was shown to provide the beneficial effects of estrogen in protecting bones against osteoporosis while also reducing the risk of breast cancer. Phytoestrogens are natural SERMs and can be readily obtained from eating the right foods.

More than just phyto-hormones

Early researchers noted very low rates of breast cancer and prostate cancer in Japanese who regularly consume soy foods. In a ground-breaking paper published by the *American Journal of Clinical Nutrition* in 1984, Dr Kenneth Setchell, co-author of this book, and co-workers first proposed that the phytoestrogens in soy could be important natural anti-cancer agents. It was suggested they reduced cancer risk simply by blocking the actions of estrogen, just as.we have explained. Later experiments by Drs Greg Peterson and Stephen Barnes at the University of Alabama in the US showed that phytoestrogens could also prevent the growth of breast cancer cells that did not have estrogen receptors. This indicated that phytoestrogens must also work in other ways to stop tumours from growing. Since these early studies, thousands of scientific publications have emerged showing that phytoestrogens have many other important properties not linked to hormone action that can regulate the way cells grow and multiply. These actions are beginning to explain the many beneficial effects of diets rich in phytoestrogens.

Controlling cancer enzymes

Enzymes are the on–off switches that control many reactions taking place in the body. Phytoestrogens inhibit the actions of enzymes that cause tumour cells to multiply.

In a landmark discovery, Dr Tetsu Akiyama and his team of researchers in Japan first showed that genistein, the phyto-estrogen found in soy, potently inhibits enzymes called protein tyrosine kinases that regulate the way many growth factors work in cells. Being able to block these gives us another way to prevent cancer cells from growing. The same enzymes are involved in inflammation—an important early stage of cancer. Inflammation plays a central role in many other conditions, such as heart disease, rheumatoid arthritis, psoriasis and inflammatory bowel disease. Several studies have now found that phytoestrogens are anti-inflammatory and may therefore have a positive effect on such conditions.

Phytoestrogens can also block an enzyme called aromatase which is responsible for changing testosterone into estrogen. As mentioned previously, excess estrogen can promote the growth of cancers, so blocking aromatase is desirable. New breast cancer drugs have been developed to inhibit this enzyme—one recently showed promising results in a clinical trial of breast cancer patients. Phytoestrogens already do this naturally!

In treating prostate cancer, drugs are used to block an enzyme that turns testosterone into a more potent hormone called dihydrotestosterone (DHT). Research from the Tenovus Cancer Research Centre in the UK has shown that phyto-estrogens from soy foods inhibit this enzyme in the prostate gland. Interestingly, Japanese men who consume a high phyto-estrogen diet have low rates of prostate cancer. And a recent study of American men found that drinking soy milk more than once per day was strongly linked to a reduction in prostate cancer by a whopping 70 per cent.

THE MANY FEATURES OF PHYTOESTROGENS

Phytoestrogens have a multitude of positive effects on the body. They can mimic the beneficial effects of estrogens, or behave like anti-estrogens to stop the estrogen's harm-ful effects. They also have other actions that are not related to hormones. They are antioxidants; they control the activ-ity of many disease-related enzymes; and they may even guard against the damaging effects of some synthetic estrogens or pollutants. They are 'smart molecules' of nature, designed to protect us from many degenerative diseases.

Research on Phytoestrogens—nature's way of combating many diseases

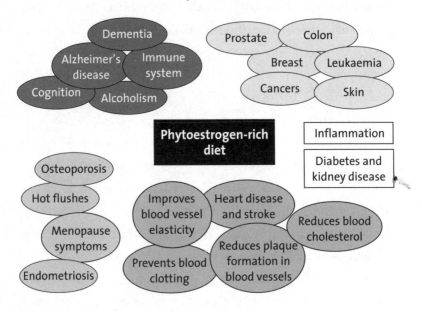

Antioxidants

Most people have heard of antioxidants such as vitamins C and E, but few realise that phytoestrogens are useful antioxidants. Antioxidants protect us by mopping up 'free radicals' in the body, which damage our DNA, fats and proteins—increasing the risk of cancers, heart disease and cataracts, and probably accelerating ageing.

A study of healthy men showed that those who drank a litre of soy milk daily had less damage to their DNA than those who drank the same amount of dairy milk or rice milk. Soy milk is a 'rich-source' of phytoestrogens and manufacturers are now beginning to label such products with their isoflavone content. Researchers believe that the antioxidant properties of phytoestrogens may be one of the most important factors in

PHYTOESTROGEN FOOD CATEGORIES*	
Rich source	More than 15 mg phytoestrogens per serving
Good source	5–15 mg phytoestrogens per serving
Source	Up to 5 mg phytoestrogens per serving

* We have defined these categories based on our experience with foods and how they
influence the phytoestrogen levels in the body. For a detailed listing of foods in each
category see Table 12.1, pages 148–151

helping to prevent cholesterol from being oxidised and laid down in the arteries.

Preventing the spread of tumours

Preventing tumours from spreading throughout the body continues to be one of the challenges of cancer research. Solid tumours cannot grow and spread without first developing a blood supply. In a series of scientific papers that received media attention some years ago, researchers at the University of Heidelberg found that phytoestrogens prevented blood vessels forming in and around tumours.

Pollution protectors

Our environment is swamped with synthetic estrogens that are able to dock to estrogen receptors in the body and cause harmful effects. These come from many sources, including plastic food containers, babies' teething rings, detergents, electrical transformers, hydraulic fluids and flame-retardants—to name just a few. They can be found in drinking water and in the air—they are literally everywhere. Many are by-products of the chemical industry. In her acclaimed bestselling book, *Our Stolen*

Future, Dr Theo Colborn drew public attention to the dangers of environmental estrogens, which led to legislative measures being implemented by the US congress to monitor the levels of many of these toxic compounds. What makes synthetic estrogens especially harmful is that they take decades to be removed from the body and can build up, especially in fatty parts of the body such as the breast.

Researchers have found that a phytoestrogen-rich diet may be able to protect against some of these synthetic estrogens. Several pesticides have been shown to be less able to stimulate the growth of breast cancer cells when soy phytoestrogens are present. The phytoestrogen genistein and another substance called curcumin, an active ingredient of curry, were found to counter the negative effects of pesticides in a laboratory study at Boston's Tufts University. Research from the Department of Environmental Genetics at the University of Cincinnati showed that soy phytoestrogens block the highly dangerous pesticide dioxin from binding to a receptor in the body. They also block an important enzyme in the liver that activates cancer-causing substances. It is possible that harmful synthetic estrogens may be of little concern provided you regularly eat a phytoestrogen-rich diet to block their effects.

chapter 3

How the body absorbs phytoestrogens

If you want protection from degenerative diseases, it is not enough to have phytoestrogens on your plate—you need high and steady levels of them in your blood. This chapter explains how your body digests and absorbs them so that you can plan the best possible diet.

Chomp, then what?

Your body digests phytoestrogens like any other food. As they move from your mouth to your stomach they are mixed with various digestive juices, but the critical time for their digestion is when they reach the intestines. Enzymes in the intestines and certain strains of the many bacteria that live there play an important role in activating phytoestrogens so they can be absorbed by the body. The end result is that two things happen. First, sugar molecules that come naturally attached to phyto-estrogens in most plant foods, are removed. New forms of phytoestrogens are then made that may have even greater health effects.

Keeping good bacteria to activate phytoestrogens

There are literally millions and millions of bacteria living in the large intestine. Some of these can convert the phytoestrogens into a range of other substances called metabolites. These metabolites and the bacteria responsible for making them are now being carefully studied. One particular metabolite called 'equol', formed in the intestine when you eat soy foods, is now creating big news because it seems that it has even greater health benefits. A recent study examining the effectiveness of soy phytoestrogens in preventing bone loss in postmenopausal women found that those who could make equol actually gained the most bone. Since only 30 to 50 per cent of people can make equol scientists are curious to find out why. It seems that the higher the carbohydrate and lower the saturated fat intake the greater chance there is of you being an equol producer.

Keeping your intestines healthy is important for this process. Many people don't realise that antibiotics kill off intestinal bacteria and thus reduce the ability of phytoestrogens to be converted to equol or other metabolites. After a course of antibiotics it can take many months for the natural balance of your intestinal bacteria to be restored. Long-term use of antibiotics has been linked with increased breast cancer risk. Probiotics, such as yoghurts that contain *Lactobacillus* and *Bifidus* bacteria, can help you to re-establish this balance. A diet rich in wholegrains is also beneficial because it offers the helpful bacteria an ideal food source.

Fermented foods: phytoestrogens to go?

You may have tried tempeh or miso, the fermented foods from Indonesia and Japan. As well as an exotic taste, they offer phytoestrogens in a form the body can absorb immediately as the fermentation process used to make these foods has already done the job of removing the sugar molecules from the phytoestrogens.

One company that markets a fermented soy supplement has claimed that fermented phytoestrogens are more 'bioavailable', meaning available to the body. Some people believe that fermented soy foods might be even better than non-fermented ones—but studies have shown that this is not necessarily true. Tests with the pure phytoestrogens have shown that you are probably better off eating the forms of phytoestrogens found in non-fermented foods, because their bioavailability is actually greater. Leaving the sugar molecules attached seems to help

---

DIGESTING ALL OF THIS

To protect yourself from degenerative diseases, you should maintain high and steady blood levels of phytoestrogens. You can do this by including phytoestrogen-rich foods on two or more occasions during the day, such as a glass of soy milk at breakfast and two slices of soy and linseed bread at lunch. We give many more tasty examples of phytoestrogen foods on pages 172–280. Avoid taking antibiotics unless this is necessary. And keep your intestines healthy by regularly eating wholegrain foods and including some probiotic yoghurts.

protect the phytoestrogen from being degraded too much by the intestinal bacteria.

Until we know more about the effectiveness of these phytoestrogen metabolites produced by bacteria in the intestine, it is difficult to conclude whether fermented foods are healthier than non-fermented foods. Both deliver phytoestrogens to you, although the non-fermented foods give you more of the type found naturally in plants. We suggest eating both kinds.

Absorbing regularly

The body is amazingly efficient. Just six to eight hours after eating phytoestrogen-rich foods, blood levels of phytoestrogens soar, and this provides a wide range of potential health benefits. It then takes another eight hours for the blood level to drop by half. So to maintain a high and constant blood concentration of these protective substances, it is best to eat phytoestrogen-rich foods several times during the day rather than just reserving them for one meal. This is, in fact, how they are traditionally eaten by cultures that consume a lot of soy foods.

 Eating phytoestrogen-rich foods at every meal will give you maximum health benefits.

Phytoestrogens in blood

The aim is to raise blood levels of phytoestrogens. If you consume even modest amounts, say one glass of soy milk or a couple of slices of soy and linseed bread, your blood levels will soon soar 1000–5000 times higher than the level of your own estrogens. Even though phytoestrogens are less potent than estrogens, you can expect positive health benefits at such high levels. If you have a poor phytoestrogen intake, your very low blood levels of these compounds mean you will miss out on the protection they could give you. A vegetarian or macrobiotic diet will provide similar blood levels to the traditional Japanese diet, which is associated with very low rates of major Western diseases.

The body disposes of phytoestrogens in the same way it disposes of its own hormones and some nutrients such as vitamin C. They are filtered through the kidneys and continually passed out in urine. In fact, phytoestrogens were first discovered 20 years ago by accident, when we were developing new techniques for measuring steroid hormones in urine.

It has been consistently shown that patients with breast cancer have relatively low levels of phytoestrogens in their urine, as do people who consume Western-type diets. A recent study from Shanghai found that women with breast cancer had 50–65 per cent lower levels of phytoestrogens in their urine compared with healthy Chinese women. A low urinary level of phytoestrogens has been proposed as a risk marker for breast cancer. Several studies have also confirmed that heart disease risk is lowest in people with the highest urinary levels of phytoestrogens. These studies attest to the importance of getting protected with phytoestrogens.

High levels of phytoestrogens in urine indicate a healthy diet and are a sign that you are being phytoprotected. Even if you do not follow an Asian, macrobiotic or vegetarian diet, simply drinking a glass of soy milk per day, can increase your urinary levels of phytoestrogens by more than 1000 times.

Can you overdose on phytoestrogens?

If blood and urine phytoestrogen levels get so high, can you have too much of a good thing? The simple answer is, no—if you get your phytoestrogens from foods and consume a varied diet. However, it may be possible that phytoestrogen supplements or pills, and high protein soy powders which are relatively new forms of consuming them, could supply too much. Even so, to our knowledge, there are no reported cases of overdoses.

New evidence shows that eating more and more phyto-estrogen-rich foods does not guarantee you will achieve proportionally higher levels in the blood. It seems there is a limit to how much the body can absorb at any one time. This is not surprising, as this is how the body regulates the uptake of some other nutrients. From a safety point of view, it's certainly reassuring.

On the other hand, if you take very large doses of supplements, absorption into the body may not be limited and phytoestrogens might then behave like drugs. There are many examples of negative effects in animals that have resulted from extremely high intakes of phytoestrogens—doses that are not achievable from a human diet. A study funded by the National Cancer Institute in the US examined the effects of feeding for one month a purified soy isoflavone supplement to healthy women at amounts 10–20 times those usually consumed in foods and found minimal toxicity. Caution is advised, and if you are taking supplements you should limit your intake to no more than 50–60 mg of phytoestrogens per day until more is known about their safety.

part II

The power of phytoestrogens to fight disease

chapter 4

Eat to avoid cancer

*'The Chinese do not draw any distinction
between food and medicine'*
Lin Yutang

Cancer is one of the most feared diseases, and it is so common that Westerners almost accept it as an inevitable part of life. Yet some groups of people enjoy extremely low cancer rates. For example, women living in Japan and China have a three- to six-times lower risk of breast cancer than women in the UK. And men in Japan are about four times less likely to die of prostate cancer than British men.

Japanese people who migrate to a Western country soon lose this advantage, mainly because they adopt the phyto-estrogen-deficient Western diet. A lack of phytoestrogens raises the risk of cancer—particularly those that grow as a result of hormone imbalance. As we saw in Chapter 2, phytoestrogens are 'smart molecules' that discourage cancer growth in many ways. So you can help protect yourself against cancer by eating phytoestrogen-rich foods every day. Of course, your diet is not the only risk factor for cancer, but it is one that is within your control. Along with regular exercise, weight control, not smoking and stress management, wise eating choices mean you have much improved chances of avoiding cancer—a reassuring feeling.

This chapter shows why researchers believe a phytoestrogen-rich diet reduces your risk of:

- breast cancer;
- prostate cancer;
- bowel cancer;
- skin cancer; and
- possibly other cancers.

The search for cancer clues

For years, scientists have searched for the 'lone gunman', a cancer-causing dietary component. Many carcinogens have been identified but they fail to explain most of the cancers seen in Western countries.

More recently, researchers have thought the problem may be a lack of something in the Western diet. Over 200 scientific studies have found that people who eat diets rich in vegetables and fruits have the lowest rates of almost all types of cancer, and so research attention has shifted to phytoprotectants. Phytoprotectants are the protective components found in plant foods. Ongoing research has found hundreds of them, suggesting the importance of eating a variety of vegetables, fruits, wholegrains, legumes, nuts and seeds.

Of all the phytoprotectants currently known, phytoestrogens stand out as probably the most important protectants against common Western cancers such as breast, prostate and bowel cancer. Phytoestrogens are found everywhere in the plant food kingdom, though they are highly concentrated in most soy foods and linseeds. By eating foods containing phytoestrogens, you automatically benefit from hundreds of other phytoprotectants that come packaged in the same foods.

In the 1980s Dr Kenneth Setchell, when working at the Medical Research Council's Clinical Research Centre in Harrow, was the first in the world to propose that phytoestrogens should be considered to be important natural anticancer agents, and that these protectants were missing from our modern-day Western-style diet. This conclusion was based on circumstantial observations that patients with breast cancer had low levels of phytoestrogens in their body, while people living in Japan, where cancer rates are low, tend to have consistently high levels.

> >> A lack of phytoestrogens and other phytoprotectants in Western-style diets is an important risk factor for cancer. <<

How phytoestrogens block cancer

Cancers take many years to develop, and phytoestrogens can work in many ways to discourage cancers at different stages of their growth. As we saw in Chapter 2, they can:

- block estrogens that stimulate cancer cell growth;
- work as antioxidants, preventing pre-cancerous damage to the body's fats, proteins and genetic material;
- switch off key enzymes involved in cancer growth;
- restrict the spread of tumours; and
- speed up the disposal of abnormal cells, preventing them from turning cancerous.

CANCER-PREVENTING FOODS

Barley*	Cucumber*	Parsnip
Berries*	Eggplant	Rockmelon*
Broccoli*	Garlic*	Rosemary
Brown rice*	Ginger	Sage
Brussel sprouts*	Licorice*	Soybean*
Cabbage*	Linseed*	Thyme
Capsicums*	Mint	Tomato*
Carrots*	Oats*	Turmeric
Cauliflower*	Onion*	Wholemeal*
Celery*	Oregano	
Citrus*	Parsley	

All these foods contain phytoprotectants. Those marked with an asterisk * contain phytoestrogens; the others have yet to be analysed for their phytoestrogen content.

Phytoestrogens may also help control the abnormal cell division that leads to cancer. They attach themselves to the newly discovered estrogen receptor beta, which is thought to control abnormal cell growth.

Breast cancer

Breast cancer is the most common cancer in women from most Western countries, including the US, Britain and Australia. Its cause is not totally clear, although early onset of menstruation and late menopause are risk factors—and both are linked with longer exposure to estrogen over a woman's lifetime. Strangely, most breast cancers are seen after the menopause when estrogen levels are low, and yet they probably developed over earlier decades when estrogen levels were at their highest.

The good news is that there are ways to reduce your risk. We know that two-thirds of all breast cancers are estrogen-dependent, which means that estrogens stimulate their growth by attaching to estrogen receptors. Yet phytoestrogens have the ability to block estrogens from attaching to these receptors. They work in a similar way to the commonly used breast cancer drugs, Tamoxifen and Raloxifene, which reduce the chances of getting breast cancer for women in the high-risk category. High risk means women with a family history of breast cancer, or who have previously had this disease.

>> **High phytoestrogen levels protect against breast cancer.** <<

Studies have found much lower risks of breast cancer in Asian women who eat traditional, phytoestrogen-rich diets. And even among populations where phytoestrogen-rich foods are not common, the women with high concentrations of phytoestrogens in their bodies have the lowest risk of developing cancer.

As discussed earlier, the Asian advantage is not just due to good genes, because Japanese women who move to the US acquire American statistics within just two generations as their diets change. Genes can't change that quickly. In fact, faulty genes explain just a small proportion of breast cancers. Women with a family history of breast cancer have a higher risk because of mutations in two important genes called BRCA-1 and BRCA-2. But only 5–10 per cent of breast cancer cases are due to these mutations. Lifestyle, and particularly diet, is much more influential. Some researchers even believe that a phyto-estrogen-rich diet may also prove to be helpful to those women who have a family history of breast cancer.

Early prevention

Studies show that feeding phytoestrogens to newborn animals gives them considerable resistance to breast cancer later in life. This is not surprising, because part of the Asian advantage is that women are fed phytoestrogens from early childhood. It seems that the earlier you start, the greater your protection in later life.

Phytoestrogens improve the architecture of the developing breast, making it more resistant to cancer. A girl's breast develops like a tree, branching in from the nipple until the branches end in bud-like structures called terminal end buds (TEBs) and ducts. This is where cancer usually forms because they are highly sensitive to cancer-causing substances.

As a healthy breast develops, many of these TEBs and ducts change into structures called lobules. Under the microscope these look like opening flower buds. Lobules are much safer because they are stable and rarely turn pre-cancerous, so ideally you want as many TEBs as possible to change into lobules. How do you help that happen? Dr Coral Lamartiniere and Dr Nadine Brown from the University of Alabama were the first to show that when the soy phytoestrogen genistein is given to animals at an early age, their TEBs are encouraged to become lobules. In other words, when phytoestrogens are taken early in life, they give breasts a permanent protective effect from cancer-causing agents later in life. This exciting discovery has not been confirmed in human studies because it is ethically impossible to do, but these animal studies are considered a good model for normal breast development in humans.

The normal architecture of the breast

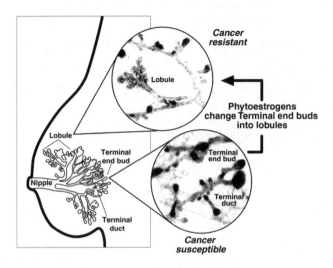

Research into phytoestrogens and breast cancer

There is compelling evidence from animal and laboratory studies that phytoestrogens are powerful anticancer agents, but it may be years before scientists can prove beyond doubt that these natual protectants prevent breast cancer in humans. Studies will inevitably be carried out in the future to see if phytoestrogens can also prevent a recurrence of breast cancer. In a new population-based study of women in China, it has been shown that those who consumed the largest amount of soy foods as adolescents had a 50 per cent lower risk of breast cancer as adults! Other than infancy, scientists now recognise that adolescence is also a sensitive period to 'prime' the breast against disease. The early changes made by phytoestrogens to make the breasts more robust against cancer later in life may be the single most important reason why the breast cancer rate is so low in women who have been raised on a phytoestrogen-rich diet.

SUMMARY OF KEY FINDINGS: PHYTOESTROGENS AND BREAST CANCER

There is a wealth of evidence that phytoestrogens are protective against breast cancer. Here are results from the latest key studies:

> Chinese women with the highest levels of soy phyto-estrogens have an 85 per cent reduced risk of breast cancer compared with those with the lowest levels.

> Japanese women enjoy a three times lower rate of breast cancer than Americans, and consume 10–50 times more phytoestrogens.

> Genistein, a phytoestrogen in soy, stops all types of breast cancer cells from growing in laboratory studies.

> Soy phytoestrogens prevent dangerous pesticides and synthetic chemicals from stimulating the growth of breast cancer cells in laboratory studies.

> Soy protein, linseed and purified phytoestrogens reduce the number and size of breast tumours in animals.

> A higher daily intake of soy products in premenopausal Singaporean women has been linked with significant reduction in breast cancer risk. Most soy products are rich in phyto-estrogens.

> Women with breast cancer and those in the high-risk category have low levels of phytoestrogens compared with healthy women.

> Tofu eaten at least weekly reduces breast cancer risk by 15 per cent in Asian–American women.

> British women consuming 60 g daily of textured vegetable protein (TVP, a rich source of phytoestrogens) lengthen their menstrual cycle by several days. This is a positive change because a longer menstrual cycle is protective. Japanese women have low rates of breast cancer and an average cycle of 32 days compared with 28 days for Western women.

> Premenopausal Japanese women who add soy milk to their daily diet lower their levels of cancer-promoting estrogens.

> Young women with a certain type of genetic makeup that affects the way their body metabolises estrogens—placing them at increased risk for breast cancer—reduced their risk with a high intake of lignan-containing foods. Such foods are fruits, vegetables, grains, nuts and seeds.

> Young women who add soy foods to their diet reduce their levels of estrogens, especially those estrogens that damage genes.

> Phytoestrogens block cancer by attaching to estrogen receptors in the breast in a similar way to new anticancer drugs, Tamoxifen and Raloxifene. In two animal studies, the phytoestrogen-rich foods miso or soy protein, given together with Tamoxifen, had an even greater anticancer effect than Tamoxifen alone on breast cancer.

Among all the research indicating that a phytoestrogen-rich diet is likely to be beneficial in preventing breast cancer, two studies have raised some questions regarding soy. A small study of women undertaken at the University of California found that adding a soy protein powder daily to their diet for nine months increased the amount of fluid that could be obtained under suction from the nipples—called nipple aspirate fluid (NAF). This is thought to modestly increase the risk of breast cancer, particularly when abnormal cells are found. However in this study no abnormal cells were detected and the results were influenced by the fact that only women who produce this fluid could be studied. Generally, only half of women in the population make NAF, so it is difficult to know what this means for healthy women consuming soy foods. The authors cautioned against overinterpreting this study because of the many limitations in its design and the small number of women involved. Another study from the University Hospital of South Manchester in England of 84 premenopausal women with a variety of breast diseases, including cancer, failed to show any effect on markers of breast cell growth after two weeks of eating textured vegetable protein daily. This latter finding is consistent with findings in female monkeys where soy did not adversely affect the breast. Also, when rats with breast cancer were fed genistein, this did not stimulate tumour growth.

When human breast cancer cells are grown in test tubes, genistein stimulates their growth under artificial conditions where none of the body's natural estrogen is present. However, when estrogen is present—as occurs normally in the body— this phytoestrogen actually inhibits growth of the cancer cells.

The speculation that soy and its phytoestrogens could be bad for breasts doesn't fit with the huge reduction in breast cancer risk seen in women who consume the most soy. Phytoestrogens have important differences from estrogens. As we saw in Chapter 2, they are selective in their actions and do not have the deleterious side effects of estrogens. In a study of women with breast inflammation (a sign of early breast disease), taking 24 g soy protein daily for six months dramatically reduced the inflammation.

Doctors are now researching whether this phytoestrogen-rich food could also reduce the recurrence of breast cancer. In principle it should because phytoestrogens act like SERMS which we know protect the breast from cancer. If you are a healthy woman there is no reason to be concerned about consuming phytoestrogen-rich foods. If you already have cancer or pre-cancerous changes in the breast, these foods may actually be helpful in fighting the disease, but more research is needed.

In Japan, where hamburgers are replacing traditional soy foods such as tofu, the once-low breast cancer rates are now on the rise. It is difficult to ignore the mountain of evidence indicating that phytoestrogens are linked with preventing rather than causing breast cancer.

Prostate cancer

Prostate cancer is the most common cancer in men living in Western countries, such as Australia and the US. In the UK, the cancer most common in men is lung cancer, closely followed by prostate cancer. However, lung cancer rates have been falling in men since the 1960s while prostate cancer rates continue to rise. In the US, African–Americans have the highest rate, while Japanese men have very low rates. This difference is partly due to hormones. African–Americans have higher levels of androgens (male hormones) than do Caucasians or Japanese, and androgens encourage prostate cancer cells to grow. Prostate cancer is treated by resetting hormone balance—and this is precisely where phytoestrogens may help.

Asian men—brought up on phytoestrogen-rich diets— have the lowest death rates from prostate cancer. A 20-year Japan–Hawaii Cancer Study of 8000 Japanese men revealed that those who consumed tofu daily were three times less likely to contract prostate cancer.

Phytoestrogen-rich foods can be just as beneficial for non-Asian men. A Californian study of 12 000 Seventh-day Adventist men showed that drinking soy milk is linked with a reduced risk of prostate cancer. Men who drank soy milk once a day had a 30 per cent reduction in risk, while those who drank it more often had a 70 per cent risk reduction!

Prostate cancer death rates

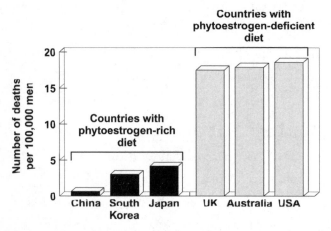

Globocan (International Agency for Research on Cancer, WHO) 1998 Age Standardised Rates (World)

Preventing prostate problems

The prostate is a small gland that adds fluid to sperm. It is positioned at the base of the penis beside the urethra, the tube that carries urine. The prostate becomes larger with age, a condition called benign prostatic hyperplasia (BPH), putting pressure on the urethra and making it difficult to pass urine. BPH is not deadly, but it is usually an early step on the path to prostate cancer.

BPH happens to most men around the world in much the same way—it comes with ageing. In Japanese men it rarely progresses to prostate cancer but it commonly does in Westerners.

We believe this difference is due to the phytoestrogen-deficient diet. In one study, researchers looked at a particular breed of rat that spontaneously contracts prostate cancer, and showed that feeding them phytoestrogens delays the appearance of prostate cancer. Soy protein prolonged the time they were cancer free by 27 per cent. In a recent study, genistein fed to rats reduced the size of the prostate (a good feature where prostate cancer is concerned) and it was not toxic. The opposite occurred when androgens were given. There are similarities between the human and rat prostate and this is why researchers use these experimental models. Soy products could have similar beneficial effects in men.

CASE STUDY   PHILLIP'S STORY

Phillip, a 75-year-old retired food industry executive, was diagnosed with prostate cancer and given radiation therapy. Over a five year period his blood PSA level—a marker of tumour size—rose from 10 ng/mL to 39 ng/mL (normal levels being less than 4 ng/mL), and there was concern that surgical or chemical castration would be required. His doctor advised him to try a phytoestrogen-rich vegetarian diet with soy foods every day. With the dedication of his wife in creating an interesting menu, he brought his PSA down into the 20–25 ng/mL range over a period of five months and held it there for the next seven years of his life. Sadly, he died unexpectedly of an unrelated stroke at the age of 82. This was probably associated with the use of Warfarin on which he had been placed because of a blood-clotting problem of genetic origin. His change to a phytoestrogen-rich diet arrested any further rise in PSA level and saved him from major surgical and drug treatments.

How phytoestrogens protect the prostate

Researchers have uncovered many ways in which phytoestrogens shield the prostate from turning cancerous. They prevent inflammation, block the formation of growth factors and hormones associated with cancer and help to correct the hormone imbalance that occurs with ageing. Let's look at these in turn.

- *Preventing inflammation* Inflammation is an early step in almost all cancers but phytoestrogens protect against it, according to animal studies. Researchers at Johns Hopkins University in the US tested rats with soy protein added to their diets, and compared them with a control group. The rats eating soy protein had much less inflammation of the prostate and after 11 weeks they were the only ones free of inflammation.

- *Blocking production of growth factors* Growth factors such as Epidermal Growth Factor (EGF) stimulate the growth of the prostate and high levels are found in men with prostate cancer. Phytoestrogens interfere with EGF production. Studies have shown that feeding the phytoestrogen genistein to male rats lowered the level of EGF in the prostate.

- *Blocking production of damaging hormones* Phytoestrogens can protect against the potent hormone dihydrotestosterone (DHT). High levels of DHT cause uncontrolled growth in the prostate, and this hormone also breaks down into other, more potent prostate-damaging hormones called *androstanediols*. Drugs are now available to stop DHT being made, but phytoestrogens do this naturally by blocking the enzyme that is needed to make DHT from testosterone in the body.

- *Restoring hormone balance* Ageing changes a man's hormonal balance. Testosterone levels decline while estrogen levels do not, so the balance tips towards female hormones. While estrogens are important for men's health, this imbalance may be a reason for the increase in size of the prostate gland with age. Phytoestrogens can oppose the negative effect of estrogen on the prostate, which is further reason why they are important for men and not just women. Real men should eat phytoestrogens!

SUMMARY OF KEY FINDINGS: PHYTOESTROGENS AND PROSTATE CANCER

Here is a list of research findings indicating why phytoestrogens are an important weapon against prostate cancer.

> Asian men have high phytoestrogen levels and the lowest death rates from prostate cancer.

> In Japan, China and other Asian countries where soy is a food staple, the pre-cancerous condition called benign prostatic hyperplasia (BPH) rarely progresses to full-blown prostate cancer.

> The phytoestrogen genistein completely blocks the growth of prostate cancer cells in the laboratory.

> Prostate cancer risk was reduced 30 per cent by drinking soy milk once daily, and 70 per cent by drinking it more often, according to a Californian study of Seventh-day Adventists.

> Japanese men who eat tofu every day are three times less likely to get prostate cancer than those who don't.

> Phytoestrogens become concentrated in the prostate gland, which may explain why they are protective. Chinese men have

15 times more daidzein, a phytoestrogen found in soy, in their prostatic fluid than do Europeans.

> The enzyme responsible for making the potent hormone DHT that causes the prostate to grow is less active in the prostate of Japanese men than in American men.

> Prostate cancer patients given a supplement of 100 mg isoflavones daily for a minimum of three months experienced a slowing down in the rise of PSA levels (PSA is a marker of tumour growth).

> The onset of prostate cancer is delayed in rats fed soy protein containing phytoestrogens.

> Inflammation of the prostate is reduced when rats are fed a phytoestrogen-rich diet. Inflammation is an early step in triggering cancer.

> Rats fed the phytoestrogen genistein developed a smaller sized prostate gland and had reduced levels of testosterone as they aged—lowering the risk of prostate cancer.

Bowel cancer

Cancer of the bowel is rapidly becoming more prevalent in Western countries. Yet low rates exist in China and Japan and generally among vegetarians who have a diet high in phytoestrogens.

Studies of Japanese people have found high intakes of soybeans and tofu give an 80 per cent reduced risk of cancer of the rectum or lower bowel. Eating one to two servings of soy each week was also highly protective against cancer of the colon, according to these research findings.

Phytoestrogens can reduce the number of aberrant crypts, the microscopic changes in the lining of the bowel that give early warning that cancer may be on its way. Dr Lillian Thompson of the University of Toronto has shown that consuming linseeds, a 'rich-source' of phytoestrogens, reduced the number of aberrant crypts in rats. Another study showed that soy phytoestrogens have the same protective effects.

Dr Maurice Bennink of Michigan State University looked at people who were in a high-risk category for colon cancer. He supplemented their diets with 39 g of soy protein each day for a year and found favourable changes in the cells lining their colon, indicating that their risk of colon cancer was reduced.

A few studies, including one by the co-author of this book, have found that feeding linseeds to rats with colon cancer did not reduce the number of actual tumours in the bowel. This suggests that for bowel cancer, phytoestrogens may be effective only in blocking the early, rather than the late stages. If this is true it would be yet another good reason to start including these phytoprotectants into our diets from early life.

It is not known exactly how phytoestrogens protect the bowel, but they may provide beneficial hormone-like effects. Estrogen receptors exist in the bowel, and one benefit of hormone replacement therapy is that it protects postmenopausal women from colon cancer, reducing their risk by 30 per cent.

The other possibility is that phytoestrogens simply stop cells from dividing and growing into pre-cancerous or cancerous cells. The National Cancer Institute in America has tested thousands of natural plant substances, including lignans (a family of phytoestrogens), for their anti-cancer activity. A lignan isolated from the root of the North American mandrake plant was first used to make two drugs for treating testicular cancer and a rare form of lung cancer. Interestingly, cyclist Lance Armstrong, a survivor of testicular cancer, was treated with one of these lignan drugs and he then went on to win the Tour de France four times. It was the anticancer activity of such lignans that prompted our interest in linseed, a very rich edible source of lignans. Lignans are also found in wholegrains and vegetables and reach high concentrations in the bowel.

SUMMARY OF KEY FINDINGS: PHYTOESTROGENS AND BOWEL CANCER

Here are some of the major research findings supporting a role for phytoestrogens in protection from bowel cancer.

> Vegetarians and others who have high levels of lignans have low rates of colon cancer. Lignans are one family of phytoestrogens.

> In areas of Finland with low rates of colon cancer, people eat greater amounts of lignans than those in high cancer areas. Finns get lignans from rye bread, berries and other plant foods.

> Japanese regions with the highest tofu consumption have the lowest rates of colon cancer.

> Americans at high risk of colon cancer who ate soy protein daily for a year were found to have beneficial changes in their bowel, showing a reduced risk.

> Californians who ate more tofu, soybeans, fruits, vegetables and grains had fewer bowel polyps than average. Bowel polyps, if left unchecked, frequently turn into cancer.

> > Feeding rats with phytoestrogens from various sources—soybeans, soy flour, isoflavones and linseeds—reduced the number of pre-cancerous changes to the lining of their bowels.
>
> > Laboratory tests show that two lignans formed in the bowel stop the growth of four types of human colon cancer cells.

People on plant-based diets have the lowest rates of bowel cancer and the highest levels of phytoestrogens, suggesting that a phytoestrogen-rich diet is helpful in this disease. Keeping physically active and limiting your intake of red meat and alcohol is also important.

Skin cancer

Skin cancer is not the Western world's biggest killer but it is rapidly on the increase, with the highest rates found in sunny Australia. Experiments in mice have shown that phytoestrogens can protect against the harmful effects of UV radiation from sun exposure. In a study performed by the US Army it was found that rats exposed to lethal doses of X-rays all survived if they were fed phytoestrogens in their diet, whereas those eating regular food all died. The burning question is: could similar benefits be anticipated in humans?

A study from Australia's Commonwealth Scientific and Industrial Research Organisation (CSIRO) Division of Human Nutrition showed that the soy phytoestrogen genistein blocks the growth of skin cancer cells called B16 melanoma cells in mice. The researchers also found that when healthy mice were fed genistein they experienced a 50 per cent reduction in the size of transplanted solid tumours within just seven days.

Similar tumour shrinkage has been demonstrated in mice that were fed phytoestrogens in the form of linseeds. One study from Creighton University School of Medicine in the US found a 63 per cent reduction in the size of tumours.

Phytoestrogens can stop skin cancers from growing, make them shrink and even prevent them from spreading, according to animal research. It remains to be seen if they can be equally effective against skin cancer in humans.

Of course, it is still important to take other precautions against skin cancer. You need to minimise your exposure to UV radiation by using sunscreen and wearing a hat and shirt if you spend significant periods in the sun.

It is not surprising that phytoestrogens might protect the skin from the harmful effects of UV radiation. Soy, our richest source of phytoestrogens and many other protective phytochemicals, has long been known in Asia to be good for the skin. The Empress Dowager in China is said to have enjoyed the skin-care benefits of soy by bathing in soy milk!

Early scientific tests suggest that a manufactured soy 'cream' can smoothe and moisturise the skin. This fits with folklore in China where it is said that women who work in tofu shops have the best skin. This soy cream has also been shown to reduce the redness and peeling caused by sun damage, and to lighten skin blotches. When we visited Seoil Farm in South Korea where traditional soybean paste is made we were told that women given the task of transferring cooked steaming soybeans into large vats observed a fading of their skin pigmentation caused by sun damage. Interestingly, before this amazing discovery it was difficult to recruit workers for the job because it involved hard labour, but afterwards there was no shortage of volunteers!

Other cancers

Since genistein has been shown to block various enzymes and growth factors that are common to all cancers, phytoestrogens may have much wider anti-cancer effects than we think. Here are some intriguing early findings on a range of cancers.

Cancer of the uterus

According to a study from the University of Hawaii, women who ate the most phytoestrogen-rich foods, such as legumes and tofu, had a 54 per cent reduction in risk. Eating more soy products in general and wholegrains also reduces the risk of this cancer. Cancer of the womb or uterus is also known as endometrial cancer. A red clover phytoestrogen extract was found to have beneficial effects on the endometrium—reducing the level of a protein called Ki67 used to measure overactive growth of cells.

Stomach cancer

A Japanese study from the National Cancer Center Research Institute in Tokyo found that eating miso soup each day reduces the risk of stomach cancer. Miso soup is made from soybean paste, a traditional source of phytoestrogens in the Japanese and Korean diets.

Regions in Japan that have a high tofu intake have the lowest rates of stomach cancer, according to a nationwide nutrition survey conducted by the Japanese Ministry of Health.

Lung cancer

A higher consumption of tofu is one of the factors that protect against lung cancer, according to a study of Hong Kong Chinese women who have never smoked.

Thyroid cancer

A study of women has found that both Americans and Asian immigrants to the US consuming the highest amounts of phytoestrogen-rich soy foods had a 36 per cent lower risk of thyroid cancer compared to women with low intakes of these foods. Thyroid cancer is three times more common in women than men and appears to be linked to hormones. It is one of the five most common types of cancer occurring in women between puberty and menopause.

Bladder cancer

Laboratory studies from the Harvard Medical School show that soy phytoestrogens stop the growth of bladder cancer cells. Feeding animals with modest amounts of soy protein isolate, soy extracts or genistein also reduces the growth of transplanted bladder cancers.

Neuroblastoma

This is a common childhood cancer of the autonomic nervous system. The phytoestrogen genistein has been shown to stop neuroblastoma cells from growing in laboratory tests conducted at the University of Alabama and Mount Sinai School of Medicine, New York.

Leukaemia

Studies from the University of Minnesota showed that genistein when attached to special antibodies killed human B-cell precursor leukaemia cells that had been transplanted in mice. This is the most common form of leukaemia in children and second-most common in adults.

Can phytoestrogens treat existing cancer?

It is not yet known whether phytoestrogens can be used to treat or cure people with existing cancers. In rats with breast cancer treated with the drug Tamoxifen, soy improved the drug's effectiveness. Tamoxifen alone reduced tumours by 29 per cent, but when soy was also added to the diet, tumours dropped by a huge 62 per cent. Importantly soy does not appear to interfere with this drug and, in contrast to Tamoxifen, it protects the uterus. Preliminary clinical findings in several American women suggest that soy may also be helpful in preventing the recurrence of breast cancer. A large study is now planned to investigate this at the Camelot Foundation in Nebraska.

The real value of a phytoestrogen-rich diet, we believe, is in prevention, its ability to protect against cancer in the first place. Phytoestrogens are more likely to do this if you start early and consume them regularly—but it's never too late to start.

Finally . . .

A phytoestrogen-rich diet is a great natural defence against cancer. People who eat the most phytoestrogen-rich foods have the lowest rates of breast, prostate and bowel cancer, which are major killers in the Western world.

This diet will also supply you with an abundance of other important nutrients: thousands of phytoprotectants, dietary fibre, vitamins and minerals which all help to keep cancer at bay. Many of these substances can be purchased as pills and supplements but current research suggests that it is better to obtain your phytoprotectants naturally and from foods. We recommend including each day at least one food or drink that provides a 'rich-source' of phytoestrogens. In Part III of this book, we'll show you just how easy this is.

chapter 5

How to hijack heart disease

'The trouble with heart disease is that the first symptom to deal with [is] sudden death'
MICHAEL PHELPS

Many of us are sitting on a time bomb. Every two minutes, someone in the UK dies from cardiovascular disease, the nation's biggest killer. Death rates from heart disease in the UK rank among the highest in the world, even though they have declined almost one-third in the last decade. In the year 2000 heart disease accounted for 36 per cent of all premature deaths of men and 28 per cent of women, according to statistics from the British Heart Foundation. While risk factors exist, warning signs are rare. Death is the first symptom for 57 per cent of men and 64 per cent of women, according to the American Heart Association.

Heart disease is a slow and silent assassin. It starts in the blood vessels during childhood. Fats are deposited, causing significant damage and paving the way for a blockage and heart attack to occur later in life. If you are 'lucky', you might be alerted by the presence of high blood pressure or chest pain that there is something seriously wrong. But by this stage, the best you can do is to go into damage control. It is much easier to prevent heart and blood vessel disease from developing, rather than trying to deal with it once you have it.

While many people see it as a man's disease, in the UK each year, more women die from cardiovascular disease than men. But men die from it earlier. The reason for this is because women are protected by their higher levels of estrogen, that is until they reach menopause. Estrogen is like a tonic for the blood vessels, helping to keep them healthy. After the menopause when estrogen levels drop, women are no better off and they become even more prone to heart disease than men.

One of the reasons postmenopausal women have in the past been prescribed HRT is because estrogen plays an important role in regulating blood cholesterol levels. It was long thought, therefore, that it would protect against cardiovascular disease. The recent findings from the Women's Health Initiative study of 16 806 postmenopausal US women of a significantly increased risk of heart disease, stroke and blood-clotting from HRT—specifically the combined estrogen and progesterone form—has shocked health professionals and women throughout the world. The findings are perhaps not surprising because one of estrogen's bad effects is to increase the thickness of blood, so that blood clots are more likely to occur. This was known a long time ago when oral contraceptives were first introduced and it probably undoes any beneficial effects estrogen has on blood cholesterol. The North American Menopause Society is now advising physicians against using HRT for long-term prevention of cardiovascular disease and recommending that alternative strategies be used.

In countries where phytoestrogen-rich diets are consumed regularly, heart disease rates for both men and women are much lower than in the UK and other Western countries. Phytoestrogens offer many of the advantages of estrogens, but also protect your heart and blood vessels in other ways. In this chapter we explain how phytoestrogens help to:

- control cholesterol
- boost antioxidant levels
- reduce size of fatty deposits in blood vessels, called plaque
- improve flexibility of blood vessels
- prevent blood from clotting
- lower blood pressure

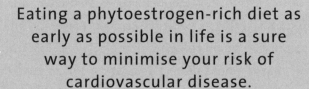

>> Eating a phytoestrogen-rich diet as early as possible in life is a sure way to minimise your risk of cardiovascular disease. <<

Why people get heart disease

Many risk factors work together to determine whether you will develop heart disease. Among the top three risk factors is a high level of cholesterol, which causes the arteries to become clogged with plaque, a condition known as atherosclerosis.

Most people are born with a normal cholesterol level, but this soon rises if you live in a Western country where the diet is typically rich in animal fats, cholesterol, animal protein and, in particular, deficient in phytoestrogens. For most people, therefore, high blood cholesterol is diet induced. In the year 2000, two-thirds of all adults in the UK over the age of 25 years had blood cholesterol levels higher than 5.0 mmol/L, the upper limit of normal recommended by the British Heart Foundation. Ten to 15 per cent have a genetic disease that accounts for their abnormally high cholesterol level. By contrast, statistics from the World Health Organization (WHO)/MONICA project show that only 20 per cent of Chinese adults had blood cholesterol levels above 5.2 mmol/L. Even if your cholesterol is not excessively high, you should take it seriously. More than half of all heart attacks occur in people who have only a moderately raised cholesterol level, according to the WHO.

Lifestyle is the most influential way of keeping the majority of risk factors in check. For example, by keeping physically active and being a non-smoker you significantly reduce your risk of heart disease. A phytoestrogen-rich diet is also an effective way to control some of the key risk factors—high blood pressure and high blood cholesterol.

IMPORTANT RISK FACTORS FOR HEART DISEASE	
• High blood cholesterol	• Inactivity
• High blood pressure	• Diabetes
• Smoking	• Family history of heart
• Obesity	disease

How phytoestrogens can help

Control cholesterol

Phytoestrogen-rich foods such as linseed and soy lower the levels of the harmful form of cholesterol, called LDL-cholesterol, by 7–24 per cent. This is beyond that which is usually achieved by just sticking to low-fat and low-cholesterol diets, commonly recommended by many health professionals. In some people with high cholesterol levels, phytoestrogen-rich foods such as soy protein can be very powerful. They can even work as effectively as the most potent cholesterol-lowering medications—the statins. The graph below shows a comparison of the drug versus the dietary approach. Other foods that provide a source of phytoestrogens, such as oat bran, psyllium, nuts, garlic and beans, lower LDL-cholesterol by 5–15 per cent. Importantly, the cholesterol-reducing effects of phytoestrogen foods are thought to add to the benefits of a low-fat and low-cholesterol diet. The two types of diet complement each other. According to the Nutrition Committee of the American Heart Association, 'it is prudent to recommend including soy protein foods in a diet low in saturated fat and cholesterol to promote heart health'.

In the US the Food and Drug Administration (FDA) approved the use of a new food health claim in 1999 that soy protein reduces the risk of heart disease. In 2002, the Joint Health Claims Initiative (JHCI) in the UK followed suit, approving a similar claim for the cholesterol-lowering property of soy protein. This was based on the evidence from more

Effectiveness of diets and drugs in reducing blood LDL-cholesterol levels

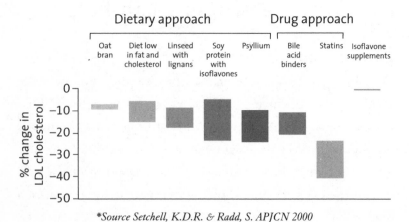

Source Setchell, K.D.R. & Radd, S. APJCN 2000

than 50 clinical studies showing that soy protein lowers high cholesterol levels in men, women and children. Some studies have also found that soy protein can improve the profile of blood fats, even in those people without high cholesterol levels.

On average, soy protein lowers LDL-cholesterol by 12.9 per cent, according to Dr James Anderson at the University of Kentucky, USA, who published his findings of a critical review of 38 scientific papers in the *New England Journal of Medicine*. In some people the reduction can be as high as 24 per cent! The greatest cholesterol-lowering effect is seen in people with the highest levels. So, if you have a normal cholesterol level, the reduction won't be so great. Many food products in the US that provide at least 6.25 g of soy protein per serve are now displaying this soy protein health claim.

To lower high cholesterol levels, the FDA states you need to consume a total of 25 g of soy protein each day in conjunction with a diet that is low in saturated fat and cholesterol. Over the page we provide you with a table listing the soy protein content of some common soy foods. Note that soy sauce and soybean oil do not contain soy protein.

For information on specific products, check the food labels or contact the manufacturer. In some countries many products highlight their soy protein content. One way to get 25 g of soy protein would be to add soy milk to your cereal each morning, snack on a handful of soy nuts during the day and include a soy burger for lunch or your evening meal, for example.

Phytoestrogens do not seem to lower cholesterol on their own, so supplements and purified extracts are not likely to be effective unless they also contain adequate amounts of soy protein. Nevertheless, it is important for phytoestrogens to be present in food because soy protein stripped of its phytoestrogens does

SOY PROTEIN CONTENT OF SELECTED FOODS

Soy food	Grams of soy protein
Soy protein powder, 2 scoops (28 g)	23
Soy burger, 1 pattie (90 g)	17
Soy protein shake, 1 scoop (35 g)	14
Soy protein bar, (61.5 g)	14
Soy flour, ⅓ cup (30 g)	13.5
Textured vegetable protein (TVP), ½ cup rehydrated (57 g)	12
Soy nuts, ¼ cup (30 g)	11
Tempeh, ½ cup (70 g)	10
Tofu, ½ cup (90 g)	10
Edamame (green soybeans), ½ cup (75 g)	10
Soybeans, cooked, ½ cup (100 g)	9
Soy milk, 1 cup (250 ml)	8.5
Soy based deli slices, 3 slices (60 g)	8.4
Soy hot dog, 1 link (42 g)	7
Soy pasta, 2 oz (58 g)	6.3
Soy breakfast cereal, ¾ cup (45 g)	5
Soy yoghurt, 1 small tub (200 g)	5
Soy cheese, 1 slice (19 g)	4
Soy custard, 100 g	3.2
Soy & linseed bread, 2 slices (80 g)	2.8
Soy ice-cream, ½ cup (70 g)	2
Soy chips, 28 g	1

not lower cholesterol either. Scientists currently believe that phytoestrogens account for about half of the cholesterol-lowering effect of soy protein—these work together with soy protein to deliver this benefit. The extent of reduction in blood cholesterol is greater the more phytoestrogen there is in the food. It may not be necessary however to take as much as 25 g of soy protein each day to lower cholesterol if phytoestrogens are obtained from a combination of foods. In a study from Wollongong University, postmenopausal women with mildly raised cholesterol levels were asked to incorporate into their daily diet two slices of bread, one English muffin, one muesli bar and one oatcake—all enriched with soy and linseeds. After just three weeks, when the body's level of phytoestrogens was high, LDL-cholesterol dropped by an average of 12.5 per cent. Yet after 12 weeks, when levels of phytoestrogens in the body were 50 per cent lower, presumably due to a lower intake, the LDL-cholesterol reduction was only 6.5 per cent. This suggests the need to consume phytoestrogen foods on a regular basis to reap the best long-term results.

The greatest benefit of phytoestrogens may be in preventing levels of the 'bad cholesterol' from rising in the first place. In Japan, where there is a low rate of heart disease, it has been shown that blood cholesterol levels are lowest in people who eat the most soy protein foods, according to a study conducted at the Department of Public Health, Gifu University School of Medicine. Researchers have also shown that Japanese school-aged children have higher levels of the protective HDL-cholesterol compared with American or Australian children. This probably also applies to UK children but figures are difficult to obtain. About one-quarter of 16–24 year-olds in the UK have total cholesterol levels above 5.0 mmol/L, and 1 in 8 has a low HDL-cholesterol, according to the British Heart Foundation's latest figures. HDL-cholesterol, the 'good cholesterol' is the way the body packages our cholesterol so it can be removed rather than laid down in blood vessels as plaque.

CASE STUDY   DAVID'S STORY

David, a 53-year-old builder, battled for years to lower his high blood cholesterol level (6.5 mmol/L) because he found it difficult to comply with the recommended low-fat/cholesterol diet. He then made one simple but significant change to his diet: he switched from using dairy milk to soy. Previously he had used up to 1 litre of full cream dairy milk each day. He didn't make any other changes to his lifestyle. Six weeks later when he visitied his doctor he was told 'whatever you've done keep on doing it because your cholesterol has dropped'. David now loves his soy milk and consumes about 2 cups each day (500 ml) on his cereal and in drinks. He says he couldn't do without it. He has been using soy milk for over three years and his cholesterol is down to 4.8 mmol/L—well within the normal range (3.5–5.5 mmol/L).

A recent move by the US Department of Agriculture should help American children in schools and day care centres across the country start to increase their phytoestrogen intake. Federal officials worried about the fat content in school lunches revised the School Lunch Program in 1999, paving the way for the inclusion of more soy products, such as veggie burgers and tofu, to be used as meat substitutes in federally subsidised meals.

More than 26 million children in the US currently have levels of cholesterol that are above the normal range, predisposing them to premature heart disease. Large numbers of children in most Western countries, including the UK, probably also have high cholesterol levels.

Boost antioxidants

Most of us have heard how vitamins C and E are good antioxidants, but most people don't know that phytoestrogens also work as antioxidants to help protect us from heart disease. Boosting the level of antioxidants in the diet is extremely important to prevent us from making an even worse form of cholesterol, known as 'oxidised LDL-cholesterol'. This we call the 'really bad' form of LDL-cholesterol. It is the true villain because it readily deposits itself in the walls of the arteries and, once there, is extremely difficult to remove.

People who have heart attacks have been found to have low levels of antioxidants in their blood. The importance of maintaining a good level of antioxidants can therefore not be understated. Phytoestrogens found in soy and linseed are effective antioxidants. Research conducted at the University of Cincinnati College of Medicine by the co-author of this book and colleagues, found that when postmenopausal women consumed soy milk or soy nuts each day, their LDL-cholesterol became much more resistant to oxidation. Young men and women gained similar benefits by consuming phytoestrogens in soy bars in a study conducted at the University of Helsinki, Finland. And a study carried out by Dr David Jenkins at the Department of Nutritional Sciences, University of Toronto, showed that including 33 g of soy protein daily, which supplied 86 mg of isoflavones, reduced the amount of oxidised LDL-cholesterol in the blood, even in those men and women taking vitamin E supplements.

The phytoestrogens present in foods such as soy and linseeds will not only boost your antioxidant status, but will also contribute to reducing blood cholesterol levels, so that less is available to be oxidised into the really bad form. Fruits, vegetables, tea and red wine are also good sources of antioxidants. Some of these foods provide a source of phytoestrogens in the form of isoflavones, while others provide similar and closely related phytoprotectants called flavonoids. A high intake of the flavonoid antioxidants from tea, onions and apples has been linked to lowered rates of heart disease.

Reduce the size of plaques

Plaque consists of a complex mixture of cells, fats and cholesterol. As it is laid down, it thickens the walls of blood vessels, narrowing the inner diameter and restricting blood flow. Phytoestrogens can slow the rate at which plaque forms in blood vessels and reduce the amount of these fatty deposits. Our own estrogens protect blood vessels by preventing the build-up of plaque.

Several studies from the Bowman Gray School of Medicine in the US have found that giving soy protein to animals fed a high cholesterol diet leads to much lower levels of plaque formation. The phytoestrogens in soy seem to be able to counteract the harmful effects of the typically unhealthy Western diet. Consuming linseeds, similarly caused a 46 per cent reduction in the size of plaques that would ordinarily form with a high cholesterol diet, according to research published in the medical journal *Atherosclerosis*.

Improve flexibility of blood vessels

As plaque accumulates with the ageing process, blood vessels tend to stiffen and become more rigid, which makes them less capable of responding to the sudden changes in blood pressure that occur in times of stress.

Estrogens help to keep blood vessels flexible, and new evidence shows that phytoestrogens can also restore their normal responsiveness. A daily supplement of 80 mg of isoflavones given to women improved the elasticity of their blood vessels by 26 per cent in a study conducted at the Baker Medical Research Institute and the CSIRO Division of Human Nutrition in Australia. This is an improvement similar to that reported for estrogen. Female monkeys consuming a typical Western high fat and cholesterol diet also benefited by having phytoestrogens added. Their blood vessels were more relaxed when phytoestrogens were consumed and more restricted when phytoestrogens were absent.

The latest research from London's Imperial College School of Medicine and the University of Sydney has shown that genistein has an additional effect on improving the flexibility of blood vessels—likened to the function of 'digitalis', an old remedy for heart failure obtained from the purple foxglove plant. In fact, it has been suggested that phytoestrogens may be the 'digitalis glycosides' of the 21st century, and that they have the potential for preventing and treating blood vessel disease. These effects occur at blood levels similar to those achieved when you drink a glass of soy milk three times a day.

Again this demonstrates that it's not just what you eat that's so important, but what you are not eating. Leaving out phytoestrogen-rich foods could mean you miss out on being protected from the harmful effects of a high-fat Western diet.

Prevent blood from clotting

A heart attack occurs when a small blood clot gets stuck in a blood vessel that has become narrowed by plaque. Blood flow to the heart is reduced or blocked and the heart muscle dies because it can't get enough oxygen. Similarly, if a clot forms in the small blood vessels of the brain, a stroke results. An increased occurrence of blood clots, stroke and heart attack was one of the major findings from the large Women's Health Initiative study of HRT use by postmenopausal women. Estrogen is a powerful steroid that thickens blood. Phytoestrogens on the other hand act differently to reduce the chance of blood clotting by stopping cells called platelets from clumping together, according to a study from the University of Guelph, Canada. The aggregation of platelets is an early step in blood clot formation. Researchers at Emory University in the US have also found that phytoestrogens inhibit the formation of a 'thrombus'—a small clot that has formed on a plaque and broken off. In this respect phytoestrogens act like fish oils, because they help keep the blood thin.

Lower blood pressure

High blood pressure increases your risk of having a stroke. When you eat phytoestrogens in foods such as soy protein, you may be able to lower your blood pressure. Healthy middle-aged women given a daily supplement of 20 g of soy protein split into two servings during the day showed a significant drop in their blood pressure according to a study by Dr Scott Washburn and his team at Wake Forest University School of

Medicine in North Carolina. In a study of men given stressful tasks to perform, 30 g of soy protein taken daily was found to reduce blood pressure. A study from Spain found that 500 mL of soy milk taken twice daily by people with mild to moderate hypertension reduced blood pressure by 16.7 mm Hg on average, compared with only 3.0 mm Hg when cow's milk was consumed. Those with the highest genistein levels in their urine —an indicator of phytoestrogen intake—had the largest reductions in blood pressure.

Other phytoestrogens that originate from wholegrains, berries and vegetables, may also help prevent rises in blood pressure. A study from the University of Kuopio and the University of Helsinki, Finland, found that men with low blood levels of a particular lignan had the highest blood pressure. Since blood levels of phytoestrogens are a surrogate marker of dietary intake, this study suggests that the men were not phyto-protected.

Recommendations for your heart

Asian people who regularly consume phytoestrogens from a young age have low cholesterol levels and a low risk of heart disease. We recommend introducing phytoestrogen-rich foods into your diet as soon as possible to obtain the greatest benefits for your heart and blood vessels.

If you are healthy, including as little as one serving of a phytoestrogen-rich food such as a glass of soy milk or a handful of soy nuts each day, should help to maintain blood vessels in good condition and reduce your chances of having a high blood cholesterol level. We believe the greatest advantage of phytoestrogen-rich foods is their effectiveness in preventing disease if taken well before the damage is done.

If, however, you already have an abnormal cholesterol level, taking a higher amount of phytoestrogen-rich foods may be necessary. Including 25 g of soy protein in your daily diet will reduce the amount of the bad form of cholesterol, while also protecting it from being oxidised. Alternatively, you could consume 15–20 g of linseed each day. On pages 189–280, we provide many appetising recipes using soy and linseed foods.

While phytoestrogen supplements and extracts may help keep your blood vessels flexible, current research shows that they do not provide the full range of benefits you can get from foods. There are important interactions that occur between phytoestrogens and many other components of food that are lost when phytoestrogens are extracted from their natural surroundings.

Finally, because a phytoestrogen-rich diet is also lower in animal fat, cholesterol and animal protein, you will gain more bonuses to help you remain young at heart. Other lifestyle factors such as regular exercise, weight control, not smoking, adequate rest and relaxation are also important in maintaining a holistic approach to your health.

chapter 6

Boning up—preventing osteoporosis

*'Children, you are very little, And your bones
are very brittle . . . If you would grow very
stately, You must try to walk sedately'*
ROBERT LOUIS STEVENSON

Osteoporosis is a killer that rarely makes the headlines. It quietly removes calcium from bones until they are brittle, allowing hip fractures and their complications to kill more Western women than breast cancer does each year. About three million people in the UK suffer from osteoporosis according to the National Osteoporosis Society. Every three minutes someone fractures a bone due to osteoporosis, and the annual cost to the National Health Service is about £5 million a day. About one in five people who have a hip fracture die within six months and it has been predicted that by the year 2020, one in three hospital beds will be occupied by elderly women with fractures.

You can minimise your risk of osteoporosis by:

- maintaining estrogen levels in your body;

- keeping physically active;
- not smoking;
- not drinking alcohol, or limiting the amount if you do;
- getting enough calcium, vitamin D and vitamin K;
- eating plenty of green vegetables;
- cutting down on salt;
- eating less animal protein; and
- avoiding or minimising caffeine intake.

This chapter presents exciting new research suggesting that phytoestrogens can provide additional benefits to help you prevent osteoporosis. These go beyond the gains you can expect by following conventional guidelines.

Why bones break

Osteoporosis means 'porous bones'. It occurs when calcium is leached out of your bones, making them porous and prone to fracture. You might like to think of your skeleton as a bank account of calcium. It is extremely important to deposit as much calcium as possible when you are young, especially in the teenage years, because this will provide you with a better reserve later in life.

When the body spends more calcium than it deposits, the skeleton becomes depleted. For example, women can lose a significant amount of calcium from their bones due to the extra demands of pregnancy and breastfeeding—particularly if they go through multiple pregnancies in rapid succession. And it can take years to rebuild the supply.

Many people think their bones are dead and merely supportive, like the wood in the frame of their house. Bone is actually a living tissue, maintained by crews of two different types of cells. Osteoclasts break down existing bone. A second type called osteoblasts make new bone to replace depleted bone.

These two cell types normally work together to maintain a constant amount of bone.

Estrogen is the body's most important bone guardian because it restrains the bone-dissolving cells. When estrogen levels fall, the bone-dissolving cells become highly active and the bones are rapidly robbed of calcium. This explains why post-menopausal women, with their plummeting levels of estrogen, are worst affected. Women lose 7–8 per cent of their total bone mass in the first three years after menopause and they keep losing it thereafter, although at a slower rate. Fifty per cent of women develop bone fractures after the age of 50, while 20–26 per cent never leave a hospital or nursing home after a hip fracture. Quite unfairly, women are three to four times more likely than men to develop osteoporosis, and for a fascinating reason. Strange as it may seem, men actually produce two to three times more estrogen than postmenopausal women. Remember, estrogen is not just a female hormone, but is equally important to men. Men also have a higher bone density, which further helps to protect them against fractures.

You might think that if the problem is loss of calcium, then the solution is to get more calcium into the body. That is important, but it's not the total answer. For example, dairy food is a good source of calcium, but countries with the highest intake of dairy foods also have the highest rates of hip fractures from osteoporosis. And Asia has a low incidence of hip fractures according to the World Health Organization, even though the traditional Asian diet is very low in dairy foods. This Asian advantage could be partly explained by the traditional phyto-estrogen-rich diet. A study from Tokyo Metropolitan Geriatric Hospital found that postmenopausal Japanese women with higher soy protein intakes had higher bone mineral densities and a lower level of bone loss from the spine. Soy protein, which is rich in phytoestrogens, was also deemed to have a more significant effect on bones than calcium intake. Calcium is good, but it alone is not enough. A similar Japanese study confirmed that postmenopausal women who consumed the most soy products such as soybean curd, fermented soybeans and soybean paste had the highest bone mass.

When it comes to calcium, the important issue is not just how much you eat, but how much you retain in the body. High intakes of animal proteins can cause you to lose calcium from the bones by eliminating it through the kidneys into the urine. This takes place because protein can increase the pressure at which blood is filtered through the kidneys. Meat, poultry, fish, egg or dairy proteins can cause this calcium loss, but red meat is thought to be the worst, as it puts the greatest pressure on the kidneys. Vegetable proteins do not seem to have this bad effect. Soy protein, for example, does not leach calcium from the bones according to two studies from the US.

One way to maintain healthy bones is to take some form of estrogen to prevent estrogen levels from declining. Estrogen replacement therapy (ERT) and hormone replacement therapy (HRT) are proven to slow the rate of bone loss during menopause. Yet these drugs do not appeal to all women because of their numerous side effects and they have been linked to an increased risk of breast and ovarian cancer and more recently strokes, blood-clotting and heart attacks. HRT, of course, is not usually taken by men! Is there another source of 'safe estrogen'? You guessed it—a phytoestrogen-rich diet.

>> Estrogen is one of the most important factors in protecting you from osteoporosis. <<

How phytoestrogens help bones

Phytoestrogens will slow your rate of bone loss, although not as effectively as estrogens do. Like estrogens, they make the bone-dissolving osteoclasts less active. But they provide an added bonus—something HRT cannot do. They seem to stimulate the bone-making cells to build new bone. Here are the latest research findings.

Prevent bone loss

Perimenopausal women (those entering the menopausal period) prevented bone loss in their spine by taking phytoestrogens in the form of a food supplement, according to a study published in the *American Journal of Clinical Nutrition*. The women consumed 40 g of soy protein daily over a six-month period, which provided them with 80 mg of isoflavones. Isoflavones are the family of phytoestrogens found in soy.

Soy protein was earlier reported to prevent bone loss in animal studies that simulated the postmenopausal period in women. Several studies have confirmed that the phytoestrogen genistein is almost as effective in preventing bone loss in animals, as Premarin, the most commonly prescribed form of HRT.

Beneficial effects on bone cells

Phytoestrogens are proven to slow down the bone-dissolving cells and make the bone-building cells more active. Seventeen separate studies on bone cells and 24 different animal studies of osteoporosis agree in their findings—phytoestrogens have beneficial effects on bone. In 1996 at the University of Alabama, experiments performed on bone cells showed that genistein suppressed the activity of the bone-dissolving cells. Later, studies in humans confirmed this also happens in the body when phytoestrogen-rich soy foods are eaten. Postmenopausal women who consumed three cups of soy milk or a handful of soy nuts every day for three months experienced a 14.3 per cent drop in NTx, a protein marker, showing that the bone-dissolving cells were less active. The same women also had increased levels of a substance called osteocalcin, showing that the bone-building cells had become more active. These studies conducted at the University of Cincinnati College of Medicine supported the findings of research from Italy where a 24 per cent reduction in NTx was seen in postmenopausal women when soy protein was added to their diets. Eight studies now show that phytoestrogens reduce the activity of the bone-dissolving cells.

In the first study of its kind in the world, researchers from Oklahoma State University showed that phytoestrogen-rich foods may also help men's bones. For a period of three months, 64 men supplemented their usual diets with either soy protein or dairy protein. The effect of the soy was two and half times greater than that of dairy in boosting a marker of bone formation called IGF-1.

Improve mineral content and density in bones

The most striking evidence that phytoestrogens are important for bones comes from a two-year Danish study, which found that soy milk containing naturally high levels of phytoestrogens actually stops the bone loss that would otherwise occur in women after the menopause. Women who consumed two glasses of soy milk daily delivering 85 mg of isoflavones over the two years did not lose bone from their spine. By contrast, women who consumed the same amount of a soy milk specially made to be very low in isoflavones experienced over a 4 per cent loss in the bone mineral density of their spine. What was particularly significant about this study was that certain women—those who were able to make the metabolite equol from soy—actually gained 2.2 per cent in bone density in their spine. Since all women received supplements to ensure an adequate intake of calcium and other important bone nutrients, such as magnesium, zinc and vitamins C, K and D, this is the first long-term study to directly show the benefits of phytoestrogens over and above the effects of other nutrients.

In an Australian study conducted at the Royal Women's Hospital in Melbourne, postmenopausal women experienced a 5 per cent increase in bone mineral content when they ate 45 grams of soy grits every day for three months. The speed of this change is very surprising because it usually takes several years to increase bone mineral content by this amount. However, the direction of this finding is consistent with the first ever bone study in women which was conducted at the University of Illinois, in the US. Forty grams of soy protein taken each day for six months increased both bone mineral content and density in the spine.

Phytoestrogens work like osteoporosis medication

A medication named Ipriflavone was especially designed to conserve bone and prevent osteoporosis. Although it is a synthetic isoflavone, Ipriflavone is broken down in the body to produce daidzein, a phytoestrogen found in soy. So it was thought that phytoestrogens could work in a similar fashion.

While there is a wealth of evidence from animal studies that Ipriflavone protects bones, one recent study with 474 women from four different European countries didn't find any bone

CASE STUDY STELLA'S STORY

At the age of 73 Stella was diagnosed with severe osteo-porosis, having fractured her wrist and several ribs the previous year. She sought help from a nutritionist because her bone mineral density was so low—55% of a similarly aged woman—that she had been refused entry into a clinical trial of a new osteoporosis drug. She had always exercised regularly and eaten a diet that included calcium (though she was a lifelong coffee drinker —four cups a day—which promotes calcium loss). She had even taken a broad-spectrum daily vitamin and mineral supplement for the last 20 years. The major reason for her osteoporosis was that she went through menopause early at the age of 43. She tried hormone replacement therapy (HRT) for some months, but quit this due to mood swings and breast tenderness. No other options were offered by her doctor to compensate for her menopausal estrogen loss. The nutritionist advised Stella to increase the phytoestrogen content of her diet by including 500 mL of whole-bean soy milk daily. After drinking this for three months, Stella reported that it cleared her life-long constipation, improved her quality of life and lifted her mood. Importantly, scans done one and two years after starting with the soy milk revealed a gain of 2.1% and 2.5% respectively in bone mineral density of the spine (a total gain of 4.6% in two years) and that the bone density in her hip was stable during this time. After three years on her phytoestrogen-rich diet Stella maintains good health. She tolerates her soy milk very well and says she will never let go of it again. She claims to have an improved memory and is socially active. Remark-ably she has had no further fractures.

benefits from this synthetic isoflavone over a four-year period. Nevertheless, the early research on Ipriflavone provided the stimulus for scientists to consider that soy isoflavones may have beneficial effects on bone.

 Phytoestrogens protect bones in two ways—by restraining the bone-dissolving cells and stimulating the bone-forming cells.

What is not known

The ideal dosage of phytoestrogens for optimising bone health is not known. Until now, studies have given 45–90 mg of isoflavones per day, mostly to postmenopausal women, and not all have reported bone improvements—the reason being that most were not long term studies. Recent evidence from experiments with bone cells suggests that small amounts of phytoestrogens might be effective. This news is very encouraging for the prevention of osteoporosis.

Currently, there is one long-term study showing convincing evidence that phytoestrogens have bone-sparing effects in postmenopausal women. But more research is needed, particularly to determine whether these protectants reduce the number of fractures caused by osteoporosis, since this is the ultimate goal.

It is not known whether adherence to a phytoestrogen-rich diet earlier in life, especially before a woman enters the menopause, could be the most effective strategy for preventing osteoporosis. It is likely, on two counts. First, the substitution of vegetable protein for animal protein will conserve calcium in bone, and secondly, the phytoestrogens will favourably influence the activity of the bone-forming and bone-dissolving cells.

Boning up ... what we recommend

Both men and women are at risk of osteoporosis, though older women are most vulnerable because they have the lowest levels of estrogen and a much lower initial bone mineral density compared with men. Phytoestrogens can help to reduce bone loss, but based on studies where they have been taken just in the menopausal period, they cannot compete with the powerful effects of HRT. What is appealing to women electing not to use HRT is that phytoestrogens can offer at least some of the positive effects of estrogen without its side-effects.

We recommend a phytoestrogen-rich diet together with other lifestyle choices for building and maintaining healthy bones. These include being physically active, not smoking, drinking alcohol only in moderation if at all, cutting back on salt, animal protein and caffeine, and getting enough calcium, vitamin D, vitamin K and green vegetables. Finally, as convenient as phytoestrogens extracts or supplements seem, so far there is no convincing evidence that they provide the same bone benefits as phytoestrogen-rich foods.

chapter 7

Menopause made easier

'*Life is estrogen-dependent—ask any woman going through menopause*'
Dr Kenneth D.R. Setchell, 1995

No woman looks forward to menopause, yet the unpleasant symptoms can be vastly reduced by providing an alternative source of estrogen—phytoestrogens. These are natural estrogen mimics which help make up for the loss of estrogen enabling a smoother transition to postmenopausal life.

Phytoestrogens are the most widely studied of all natural therapies for managing the menopause. This chapter will show you how they can:

- reduce hot flushes
- keep the vagina from becoming dry
- maintain healthy cholesterol levels
- protect bones from osteoporosis

- possibly help maintain good skin condition
- possibly maintain brain function

What happens in menopause

Menopause occurs naturally when the ovaries cease producing their usual amounts of estrogen. It is accompanied by a 70 per cent drop in the body's estrogen levels. Menopause can also be induced in younger women by the surgical removal of the ovaries, and in such cases it can be extremely severe. Hot flushes are among the first noticeable results, yet there are even more serious long-term consequences—a greatly increased risk of heart disease and osteoporosis.

Hormone replacement therapy (HRT) is highly effective in correcting the estrogen deficiency of menopause. It counters the immediate symptoms and the long-term effects by replacing the body's estrogen with closely related estrogens—commonly obtained from the urine of pregnant horses. Yet many women reject HRT for fear of increased risk of breast cancer or because of the many side effects caused by these powerful drugs. Only 17 per cent of women in the UK use HRT when entering menopause, and the duration of use is relatively short for most. This is true for many other Western countries including the US. Surprisingly, 40 per cent of Australian women use HRT although most stop taking it after two to four years. Following the damaging findings on HRT from the Women's Health Initiative study—a significantly increased risk of breast cancer and no cardioprotective effects—many women have abruptly stopped taking HRT. Most physicians are now advised to prescribe HRT to healthy postmenopausal women only for treating hot flushes. Long-term use for prevention of heart disease and osteoporosis is generally being discouraged. Women are now seeking alternatives and research into alternative therapies is at an all-time high.

Phytoestrogens have caught the attention of health professionals because they are logical candidates as estrogen substitutes and they don't have the negative side effects of the estrogens in HRT. Phytoestrogens can be conveniently included in any diet through a range of tasty foods—and we show you how in Part III.

How phytoestrogens help

Hot flushes

Hot flushes are one of the classic symptoms of the menopause. They are particularly distressing because you have no control over where or when they occur. You could be enjoying dinner or the theatre and suddenly feel overwhelmed and in need of a shower.

Estrogen is a powerful regulator of the body's temperature. But when estrogen levels drop or fluctuate wildly as they do in middle-age, the body has difficulty regulating its heating and cooling. Fortunately for most women, hot flushes eventually disappear naturally as the body adjusts to living with low estrogen levels. Yet, 10 per cent of women will have them for the rest of their life.

Hot flushes are rare in women living in some countries. While 85 per cent of North American women will experience them, only 14 per cent of Singaporean women do. According to Dr Margaret Lock from McGill University, Canada, there is no specific word in the Japanese language used to describe hot flushes related to the menopause. A recent study from Fukuoka, Japan, reported less than 5 per cent of Japanese women felt hot flushes were a problem of menopause.

Researchers believe a diet rich in phytoestrogens accounts for the differences, because these compounds can act like estrogens.

In a six-year study of more than 1100 Japanese women tracked between the premenopausal and postmenopausal period a strong link was found between a high intake of soy products and isoflavones and a low occurrence of hot flushes. There is also anecdotal evidence that vegetarians who have high phyto-estrogen intakes cope better with the menopause.

Eleven out of 18 studies conducted around the world have shown that phytoestrogens influence the frequency or severity of hot flushes. Many have been criticised because there is a strong placebo effect, meaning almost anything can relieve hot flushes—and they go away with time, anyway. Not all studies have adequately taken this into account.

SUMMARY OF KEY FINDINGS ON PHYTOESTROGENS AND HOT FLUSHES

> Adding 40 g of soy flour per day to the diets of Australian women showed a 40 per cent reduction in hot flushes in just six weeks. A 25 per cent reduction occurred by adding the same amount of refined, unbleached wheat flour.

> There was a 45 per cent reduction in the intensity and severity of hot flushes after three months when a group of Italian women added 60 g of soy protein per day to their diet.

> Adding 20 g of soy protein each day for six weeks to the diets of American women reduced the intensity of hot flushes.

> In the only study of linseeds a 41 per cent reduction in hot flushes was reported after three months in postmenopausal women who consumed 45 g a day added to bread.

The studies using phytoestrogen-rich foods or diets have typically shown a 40–54 per cent reduction in symptoms, compared with a 25–35 per cent reduction if nothing is taken, or an amazing 80–90 per cent reduction with HRT. The effect of phytoestrogens is therefore modest, but many women swear they are helpful.

Phytoestrogens may not be effective in all women. Recent evidence from a Japanese study indicates that women who are able to produce equol when eating soy have very few hot flushes. The lack of effect in many studies could be related to the way isoflavones are handled by the body and particularly whether or not you are an equol producer (see Chapter 3). Far fewer people in Western countries are equol producers compared to the Japanese.

Tests on commercial phytoestrogen supplements and isoflavone extracts show generally disappointing results, despite advertising claims that they reduce hot flushes. Some studies have found no effects at all; others have found some reduction. A study from the Mayo Clinic in the US reported that a high-dose phytoestrogen supplement, 150 mg per day, did not relieve hot flushes in breast cancer survivors undergoing treatment with Tamoxifen or Raloxifene. However, these women are not representative of healthy women going through the menopause, so it is not surprising that phytoestrogens failed to counteract hot flushes caused by these powerful anti-estrogen drugs.

Soy and clover supplements are a convenient source of phytoestrogens, but evidence indicates that they seem unable to match the overall benefits of phytoestrogen-rich foods.

What is not known is whether consuming a phytoestrogen-rich diet well before reaching the middle years will provide even greater effects in relieving menopausal symptoms. This is, after all, the way Asian women and vegetarians typically consume phytoestrogens.

CASE STUDY MARIA'S STORY

Maria, a 55-year-old Italian woman, had been complaining of severe hot flushes for almost seven months. She had tried hormone replacement therapy (HRT) but stopped because of worsening migraines, weight gain and a rise in her blood pressure. Her flushes were now getting her down particularly because they were keeping her awake at night. She tried several other remedies, such as antidepressants and progesterone, but these weren't helpful either. Maria then heard about a trial of phytoestrogens for the prevention of hot flushes and volunteered to take part. She was given a powdered beverage each day for three months not knowing if she was taking one rich in phytoestrogens—this was soy based and contained 76 mg of isoflavones—or a placebo. She completed the study feeling very well. The frequency of her flushes decreased from 15 episodes each day before she started to only 1–2 a day during the trial. However, as soon as she completed the trial and stopped taking the powdered beverage her hot flushes came back with a vengeance. Again she tried different forms of HRT in an attempt to find relief but without any success. When the researchers finally broke the code, Maria discovered that she was one of the women who had received the phytoestrogen treatment. She was then convinced that it was soy with the phytoestrogens that helped relieve her flushes!

Vaginal dryness

The vagina naturally responds to sexual stimulus by becoming moist and lubricated. The cells that produce this lubrication are in turn stimulated by—guess what?—estrogen. When estrogen levels fall, as they do in menopause, the vagina becomes dry and sex can be painful and irritating.

Yet the cells that produce lubrication can actually be maintained by eating phytoestrogen-rich foods. A 1990 Melbourne study conducted by Dr Gisela Wilcox and Professor Mark Wahlqvist reported that women who included soy flour or linseeds in their diet for six weeks had more of these cells. Other studies have shown similar effects from soy protein and other phytoestrogen-rich foods such as tofu, soy milk and miso.

Cholesterol level

Heart disease is the number-one killer of women over 45 years of age. The risk rises dramatically during menopause because of rising cholesterol levels and the deterioration of blood vessels, both of which are linked to a decline in estrogen.

Phytoestrogen-rich diets can help maintain healthy cholesterol levels. A World Health Organization study found that the average blood cholesterol of Chinese adults is low (4.5 mmol/L) and only 20 per cent of those people have abnormal levels. Research suggests that Japanese people with the lowest blood cholesterol levels are the ones who eat the most soy protein. Western women can also benefit from soy. Studies have shown that postmenopausal women who supplemented their diets with soy protein experienced a 14 per cent improvement in levels of 'good' HDL-cholesterol in four weeks; and that an 8 per cent decrease in 'bad' LDL-cholesterol occurred in women who ate linseeds each day.

In the body, soy phytoestrogens are also good antioxidants. Evidence from research suggests that when phytoestrogens are consumed in food, they prevent cholesterol from oxidising into the really damaging form that is readily deposited in arteries and used to make plaque. Cholesterol in the blood of post-menopausal women was much less likely to become oxidised when the women drank soy milk or ate soy nuts daily. For more on how phytoestrogens benefit the heart and blood vessels, see Chapter 5.

Osteoporosis

Estrogen is vital to bones. It limits the activity of the cells that dissolve calcium from the bone, preventing the onset of osteoporosis. Osteoporosis places you at great risk of fracture as you age; the complications arising from hip fractures cause long-term disability and death. More women die each year following hip fractures than from breast cancer. So you can see how important it is to find a source of estrogen, especially if you are menopausal. Phytoestrogens have bone-sparing actions and this has been proven in animals where menopause has been simulated, and also in several human studies. Phytoestrogens are therefore an ideal alternative for women who can't or don't want to take HRT.

Bone cell activity was positively affected when post-menopausal women drank soy milk and ate soy nuts every day for 12 weeks, according to a recent study published in *Menopause*, the journal of the North American Menopause Society. Bone-dissolving cells became less active while bone-forming cells stepped up their activity. Similar findings have been reported in seven other human studies. Importantly, phyto-estrogens have also been found to be beneficial in the transitional period to menopause, called the perimenopause. Perimenopausal women prevented bone loss in their spine by supplementing their diets with soy protein over a six-month period, as reported in the *American Journal of Clinical Nutrition*.

In the latest two-year study from Denmark, soy milk containing naturally high levels of isoflavones prevented the loss of bone in the spine of postmenopausal women, yet soy milk specially formulated for the purposes of this study to contain very low isoflavone levels was ineffective. In the same study, natural progesterone cream similarly prevented bone loss. However, the combined treatment of phytoestrogen-rich soy milk and natural progesterone cream showed a negative interaction, resulting in loss of bone! This finding should caution women against combining both of these natural therapies as a substitute for HRT to gain bone protection.

For more detail on how to prevent osteoporosis, see Chapter 6.

Other benefits

Researchers speculate that phytoestrogens probably have many more benefits for women. This is based on our knowledge of what estrogens do, and from circumstantial evidence of studies in the following areas:

- *Healthy skin* Estrogen therapy helps keep skin moist and young looking, as well as maintaining its natural thickness. When estrogen levels drop, the skin becomes thinner, rougher and less elastic. Studies are now being carried out to see if phytoestrogens have any beneficial effects on the skin.

Early clinical trials of one manufactured soy cream have found it smoothes and moisturises the skin. See page 50.

- *Brain and reasoning* Cognition, the brain's ability to remember and process information, declines with ageing. The estrogens in HRT improve cognition and prior use of HRT lowers risk for Alzheimer's disease and dementia later in life. Phytoestrogens travel quickly to the brain, so there is reason to believe they could protect the brain in a similar way to estrogen.

- *Bladder control* Many postmenopausal women feel the urgent need of repeated trips to the bathroom. This is because menopause, a period of declining estrogen levels, causes muscles in the pelvic floor to lose their tone. As a result, urinary tract infections become more common. Since estrogens appear to help correct some of these problems, researchers have questioned whether phytoestrogens may be helpful—but it's too soon to know.

Alternative therapies

The use of alternative therapies is prevalent in England. Almost one in two adults has visited a natural therapist or used complementary medicines at some stage in their life, according to a 1998 study from the University of Sheffield. The annual out-of-pocket spending is estimated to be £450 million. Great claims are made for products such as dong quai, black cohosh, wild yam, progesterone creams, evening primrose oil, ginkgo biloba, bioflavonoids, vitamin E, licorice, sage, and vervain for the relief of menopausal symptoms. However, these claims are based on scant evidence. By contrast, phytoestrogens have been the most extensively studied of all the natural therapies over the past decade and the evidence for their role in the menopause is stronger.

Not all products that promise phytoestrogens actually deliver—some simply create 'expensive urine'. When we analysed 34 different 'menopause products' at the University of Cincinnati, almost half did not contain what the label promised and a few had almost no phytoestrogens at all. If you choose to use these supplements select those marketed by the major pharmaceutical companies because these are more likely to be labelled correctly. See pages 288–9 for a list of the supplements tested.

Menopause without drugs

Today's women can expect to live 30–40 per cent of their time after the menopause. To avoid the minefield of health problems that occur during this period of estrogen deficiency, we believe that all women should take some form of estrogen.

What you take is your choice, but it is important to discuss all the options with your GP first. Phytoestrogens taken in foods, although less effective than the potent estrogens in HRT, offer a natural alternative without side effects, unless you take unusually large quantities on a regular basis. There may be more to gain by eating phytoestrogen-rich foods well before entering the menopause. This is the normal dietary practice in countries with low rates of menopausal problems.

Eat and drink phytoestrogens more than once per day so that your levels stay 'topped-up'. Natural food sources are best. While they are convenient, phytoestrogen supplements do not offer all the benefits of foods. The North American Menopause Society's recent Consensus Opinion paper on isoflavones in menopausal health recommends that it is preferable to con-sume isoflavones from whole foods to gain potential health benefits. You can get phytoestrogens from a great variety of meals and snacks, such as stir-fried vegetables with tofu, soy burgers, strawberry soy shakes, or a bowl of sweet-tasting Edamame. The recipes on pages 189–280 show just how deli-cious and easy this can be.

chapter 8

Ageing without losing your marbles!

'Old age isn't so bad when you consider the alternative'
MAURICE CHEVALIER

Most of us know of someone with severely impaired brain function and the emotional toll this has on the family cannot be underestimated. The Alzheimer's Society estimates that there are currently over 700,000 people in the UK with dementia—with approximately 55 per cent of those having Alzheimer's disease. These numbers are predicted to rise steadily as our population ages. Worldwide, nearly 18 million people are estimated currently to have dementia, and by the year 2025 this figure is expected to rise to around 34 million. More than 70 per cent of these people will be living in developing countries.

What causes Alzheimer's disease and dementia is not known. Autopsy examinations reveal that major changes occur in the brain—it becomes riddled with abnormal proteins that entangle themselves throughout the tissue. As the disease

WHAT'S KNOWN ABOUT ALZHEIMER'S DISEASE

> There are two main forms of Alzheimer's—an early-onset form which strikes anywhere from the ages of 30 to 70 years and appears to be genetic, often running in families. More commonly, Alzheimer's disease occurs later in life and is more sporadic with no obvious genetic link.

> It is about 1.5 times more common in women than men.

> It seems to be more common in people living in urban, rather than rural areas.

advances there is a loss of the normal connections between the brain's nerve cells, so that the electrical signals carrying information cannot be successfully transmitted.

There is a clear link between hormone levels, brain function and mood. Estrogens seem to have a protective effect on the brain. In some people with Alzheimer's, estrogens slow the rate at which this disease progresses, and researchers are now investigating if phytoestrogens could offer similar benefits. In this chapter we show you early evidence from monkey studies suggesting that soy phytoestrogens might also reduce the risk of Alzheimer's disease in women.

Estrogens are important for brain function

Many substances cannot pass into the brain because we have a 'blood–brain barrier'. This is an intelligent gatekeeper because it only lets certain molecules through and protects the brain from many toxic substances. Estrogens, however, readily cross this barrier and get into brain cells. Several lines of evidence show how important estrogens are for normal brain function in women, but their role in men is less obvious. Perhaps this is because, unlike postmenopausal women, men maintain relatively constant blood estrogen levels as they age.

Scientists have shown that nerve cells in the brain can be stimulated to grow and sprout more junctions when estrogen is present. These junctions contain the essential chemicals that help electrical signals to be transmitted from one nerve to the next. In other words, these enable the brain cells to talk to each other. In the brain of people with Alzheimer's, however, these junctions are gradually lost. As a consequence, messages are unable to pass between different regions of the brain, leading to memory loss and decline in cognition. Using sophisticated Magnetic Resonance Imaging (MRI) techniques a study presented at a 1998 annual meeting of the North American Menopause Society was able to show that the brain of postmenopausal women had much higher levels of the important chemical transmitter choline if estrogen was administered. Drug companies are constantly seeking ways to increase the brain's production of choline for many brain diseases, because without it there is no way for signals to be sent from one brain cell to the next.

A multicentre survey of over 2800 postmenopausal women, coordinated by the University of Florence in Italy, found that women who had previously taken HRT were four times less likely to develop Alzheimer's disease. Several clinical studies of people with Alzheimer's disease have also shown that taking estrogen can slow the progression of the disease and improve short-term memory loss.

Yet, when women hit the menopause, there is an abrupt decline in estrogen levels, which brings with it a progressive decline in cognition for many—the ability to process information, to perceive, think and reason. Also, steep declines in estrogen during other stages of a woman's life often result in large swings in mood. Many women will readily testify experiencing mood swings with PMT, or after childbirth. So it seems that some kind of intervention is needed to influence estrogen levels and protect brain function, particularly after menopause.

Diet can affect estrogen levels

Diet has a powerful influence on estrogen status. Considerable differences in estrogen levels have been reported for vegetarians, and drinking alcohol has a marked effect in altering estrogen metabolism. In South-East Asian countries, where the diet is high in phytoestrogens, the rate of dementia is lower than in Europe, according to research published in the scientific journal *Neurology*. The type of dementia most common in Asia also differs from that seen in Western countries. In Japan, for example, vascular dementia, a form that involves the blood vessels, is more common than Alzheimer's. The risk of vascular dementia is increased by high-salt diets—one of the few undesirable aspects of the Japanese diet. However, Asians fare better when it comes to Alzheimer's, which destroys the minds of almost a quarter of all older Australians.

Do phytoestrogens protect the brain?

If estrogens are so important for the brain, can phytoestrogens in the diet have similar effects and benefits?

There are at least two reasons why phytoestrogens could be good candidates in the fight against Alzheimer's and the cognitive decline we see with ageing. First, after we eat phytoestrogens and they are absorbed into the blood, they quickly find their way to the brain. Secondly, when they get there they can dock to the brain's estrogen receptors. In Chapter 2 we explained how estrogen receptors are the 'ports' to which phytoestrogens dock to provide 'estrogen-like' effects. The brain is rich in estrogen receptors—presumably for a good reason. In particular, the brain has ample amounts of the estrogen receptor beta, to which phytoestrogens prefer to dock.

This knowledge has prompted recent research to determine whether eating a phytoestrogen-rich diet is beneficial. Although this area of research is still in its infancy, promising findings are already emerging.

American studies, for example, have shown that monkeys receiving soy isoflavones display fewer Alzheimer's-linked changes in the brain; and that soy promoted the production of a protein essential for good brain function in rats. People with Alzheimer's have significantly reduced levels of this protein. In a South Australian study of the relationship between soy and wellbeing, the people with the highest intake of soy foods such as soy milk, soy and linseed bread, soy cereal, soy sprouts and tofu were also the least confused. This finding may have significant cost implications for our ageing population, since short-term memory loss often leads to nursing home admissions.

The thousands of blood vessels that permeate the brain may be protected by high levels of phytoestrogens. As discussed in Chapter 5, phytoestrogens help to relax blood vessels, improve the flow of blood through them and protect them against the build-up of plaque. These positive effects are important in the brain because some forms of dementia are caused by restrictions in blood flow to the brain—images of the brain of people with dementia usually show extensive narrowing of the large and small blood vessels.

Improving memory

In a study of male and female students at Kings College, London, a phytoestrogen-rich diet significantly improved memory in just ten weeks, based on several psychological tests. The students were fed 100 mg phytoestrogens daily via a range of soy foods, including commercially available products such as soy milk and soy puddings, and meals prepared with textured vegetable protein and soy flour. The phytoestrogen-rich diet was also reported to reduce anxiety.

CASE STUDY   LYNN'S STORY

Lynn, a housewife aged 58 years, was getting increasingly frustrated by her forgetfulness. She noticed that she misplaced her keys more frequently and was constantly rechecking whether she had left her household appliances on. In an attempt to get some help, Lynn volunteered to take part in a clinical trial where she was asked to increase her phytoestrogen intake. In addition to her usual diet, Lynn consumed two soy bars each day. Each bar contained 20 mg of isoflavones. After 10 weeks of taking these bars, she was amazed at how much better she was coping with everyday life and had regained her self-confidence. She no longer needed to check things she had already done and was convinced that this had improved her memory.

Tofu and Alzheimer's

No study has yet been specifically designed to find out if eating phytoestrogen-rich foods can help brain function in the long term.

One general study on dementia, which considered only 27 foods in the diet, suggested that tofu contributed to early brain ageing in a particular group of American–Japanese men living on the island of Oahu in Hawaii. Men who ate tofu two or more times per week during their middle years were found to have smaller brain weights and lower test scores of brain function later in life. While initially causing some alarm, the study did not show that phytoestrogens were responsible for the declining brain function. Miso, another phytoestrogen-rich food, was also consumed by these men but was not linked to adverse brain function. In conclusion, the researchers of the study stated that age, education and history of stroke were the most important predictors of declining brain function, explaining 27.8 per cent of the difference in test scores of thinking ability. The influence of tofu was deemed to be less than 1 per cent.

Findings from the Adventist Health Study in the US have shown that meat eaters are more than twice as likely to develop dementia compared to vegetarians. Vegetarians are the ones that universally consume a phytoestrogen-rich diet—and the appearance of dementia seems to be delayed in these people.

Think about it

Estrogens are important for maintaining optimal brain function. Studies in young adults have shown that a phytoestrogen-rich diet improves memory and reduces anxiety. Early research is suggesting that soy phytoestrogens might even reduce the risk of Alzheimer's disease in women, but more research is required to confirm this. Studies are now underway at several universities to evaluate the effectiveness of phytoestrogen-rich diets for maintaining cognition and preventing dementia.

Phytoestrogens: fighters of many diseases

*'The art of medicine consists of amusing the patient while
Nature cures the disease'*
VOLTAIRE, 1788

If you eat a phytoestrogen-rich diet, the benefits may go beyond just helping to prevent cancer and heart disease, our biggest killers. Experts in the field agree that phytoestrogens have a wide range of important biological effects. They may be helpful against many less common, but just as unwelcome, conditions. In this chapter we explain how phytoestrogens might benefit:

- alcoholism—by lessening intoxication and dependence on alcohol;
- cystic fibrosis—by reducing the mucus that builds up in the lungs;
- endometriosis—by preventing and relieving painful symptoms;

- hereditary haemorrhagic telangiectasia—by stopping nose bleeds, headaches and migraines;
- inflammatory diseases—by reducing the inflammation that causes conditions such as rheumatoid arthritis and psoriasis; and
- kidney disease—by relaxing blood vessels and reducing the work load on the kidneys.

Alcoholism

For centuries, a number of traditional remedies based on plant extracts have been used in Asia to treat alcohol intoxication. The active ingredients were largely unknown until a series of scientific studies from two different groups of researchers showed that phytoestrogens lessened alcohol dependence.

Scientists at the Henan Medical Institute in the People's Republic of China fed an extract of the Chinese vine *Pueraria lobata*, also known as kudzu, to 'alcohol-dependent' rats and found they recovered very quickly from the sleep induced by alcohol. In a search for the active ingredient it was found that this edible vine has high levels of phytoestrogens. These were identified as daidzin and daidzein, the same isoflavones found in soybeans, and another closely related isoflavone called puerarin.

Tests with these pure phytoestrogens have confirmed that they work just as well by themselves. Scientists involved in alcohol research in America have shown that when either kudzu or these phytoestrogens are fed to a unique genetically bred species of rat—one that loves to drink alcohol—the animals drink about 70 per cent less alcohol.

The kudzu plant was introduced to the US in the late 1800's from China and is now growing rampantly over trees and bushes along interstate highways in the southern States. It has become a major ecological disaster because it displaces native plants, grows at up to 0.5 metre per day and is impossible to eradicate. In 1999, President Clinton signed an executive order to create a task force to eradicate non-native plants, including kudzu. But perhaps there is a potential use for the plant.

How phytoestrogens lessen alcohol dependence is unknown, but several studies have shown two effects. Phytoestrogens both slow the rate of alcohol absorption from the stomach and alter the way in which it is broken down in the liver. Interestingly, the Chinese metabolise alcohol differently and drunkenness is claimed not to be a problem in China.

All of these findings have prompted the question of whether a phytoestrogen-rich diet can reduce the effects of alcohol in people who are alcoholics. The National Institutes of Health in the US have funded clinical trials in alcoholics to see how effective phytoestrogens can be in treating such patients. Could it be that bars and pubs in the future will also offer soy drinks and soy nuts to help lessen intoxication of their customers, just like many now provide breathalysers to measure blood alcohol levels? In the UK there are many herbal over the counter products listed with the Medicine Control Agency containing kudzu for a variety of ailments.

Cystic fibrosis

Cystic fibrosis (CF) is the most common genetic disorder in Caucasians, affecting one in every 2000 newborn babies. Every week in the UK one baby is born with CF. There are presently 7500 people living in Britain with this disease and most are under 25 years of age. It is caused by mutations in the gene responsible for making a protein called CFTR, that is essential for the movement of salt in and out of cells, especially those that line the lungs and intestine. The result is that thick mucus secretions build up in the lungs making them prone to bacterial infections and causing breathing difficulties. The mucus also obstructs the pancreas stopping it from making the enzymes needed for normal digestion of food. In 1964 life expectancy for CF was just five years. Good nutrition and antibiotics have greatly improved the life of people with CF. According to the UK Cystic Fibrosis Trust, children born today with CF can expect to live into their thirties. However, much of this time is spent in and out of hospitals fighting lung disease and having the lungs cleared of mucus. New evidence is emerging suggesting phytoestrogens might be helpful in the fight against this mucus build-up.

Phytoestrogens block the harmful effects of bacteria that frequently invade the lungs of people with CF, causing more mucus to be formed. They can do this by switching off an enzyme called tyrosine kinase. Genistein, the major phytoestrogen found in soy, also seems to open an alternative passage to help salt move in and out of cells. This may further help reduce the mucus build-up in the lungs. The Cystic Fibrosis Foundation of North America is now funding studies to clarify just how helpful genistein may be to people with CF.

Endometriosis

Endometriosis occurs in about 10 per cent of women of childbearing age. It arises when cells from the lining of the uterus migrate into the pelvic cavity or abdomen—often near the ovaries—where they proceed to grow uncontrollably. In doing so, they appear to make their own supply of estrogen, which fuels their continued growth. While not life-threatening, this condition may lead to inflammation, severe pelvic or abdominal pain, and less commonly irregular periods and bleeding—it can even result in infertility.

Phytoestrogens might be effective in relieving endometriosis or helping prevent it, because of their ability to antagonise the effects of estrogens. The symptoms of endometriosis seem to be least severe when estrogen levels fall, as happens after the menopause. Smoking also lowers estrogen levels, as does exercise. And both seem to bring about relief in many women, though we obviously wouldn't recommend smoking! When all treatments fail, women may elect to have surgery to remove the large cysts that have formed, or the ovaries, thereby reducing estrogen levels (most estrogen is made in the ovaries). While high estrogen levels seem to be linked to endometriosis, interestingly pregnancy also relieves the symptoms, yet this is a period when many hormone levels are high and the body is swamped with estrogens! This paradox makes endometriosis a poorly understood disease and, consequently, difficult to treat.

Phytoestrogens might be helpful for endometriosis because of their ability to act in other ways as well. First, they block the enzyme aromatase required by the rogue cells growing outside the uterus to make estrogens. Secondly, they have anti-inflammatory benefits.

Unlike estrogens, phytoestrogens do not appear to be harmful to the uterus unless they are consumed in huge doses beyond what could be reasonably taken in foods. We are aware of a few isolated cases of uterine bleeding in women who took larger than usual doses of supplements. This reinforces our recommendation to be cautious in using supplements. Three studies on supplements showed that phytoestrogens taken in doses of 50 mg or less per day have no adverse effects on the uterus of either pre- or postmenopausal women. Similarly a study conducted at the University of Minnesota found no negative effects on the endometrium of young women who consumed high levels of isoflavones from soy protein over a three-month period. When monkeys were fed phytoestrogens at normal dietary levels and from natural foods, there was no harm to the uterus during the six months of study. One study from a research group at the Bowman Gray School of Medicine in the US, showed that soy phytoestrogens actually opposed and blunted the harmful effects in the uterus normally seen with estrogens.

So far, there have been no clinical studies performed to determine whether phytoestrogens relieve or prevent endometriosis in women, but since they do not appear to have the harmful effects of estrogens it seems logical to consider that they could be of some benefit.

Hereditary haemorrhagic telangiectasia (nosebleed syndrome)

Hereditary haemorrhagic telangiectasia (HHT) is a rare genetic disorder that causes chronic nosebleeds, severe headaches and even intestinal bleeding. These symptoms arise because of deformities in the connections between capillaries (small blood vessels), making them prone to rupture which leads to bleeding. Estrogens are usually used to treat HHT but research has found that phytoestrogens are also effective in preventing the nosebleeds and migraines.

In a study of eight people with HHT it was found that eating soy protein led to either complete relief or a vast improvement in symptoms, by reducing the number of nosebleeds these people experienced. Those who suffered persistent migraines found that soy protein completely relieved their headaches. Only one patient in the study did not appear to benefit from this phytoestrogen-rich food. Based on this study from the Yale School of Medicine it is tempting to suggest that phytoestrogens might be helpful for migraines and headaches, but it is too early to tell. More research is needed.

Inflammatory diseases

To many people, the word 'inflammation' conjures images of the painful redness and swelling they experience when grazing their skin. Inflammation is, in fact, a more complex condition. A silent and central process that occurs in the background of many diseases, it is an early stage in most cancers and is involved in the damaging of blood vessels that ultimately leads to heart disease. Diseases specifically known as 'inflammatory diseases' include rheumatoid arthritis, inflammatory bowel disease, Crohn's disease, ulcerative colitis, septic shock and the skin conditions of psoriasis, dermatitis and acne. Inflammation accounts for a great deal of distress and suffering, but how does it arise?

Inflammation is usually the result of some sort of injury to cells. If bacteria or viruses for example, attack cells, substances are released that set up a complex cascade of reactions that ultimately cause the inflammation. One of these substances is nitric oxide, a powerful and damaging free radical that attacks DNA and alters the structure of many proteins and fats in the body. To be able to block inflammation is one of the holy grails of medicine. If this could be done effectively, it would help prevent and manage many common diseases.

Phytoestrogens have anti-inflammatory properties. Genistein has been shown to act in several beneficial ways: it blocks one of the enzymes, called iNOS, that cause nitric oxide to be made and additionally behaves as an antioxidant, mopping up free radicals formed during the inflammatory process.

Kidney disease

We rarely think about our kidneys and generally only appreciate their importance when we know of someone on dialysis. The kidneys are essential for filtering out the toxins from blood. They work very hard to do this and at times we place them under a great deal of added stress. For example, eating a large piece of beef greatly increases the rate at which blood is filtered through the kidneys, more so than chicken or fish. A diet high in animal protein, as has become popular for rapid weight loss, puts a tremendous burden on the kidneys. By contrast, soy protein has a neutral effect on the kidneys and is a rich source of phytoestrogens.

In a study at Leicester General Hospital in the UK, it was found that replacing dairy protein with soy protein in the diet slowed the rate at which kidney disease progressed in rats. It also prolonged the time before dialysis or transplantation was needed for survival. Canadian researchers have reported similar observations when phytoestrogen-rich linseed was included in the diet. In another study of mice, soy protein reduced cyst development thereby preventing polycystic kidney disease. The same benefits could apply to people.

What is not yet know is whether phytoestrogens play a specific role. Phytoestrogens pass through the kidneys in relatively high concentrations on their way out of the body. A number of laboratory studies suggest kidney benefits—genistein, for example, seems to make the blood vessels in the kidneys relax.

Several studies undertaken at the University of Kentucky in the US show that soy protein containing phytoestrogens is beneficial for people with kidney disease. In one eight-week study of young type-1 diabetics, substituting soy protein for a proportion of animal protein in the diet significantly reduced stress on the kidneys by lowering the rate at which fluid is filtered through the kidneys. This rate of filtration is high in people with kidney disease, thereby causing further damage to the kidneys. In a second study, a soy protein drink containing phytoestrogens boosted the immune system in people with end-stage kidney disease. This finding has important implications because these people are prone to serious complications from a compromised immune system.

People in Japan with kidney disease have better survival rates than comparable people living in Western countries. One reason for this could be the high phytoestrogen content of the typical Japanese diet—although this is speculative. Given the rapidly increasing rate of obesity and diabetes in Western populations, and the fact that kidney disease is a major long-term complication of diabetes, increasing the dietary intake of vegetable proteins such as soy with their constituent phytoestrogens may well be beneficial.

chapter 10

Protect your child

'Death from coronary heart disease may be the price paid for
successful adaptations to undernutrition in early life'
PROFESSOR D.J.P. BARKER FRS, 2001

It's a fact—what we eat in early life may be one of the most important determinants of our susceptibility to disease when we get older. Research is also showing that what our mothers ate during pregnancy plays a large role too.

As we have discussed, Asians living a traditional lifestyle consume a phytoestrogen-rich diet, as do vegetarians. A recent study of the diets of over 4800 Japanese adults found that, on average, 56–60 g of soy foods are eaten daily. This translates to about 15–30 mg of isoflavones each day. Estimates of daily isoflavone intakes for Chinese adults have been put at 30–40 mg while even higher intakes are common in Indonesia. Of course, some people will consume less and others more.

In Asian cultures phytoestrogens are typically introduced in infancy, but the baby will have already been exposed to them in the womb. Mothers consume phytoestrogens in their diet during pregnancy and these phytoprotectants cross the placenta and reach the developing foetus. This early exposure to phyto-estrogens may explain why Asians have very low rates of many cancers. Yet those who migrate to another country, where the diet is deficient in phytoestrogens, lose this protection within several generations.

This chapter looks at exciting new evidence from animal studies showing that early intake of phytoestrogens can pro-tect the breast and prostate gland from cancer later in life.

Switching on breast protection

As we discussed in Chapter 4, Drs Coral Lamartiniere and Nadine Brown made some fascinating observations in 1994 at the University of Alabama relating to what happens if animals are given phytoestrogens early in life. Their research followed on from earlier findings by Drs Stephen Barnes and Kenneth Setchell that feeding soy protein to adult rats protected them from breast cancer caused by chemicals. These researchers asked whether giving soy phytoestrogens much earlier in life improves their already proven anticancer effects. Astoundingly, genistein ingested even for short periods of time in early life reduced the number of tumours that later formed, to a much greater extent than when it was given in adulthood. Although these studies were done with rats, scientists believe the find-ings are of relevance to women because of the similarities in the way the human and the rat breast develops.

How can the simple exposure to something in our diet have such dramatic effects in protecting against breast cancer? Studies have shown that phytoestrogens change the way the breast develops by causing a greater number of cancer-resistant structures called lobules to be formed. We described this in more detail in Chapter 4. It is now thought that these beneficial changes to the breast architecture may explain why the rates of breast cancer in Asian countries are so low.

In another comparable animal study, the same long-term benefits were seen if the body's own estrogen was given in early life. Pregnancy is a time when a woman's estrogen level is at an all-time high and it is also associated with decreased risk of breast cancer, especially if it occurs at an early age. The protective effect of pregnancy is thought to be due to the breast being stimulated by the extra estrogen to make more of the cancer-resistant lobules. This is the one time in a woman's life when high estrogen levels are actually not harmful, but good for the breasts.

Shielding the prostate

Early-life effects of phytoestrogens are not confined to the breast. Similar benefits have been found to occur in the prostate of male rats. Studies by a research team in Finland found that a phytoestrogen-rich diet fed to three-day-old rats protected the prostate from the adverse effects of a very potent drug called DES. This drug used to be prescribed to women in early pregnancy to prevent spontaneous abortions. It was withdrawn, however, because it caused severe abnormalities and cancer in the reproductive system of the sons and daughters born to these women. In separate studies at Brigham Young University in the US, feeding phytoestrogen-rich diets to either young or adult rats caused them to develop a smaller sized but nevertheless, normal prostate gland. And, in one strain of rat, the animals had lower blood testosterone levels, a factor important in prostate cancer prevention.

Research has shown that African-American men have the highest levels of testosterone and the highest death rates from prostate cancer, while Japanese men have low testosterone levels and very low death rates from this disease.

When best to get phytoestrogens

Based on the studies in this area, consuming phytoestrogen-rich diets early in life may be the key to lowering the risk of breast and prostate cancers in the long term: phytoestrogen-rich diets can be seen as providing an insurance policy against degenerative diseases. Unfortunately, the British diet lacks phytoestrogens, and infants and children are probably missing out on any potential long-term benefits. There is much to be learned from the lifestyles of those living in Asian countries.

> >   **Maximum phytoprotection = early intake of phytoestrogens + lifelong intake of phytoestrogens.**   < <

Pregnancy

Scientists at the University of Helsinki and Monash University have shown that when phytoestrogens are consumed during pregnancy, they readily cross the placenta and reach the developing baby. This is true in humans and animals. Asian and vegetarian women do not stop eating their usual diets when they become pregnant and they deliver perfectly healthy babies with good health statistics in the longer term. In the scientific journal *Laboratory Medicine* it was reported that newborn rats delivered by mothers that had been fed a diet of soy had very high levels of isoflavones in their blood, but the animals were all born normal. In fact, the food given to raise most laboratory animals contains high levels of phytoestrogens—these come from added soy protein and alfalfa. And more than 90 per cent of the soybeans grown in the US are used to produce soymeal, a high quality soy protein that is fed to livestock and other animals such as poultry and pigs.

There is no logical reason to stop consuming phytoestrogen-rich foods if you become pregnant, and certainly no evidence that they harm your unborn child.

Infants

Ideally, breast milk should be the first choice of nutrition for all babies. Other than being perfectly designed to provide for the nutritional needs of the infant, breast milk contains immune-boosting factors not found in any formulas. One published article has misleadingly suggested that breast milk is a useful source of phytoestrogens. But according to two separate studies, human breast milk has a very low content of phyto-estrogens, and even when soy foods are consumed by the mother the levels increase only ten-fold.

For babies who cannot be breast-fed, a specialised infant formula should be used. Studies show that over 80 per cent of babies are fed formula at some point in their life from one to twelve months of age. This is a large proportion. In most cases, cow-milk formula is used, but in the US 18 per cent of these infants are fed soy infant formula. In the UK and other European countries soy formula feeding is less prevalent. According to the 'Infant Feeding 2000' report from the

Department of Health, only 2 per cent of infants are fed soy formula during the first year of life.

Traditionally, very few infants were bottle-fed in Asia, but in today's urbanised societies such as Singapore and Hong Kong, it is rare for infants to be exclusively breast-fed after three months. In some countries such as South Korea around 90 per cent of infants are now bottle-fed. Again, the use of cow's milk formula predominates. Soy infant formulas have mostly been used by vegetarians and for babies with an allergy to cow's milk protein, rare genetic disorders or lactose intolerance. Since lactose intolerance is much more common in Asia, soy-based formulas have played a critical role in saving the lives of many infants.

Infants fed soy formula are unique because they ingest large amounts of phytoestrogens. In the USA and other Western countries, soy formulas are made from soy protein isolate—the natural protein obtained from the soybean. A four-month-old infant fed soy formula gets as much phytoestrogens each day as an adult eating one to two serves of soy protein-rich foods. This is considerable given the difference in size of a baby and an adult. Korean babies fed soy formula made from whole soybeans consume almost five times more phytoestrogens than Western babies. Also, the earliest soy formulas used in America were made from soy flours and these delivered much higher levels of phytoestrogens than today's formulas, where some losses occur during the manufacture of the soy protein.

For a while, it was not known if a baby could absorb the phytoestrogens from soy formula until a study from the Children's Hospital Medical Center in Cincinnati showed that a four-month-old infant had blood levels that were almost ten times higher than that of adults consuming similar amounts of isoflavones from soy foods. This is because babies are repeatedly fed formula every four to six hours, sort of 'main-lining' soy foods, so high blood levels are maintained. Adults tend to eat food at intervals. In between these times the blood levels of phytoestrogens rise and fall repeatedly, especially if soy foods are eaten just once a day.

In a 1997 article in the *Lancet*, we first proposed that if an infant has high blood levels of phytoestrogens, then biological effects can be expected. The question since then has been what type of effects. We don't believe phytoestrogens pose any threat to the infant. On the contrary, we think the phytoestrogens in soy formulas are more likely to provide positive long-term health effects of the type we have already seen from a number of animal studies described earlier. An infant fed soy formula may be advantaged by a phytoestrogen-rich diet from this early stage of life.

Since 1960, when modern-day soy formulas were introduced in the US, about 18 million American infants have been raised on soy formulas and there have been no reports in the medical and scientific literature to indicate these formulas are unsafe.

Toddlers

In Asian countries, it is the custom to introduce phytoestrogen-rich foods such as tofu early into the diet when giving solids. Asian mothers feed infants tofu because it is soft, easily digestible, inexpensive and a readily available good source of protein. Many Buddhist monks are also reared on soy products without ever tasting animal milk or any animal product. British babies, on the other hand, are rarely fed these foods unless their parents are vegetarian. On the whole, most toddlers get very small amounts of phytoestrogens in their diet, if any. Yet it makes sense to introduce such health foods to all kids. A range of phytoestrogen-containing foods could be offered when solids are given, including soft cooked vegetables, mashed or stewed fruits, wholegrain cooked breakfast cereals such as rolled oats and rich sources such as mashed soybeans and other legumes such as soft cooked lentils.

Children and adolescents

There are serious concerns over how children in Western societies are growing up today. High rates of obesity and elevated cholesterol levels, increasingly seen in children, are warning signs that disease will likely strike prematurely in adult life. Inadequate physical activity is at the core of these problems. But a diet with a large proportion of fast foods, refined snacks and fizzy drinks is a major contributor because it lacks phytoprotectants.

Children in Asian countries, where phytoestrogen-rich diets are eaten, tend to have lower cholesterol levels like their parents and obesity is less of a problem. Early exposure to these diets brings good health statistics in adult life.

A new study has shown that a high soy intake during adolescence may reduce the risk of breast cancer in later life. This study of over 3000 Chinese women found that those who had consumed the largest amount of soy foods as adolescents had a 50 per cent lower risk of breast cancer as adults, compared with women who had consumed lower levels. The self-reported intakes were in accordance with the intakes claimed by the participants' mothers, arguing against the possibility of this being a chance finding. Paediatricians now appreciate that disease programming occurs early in life and is, to a large extent, dictated by what we eat. In particular, infancy and adolescence are the two windows of opportunity in which diet can impact to reprogram our risk of disease later in life.

A phytoestrogen-rich diet is likely to have many advantages for a growing child beyond just its phytoestrogen content. The plant proteins and lower cholesterol and saturated fat content should help prevent blood cholesterol from rising, protecting the heart and blood vessels from long-term damage. Alarmingly, in the US for example, more than 26 million children have elevated cholesterol levels! Data from the British Heart Foundation show that one-quarter of all 16–25 year-olds also have high cholesterol levels.

>> Phytoestrogens and the hundreds of other phytoprotectants that come packaged in a plant-rich diet will help guard against a spectrum of degenerative diseases. <<

The high fibre content of the phytoestrogen-rich diet we promote in this book will also help with bowel regularity. Many children and adolescents suffer from constipation; this is easily relieved with an adequate fibre intake.

Promoting healthy eating habits in childhood is the key to healthy adulthood.

Are there any risks?

With the exception of a small proportion of infants (about 0.5 per cent) that have allergies to soy protein, there have been no obvious health problems associated with the intake of phytoestrogen-rich foods by infants and children living either in Asia or Western countries. Many children have been raised as vegetarians from birth and their protein source has included soy foods. And it would be difficult to convince any vegetarian that soy foods are bad for you.

But some people have questioned whether the apparent lack of negative effects may be because nobody has specifically looked for them. Common sense tells us that given the extremely large population of Asia and the estimated 18 million infants raised on soy formulas in the US since 1960, if problems existed, they would have become evident. To address the issue of whether there are any delayed negative effects of feeding soy infant formula, researchers at the University of Iowa conducted a study that examined young adults who had been fed this formula as infants. The researchers found that there was no statistically significant difference in males or females fed either soy- or cow's milk-based formula in many variables including adult height, weight, body mass index, infertility, the timing of puberty and a large number of other non-reproductive outcomes such as cancer. In response to these findings, Dr Pat Touhy, a paediatrician and advisor on soy infant formula to the New Zealand Ministry of Health, was quoted as saying 'This is the first study of its kind and as such is very important' and 'parents should be reassured'.

What about specific areas of potential concern?

• *Growth and development* Some people have suggested that soy infant formula might compromise growth and development in humans. However, numerous studies from leading medical universities on thousands of babies fed soy infant formula have repeatedly shown that their growth and development is no different from babies fed other formulas or breast milk. A recent multicentre study by the Departments of Pediatrics at the Universities of Pittsburg, Utah and Kansas confirmed that there were no differences in rates of growth of soy formula-fed and breast-fed infants, as measured from height, weight and head circumference. The American Academy of Pediatrics deems soy protein based formulas to be 'safe and effective alternatives to provide appropriate nutrition for growth and development'. The only exceptions to using soy or other standard cow's milk infant formula are for pre-term babies and newborns weighing under 1.8 kg. This is because such infants need highly specialised formulas to help their growth and development.

- *Immune function* People opposed to the use of soy formula have suggested that the immune system of soy-fed infants might be compromised. However, several studies have shown that healthy full-term babies fed soy formula have the same immune response to vaccinations as babies fed other types of milk/formula.

- *Timing of puberty* Some people have speculated that phytoestrogens might delay the onset of puberty in boys and cause earlier puberty in girls. Dr Frank Biro of the Children's Hospital Medical Center in Cincinnati, one of the world's experts in this field, states that the proportion of boys with delayed puberty is the same in America today as it was 30 years ago. In recent times, however, girls have entered puberty earlier. This is attributed to better nutrition and has no relationship to phytoestrogens. In fact, the age of onset of puberty in girls is later in Asia, where soy is a staple of the diet.

- *Gender orientation* Media stories have implied that phyto-estrogens or soy foods cause homosexuality or feminisation. This is pure speculation that has no credible basis.

- *Fertility* The suggestion that phytoestrogens may cause infer-tility in humans is totally unfounded. People in Asia do not have a problem with reproduction. In China, government regulations have for many years limited the number of preg-nancies to curb the population explosion. Reproductive problems, however, have occurred in several animal species, notably the sheep and the cheetah. In the 1940s, when sheep in Western Australia grazed on clover-rich pastures, they consumed amounts of phytoestrogens resulting in blood levels that were 100–500 times higher than what we find in babies fed soy infant formula. For humans to consume the same amount of phytoestrogens as sheep we would have to drink 1300 litres of soy milk or eat 8600 soy burgers each day—an impossibility! Cheetahs are particularly susceptible to the effects of phytoestrogens because they lack an essential enzyme that humans have to convert estrogens and phytoestrogens into forms that are much less potent and more easily removed from the body. Phytoestrogens are therefore more active in the cheetah. This latter example illustrates the need to consider carefully species differences in the way phytoestrogens are handled before jumping to conclusions about likely adverse effects in humans. Many species of monkeys, laboratory rats, horses, cattle, poultry and pigs have no reproductive prob-lems when they consume phytoestrogens as a natural constituent in their diet. Much of the negative press suggesting that phytoestrogens may cause reproductive problems comes from the adverse effects of injecting high doses into newborn rats and mice. But, these animals are not suitable models for human infant development and when given by injection, phytoestrogens behave differently in the body.

- *Thyroid function* It has been proposed that infants and adults should not eat soy foods because of the possibility that these may cause thyroid disease. Studies on rats conducted at the National Center for Toxicological Research in Arkansas, US, first showed that soy phytoestrogens can interfere with the key enzyme the body uses to make thyroid hormones, but the same researchers later found that there is so much of this enzyme in the thyroid gland that blood levels of thyroid hormones are not after all compromised. Flavonoids, abundant in many plant foods, also block this enzyme. Yet dietary guidelines around the world recommend we all eat *more* vegetables, fruits, legumes and wholegrains for their many health benefits. To put things into perspective, scientific evidence shows that thyroid function is not disrupted in healthy infants so long as their diet contains adequate levels of iodine. Before the 1960s soy formulas were deficient in iodine and problems with goitre (an enlarged thyroid) were reported in a few infants. However, soy formulas have since been fortified with iodine and, to our knowledge, only twelve cases of thyroid disease have been reported worldwide linked to the use of soy formula. In most of these cases, the infants were born with an underactive thyroid, a rare condition called hypothyroidism which affects 1 in 4000 live births.

Food regulatory bodies around the world set strict regulations on the safety and nutritional quality of soy infant formula.

A recent review by the Australia New Zealand Food Authority found no evidence that exposure of healthy infants to soy-based infant formula over some 30 years of use has been associated with any demonstrable harm. The Food Standards Agency in the UK has an active programme of research on phytoestrogens and is funding studies aimed at assessing the safety of soy infant formulas. Since manufacturers make a range of different types of infant formula based on cow's milk, goat's milk and soy milk, any suggestion that these companies have a vested interest in promoting soy formula is illogical. When it comes to selecting formula, if soy formula is not chosen, then other formulas are purchased instead. Either way the formula manufacturers win. The only consolation from any scaremongering about soy infant formula would be if it convinced more mothers to breast-feed their infants.

What we recommend

Based on the Asian experience, we believe that phytoestrogen-rich foods eaten early and throughout life will provide health benefits over a diet that is deficient in these foods. This is supported by findings from animal studies which show that the earlier phytoestrogens are consumed, the greater the advantages, at least for cancer prevention. Breast-feeding should be the first choice for newborn infants, but there is no reason why babies and children, or pregnant and lactating women should avoid soy or other phytoestrogen-rich products. The recent rise in Western diseases in Japan is intriguing as the population moves away from a traditional phytoestrogen-rich diet to a Western phytoestrogen-deficient diet, particularly in children and adolescents. If the trend continues the phytoestrogen protective shield will be lost to future generations.

chapter 11

Frequently asked questions

'. . . we shall have many opportunities of studying how preconceived theories take root: we shall often be astonished to see how accidental statements of almost no significance and often purely hypothetical have often been able to give birth to a theory of which we can no longer rid ourselves without difficulty . . . '

PROFESSOR HANS GROSS —

KRIMINALISTIK 1904

Phytoestrogens, because of their provocative name, have mistakenly been construed to be identical to estrogens. This has raised hypothetical concerns about their effects since estrogens can be double-edged swords having both positive and negative effects in the body. Yet phytoestrogens have been consumed in relatively large amounts by millions of the world's population for generations—and associated with many health benefits.

What is important to understand is that while phyto-estrogens can mimic some of the beneficial effects of estrogens they can also oppose the harmful actions of estrogens due to their subtle differences. This is what makes them 'smart molecules' as we mentioned in Chapter 2.

Following are answers to the most commonly asked questions on phytoestrogens. We cover fallacies related to an overenthusiasm about phytoestrogens that extends beyond the research findings—such as phytoestrogens making a woman's breasts bigger. We also discuss safety concerns including their effect on hormone levels, fertility and sexual development and the contentious issues of whether more vulnerable groups such as infants and pregnant women should consume phytoestrogen-rich foods. Perhaps the most controversial area is whether phytoestrogens should be taken by women with breast cancer.

Q: Will feeding soy to my young daughter help reduce her risk of breast cancer when she is older?

A: In Asian countries where the rates of breast cancer are low, females consume soy foods from an early age and throughout their lives. It is thought that the early intake of the phyto-estrogens in soy may be the most critical factor in making the breast more resistant to cancer later in life. This idea is supported by findings from animal studies in which the early introduction of phytoestrogens to the diet is much more powerful in delaying and reducing the number of breast tumours in animals exposed to cancer-causing chemicals than if they are added to the diet during adult life.

Q: Can phytoestrogen pills increase the size of my breasts?

A: Several companies are marketing phytoestrogen pills to appeal to women who want to increase their breast size with the promise that it is a cheaper alternative to silicone implants. But there is no basis for claims that phytoestrogens will have any effect on breast size. If this were true, women living in Asian countries would have the largest breasts, as they consume the most phytoestrogens!

A recent investigation of one of these products failed to find any appreciable amounts of phytoestrogens when the pills were analysed by very sensitive detection methods. In addition, when the pills were fed to animals they failed to produce any of the usual signs of estrogenicity. Despite this, the product was being sold at the time over the Internet for over US$1400 for a seven-month course—with the claim that, 'If just one pill is missed then you must start all over again' to get the benefit. Such claims are completely fraudulent.

Q: Are phytoestrogens helpful for premenstrual tension (PMT)?

A: PMT is associated with large swings in estrogen levels and the idea that a daily supply of phytoestrogens may help to buffer these hormonal changes is an interesting one. Presently, however, there is no direct evidence that this is the case, although it is often suggested in the popular press. There is evidence that a low-fat vegetarian diet can reduce period pain and premenstrual symptoms. Vegetarian diets naturally include a wide range of phytoprotectants, including high levels of phytoestrogens.

Q: Can phytoestrogens help me lose weight?

A: Phytoestrogens from red clover and soybeans are included in some popular weight loss supplements, but they have never been shown to have any special properties that promote weight loss.

Q: Will I gain weight by eating more phytoestrogen-rich foods, especially soy foods?

A: Phytoestrogens alone do not increase on body weight. Many phytoestrogen-containing foods, however, are not calorie-free. They will contribute calories to your diet, just as other foods do. In most cases, when people consume phytoestrogen-rich foods they do so at the expense of other foods. For example, you may decide to use soy milk instead of dairy milk, or a soy burger in place of a meat burger. This means that overall you will not necessarily consume more calories.

A study of healthy young women who added 50 g linseeds (around 10 teaspoons!) to their daily diet for four weeks found no significant change in body weight, despite the fact that an additional 280 calories were consumed each day. This is the number of calories you would get from a small chocolate bar. Other studies found no effect on body weight when men or women supplemented their diets with soy protein for a period of several months. So, as long as you substitute phytoestrogen-rich foods for other foods, there is no reason to be concerned about gaining weight. Moreover, Asians eating traditional diets and vegetarians generally have lower rates of obesity. Both of these groups have a much higher phytoestrogen intake than the general population in Western countries.

Q: Will phytoestrogens affect hormone levels?

A: There is some evidence that diets rich in phytoestrogens can lower estrogen levels in premenopausal women. This is thought to be highly beneficial for reducing the risk of breast cancer. Asian women have very high levels of phytoestrogens—because they eat soy and other plant foods—and have blood estrogen levels that are 20–30 per cent lower than those of Western women. Asian women have the lowest rates of breast cancer. Clearly, phytoestrogens seem to be able to alter the way the body makes and handles its own estrogen, but in a favourable way. In addition, a study of young women in the US, found that drinking soy milk with each meal reduced estrogen levels by 31–81 per cent.

In men, no significant change in blood testosterone levels was observed when linseeds, a rich source of lignans were fed for six weeks.

Q: Will phytoestrogens interfere with the oral contraceptive pill or hormone replacement therapy (HRT)?

A: Possible interactions between drugs and supplements are of increasing concern to the medical community because many herbal and botanical remedies can interfere with the way certain drugs function. In a study from the University of Minnesota of women taking the pill, the levels of estrogen and progesterone were not compromised by the daily intake of a soy beverage containing 38 mg of isoflavones over a period of two months. A separate study from the Sydney Menopause Centre of eight postmenopausal women similarly found that a diet including 28 g of soy protein did not interfere with hormone levels from the estrogen replacement therapy they were taking.

Q: Can I use phytoestrogens as a 'natural alternative' to HRT?
A: Phytoestrogens have been touted as the 'natural alternative' to HRT in managing symptoms of menopause. While evidence now exists that phytoestrogen-rich foods help to modestly reduce the frequency and severity of hot flushes, prevent bone loss and improve blood fats, their effects are not as powerful as that of estrogen. On the flipside, the advantage is that phyto-estrogens do not have the side effects of estrogens.

All women should use some source of 'estrogen' when the ovaries cease to be active. There is a lot of anecdotal evidence that phytoestrogen-rich diets taken over a prolonged period of time can offer benefits. A recent consensus article from the North American Menopause Society concluded that further work was needed to determine just how effective phytoestrogens are for the menopause. This is especially poignant now that the Women's Health Initiative study has caused a rethink about HRT.

Q: Can I stop taking my cholesterol-lowering medication if I start eating phytoestrogen-rich foods such as soy protein?
A: Many people have been able to normalise and control their blood cholesterol level by lifestyle alone. Where possible, this is far preferable to taking potent lipid-lowering drugs that interfere with the body's production of cholesterol. Foods such as soy protein may be most effective for people with a moder-ately raised cholesterol level. This probably represents about one-third of all adults living in the UK. In most cases the high cholesterol is diet-induced, the result of a lifelong diet high in animal fat and cholesterol and lacking in plant foods which supply many phytoprotectants—including phytoestrogens.

Heart disease cost the UK health care system £1600 million in 2000. One-third of this was for prescription drugs, while only 1 per cent went into prevention. A staggering 10,333,000 prescriptions were dished out for lipid-lowering drugs in the same year, representing a 35-fold increase from the 291,000 scripts written in 1981. This liberal use of lipid-lowering medication is an indication of the poor health of the nation, most of which could be improved with simple lifestyle changes. For some, it is a defect in the genes regulating the way cholesterol is handled by the body that necessitates drug therapy. However, diet is still important and helpful. Always consult your doctor before making any changes to your current medical treatment.

Q: Are phytoestrogen supplements as beneficial as phytoestrogen-rich foods?

A: There has been enormous growth in the market for phytoestrogen supplements, despite a lack of scientific research to confirm many of the claims being made for these products. Companies often promote phytoestrogen supplements based on evidence from studies in which phytoestrogen-rich foods have shown health benefits. However, several studies have found that purified phytoestrogen supplements provide only limited benefits. For example, three independent studies found that while supplements improve the elasticity of blood vessels, unlike phytoestrogen-rich foods such as soy, they have no cholesterol-lowering effects.

The current evidence suggests that there are important interactions between phytoestrogens and other nutrients in foods, and that the best way to reap maximum health benefits is to consume them in their natural state—in food.

Q: Can I overdose with phytoestrogens?

A: If your phytoestrogens come from foods and you have a varied diet, it is highly unlikely that you will be able to consume enough to 'overdose'. At the natural level that most phytoestrogens are found in plants you would have to consume buckets of plant foods each day to reach dangerously high intake levels. Recent research has also found that the body seems to be able to limit how much can be absorbed from foods. There is a long history of safe consumption of phytoestrogen-rich foods by Asians and vegetarians. Whether this holds true for supplements is unknown—caution is warranted.

Q: Is there a difference in the phytoestrogen content of regular and genetically modified (GM) soybeans?

A: Based on limited research, there appears to be no major difference between the phytoestrogen content of GM soybeans and conventionally grown soybeans.

A study conducted by scientists at the Monsanto Corporation measured the isoflavone content of GM soybeans and found it to be identical to non-genetically modified varieties. An earlier, oft-quoted study from Germany claimed that once sprayed with the herbicide glyphosate, GM soybeans actually had higher levels of isoflavones. This may be nutritionally beneficial. However, a more recent study conducted at the University of Cincinnati found a 12–14 per cent decrease in the isoflavone content of GM soybeans after they were sprayed with the same herbicide. The range of findings from these studies fit within the large natural variation in phytoestrogen content of soybeans—due to growing conditions, among other factors.

Q: Do soy foods made from genetically modified soybeans have the same health benefits as soy foods made from regular soybeans?

A: There have been no comparative studies evaluating the health benefits of GM and non-GM soybeans or, for that matter, foods made from these beans. However, studies by scientists at the Monsanto Corporation that developed the GM soybean found no obvious differences in terms of supporting growth and development in several species of animals. Most of the recent studies in America demonstrating the health benefits of soy protein in people would have used a mixture of GM and non-GM soy because more than half the crop presently grown in the US, the world's largest producer of soy, is of the GM variety.

Q: Is there a phytoestrogen advantage for me if I buy organic foods?

A: There have been no studies undertaken to assess whether organically grown foods have a different phytoestrogen content compared to non-organic foods.

Q: Do phytoestrogens reduce sperm count in men and cause infertility in women?

A: Some years ago there was much discussion in the media about a possible fall in sperm counts in men attributed to the effects of environmental estrogens. Not surprisingly, some people have asked whether phytoestrogens might also be implicated. Whether sperm counts have actually declined over the years is now a matter of disagreement among experts. With regards to phytoestrogens, there is a history of negative effects on fertility in some, but not all, animal species. The most infamous example occurred in Australia in the 1940s, when sheep grazing on a type of phytoestrogen-rich clover called *Trifolium subterraneum* became infertile. Marked abnormalities in the sperm of male sheep were noted. Much later on, it was found that phytoestrogens in soymeal caused infertility and early death of captive cheetahs in North American zoos. However, the adverse effects in both of these species of animals can easily be explained. The sheep consumed extremely high doses of phytoestrogens resulting in blood levels that are 100–500 times greater than that of humans eating phytoestrogen-rich foods. Cheetahs lack an essential liver enzyme that humans have to convert both estrogens and phytoestrogens into forms that are less hormonally active and more easily removed from the body. Phytoestrogens, therefore, are considerably more potent in the cheetah, acting somewhat like an oral contraceptive.

As for humans, there is no scientific evidence that phytoestrogens have negative effects on the reproductive system. Infertility does not appear to be a problem in countries where the diet is high in phytoestrogens, such as China, Korea and Japan. And a reduced sperm count in men has never been linked to a diet rich in phytoestrogens.

All of these examples illustrate that there are large species differences in the way phytoestrogens are handled. Care needs to be taken in drawing conclusions from the findings of animal studies when considering humans. However, these examples warn us to be cautious in the use of supplements, which can deliver extremely high doses of phytoestrogens if enough are consumed.

Q: Are phytoestrogens safe to take during pregnancy?
A: Yes, based on centuries of use of phytoestrogen-rich foods such as soy in the diets of pregnant Asian women. These

women do not stop eating their traditional foods just because they become pregnant.

According to studies of Japanese and Indonesian women, when pregnant women consume phytoestrogens in the diet, these are transferred to the developing foetus via the placenta. So the unborn child actually gets these protectants from the mother long before it is born. During pregnancy, the baby is normally bathed in a sea of estrogens—which are much more powerful than the phytoestrogens obtained from food. To guard against too much exposure, the foetus has high levels of a protein called alpha-fetoprotein. This strongly binds both estrogens and phytoestrogens, reducing their hormonal potency.

Q: Do I need to avoid phytoestrogen-rich foods while breast-feeding?

A: Human breast milk is low in phytoestrogens regardless of the type of diet the mother consumes. A litre of breast milk from women who consume a lot of soy contains only 0.015–0.030 mg isoflavones—less than 1mg! Even though these miniscule amounts of phytoestrogens can be detected in low levels in the urine of breast-fed infants, there is no evidence that they are harmful.

Furthermore, in the first days of lactation, breast milk contains substantial levels of estrogens, which accumulated in the breast during the course of the pregnancy. Environmental estrogens such as pesticides, about which we should be concerned, also find their way into breast milk.

Q: Is it safe to feed my baby soy infant formula if it contains high levels of phytoestrogens?

A: Yes, but we strongly recommend breast milk over any type of formula. There are some infants, however, who cannot be breast-fed and many women do not wish to breastfeed. In these cases formula is the only option. Recently, the safety of soy infant formula was questioned because of its high phytoestrogen content. A report from the Australia New Zealand Food Authority found no evidence that exposure of healthy infants to soy-based infant formula over some 30 years of use has been associated with any harmful effects. Adverse effects are rare and generally limited to known allergenic responses. Allergy to soy affects about 0.5 per cent of the general population and can be fatal, but the incidence of cow's milk allergy is even higher, affecting around 1.8 per cent of infants.

In the early years when soy infant formulas were introduced, problems were encountered with growth and development. Very quickly, however, the way these formulas were made was changed to meet the specific nutritional needs of a baby. This happened around 1960 and since then, numerous studies from leading university paediatric departments have shown that babies fed soy formulas grow and develop no differently from babies fed breast milk or other formulas. There have also been no abnormalities in the responsiveness of the immune system, or differences in bone density, levels of certain hormones, or the timing of puberty observed in children fed soy formula as infants. It is estimated that about 18 million infants have been raised on soy formula since the 1960s in the US alone and yet there is no evidence in the medical literature of adverse effects.

To check for any delayed effects of soy infant formula, Dr Brian Strom and his colleagues at the University of Pennsylania School of Medicine recently examined young adults who had been fed this formula as infants. The researchers found that there was no statistically significant difference in males or females fed either soy- or cow's milk-based formula in many variables studied, including adult height, weight, body mass index, infertility, the timing of puberty, and a large number of other non-reproductive outcomes, such as cancer. The American Academy of Pediatrics in their position statement on 'Soy protein-based formulas' concluded that soy infant formulas are nutritionally sound.

Q: Could phytoestrogens be responsible for delayed puberty in boys or early puberty in girls?

A: The proportion of boys with delayed puberty is no different now than it was 30 years ago. However, girls today are having their first period much earlier than girls did many years ago. The timing of this event has decreased by three to four months each decade during the last century. Most health professionals attribute this to the consumption of too much fat and too many calories from the typical Western diet. It has also been suggested that it occurs as a result of the increased use of pesticides and insecticides with strong estrogen-like properties—but this is difficult to prove. In traditional Japanese and Chinese societies, where the diet is high in phytoestrogens, girls have their first period at a later age than they do in most Western countries, so it is difficult to rationalise any link between phytoestrogens and early puberty. Studies have also found that eating more fibre from wholegrains delays the timing of the first menstrual period. Breast cancer experts believe that delaying the age of onset of menstruation significantly reduces the risk of breast cancer.

Q: Could phytoestrogens be the cause of the steady rise in malformations of the penis?

A: There is no evidence that phytoestrogens account for the steady rise in 'hypospadias'—the most common genital birth defects of the penis, observed in Western countries over the last century. The phytoestrogen content of the typical Western diet is extremely low, and if anything has declined over the years.

A study from the UK found that the rate of hypospadias in baby boys born to vegetarian mothers was five times higher than in the infants of non-vegetarians. It was speculated that phytoestrogens might be responsible because vegetarians consume higher amounts than meat eaters. However, the researchers pointed out that there was no statistically significant difference in the proportion of boys born with hypospadias among mothers who drank soy milk and who regularly consumed soy products. This finding fits with the low rate of hypospadias in Japan and China. Yet, as the Japanese diet is becoming Westernised in recent years, phytoestrogen intake is declining, and with it the rates of hypospadias are increasing. What is often not mentioned about this study is that among the non-vegetarian mothers, taking iron supplements, or having a bout of influenza in the first trimester of pregnancy, greatly increased the chance of giving birth to a baby boy with hypospadia.

The cause of hypospadias remains unknown, but the possibility that environmental estrogens such as pesticides may be responsible seems more plausible.

Q: Will feeding my baby boy phytoestrogen-rich foods feminise him?
A: The programming of sexual characteristics of the human brain occurs primarily in the womb during early development. So what you feed your baby after birth may be irrelevant in this regard. There have been no reported cases in the medical literature where feminisation of baby boys has been attributed to soy infant formula feeding.

A recent study found that phytoestrogens had no effect on two key enzymes in the brain of adult rats, called aromatase and 5α-reductase, that control the balance of hormones in the brain. An Australian study found no 'feminising effects' in men who were fed soy protein containing high amounts of phytoestrogens—their levels of male sex hormones did not change.

Q: Will phytoestrogens block thyroid hormones and cause thyroid disease?

A: Animal and laboratory studies have shown that isoflavones, at very high concentrations, interfere with an enzyme called TPO (thyroid peroxidase) that is essential for making thyroid hormones in the body. However, this does not pose a problem as there is an ample supply of this enzyme in the thyroid. Many flavonoids, which are very similar compounds found in fruits and vegetables, similarly block the action of TPO. But there is no evidence that consuming either type of these plant protectants in a varied diet causes thyroid disease in healthy people. For example, vegetarians who consume large amounts of isoflavones and flavonoids from legumes, vegetables and fruits, do not have high rates of thyroid problems or goitre (an enlarged thyroid gland). Dietary guidelines around the world stress the importance of eating *more* vegetables, fruits and legumes, as most people are not getting sufficient amounts of these protective foods.

In people who are iodine deficient or have the rare condition called hypothyroidism (an underactive thyroid gland) soy foods might promote goitre if consumed in large quantities. But so might many other well-known 'goitrogens', such as broccoli, brussels sprouts, cabbages, cauliflower, maize, kale, onions, garlic, peanuts and lima beans. The best advice is to eat a nutritionally adequate and varied diet.

Q: Should women with estrogen receptor positive breast cancer consume phytoestrogens?

A: Estrogen receptor positive breast cancer, which grows in the presence of estrogens, is the type seen in about 80 per cent of breast cancers. As a precaution, some physicians and health professionals are informing breast cancer patients that they should avoid soy foods and phytoestrogen supplements because the 'estrogen-like' effects of phytoestrogens might stimulate breast cancer cells to grow. But there is no clinical evidence to support this recommendation. Phytoestrogens act as natural selective estrogen receptor modulators (SERMs)—having subtle but important differences from estrogens. Consequently, we believe they are more likely to have beneficial effects on the breast in the same way as the SERM drugs, Tamoxifen and Raloxifene, proven to reduce the risk of breast cancer.

There is a vast amount of compelling evidence from animal and laboratory research showing that phytoestrogens are powerful anticancer agents—although in some manipulated animal models they have the opposite effect. It is also noteworthy that studies of breast cancer patients have found that they tend to have the lowest levels of phytoestrogens, while in countries where the intake of phytoestrogens is the highest, the rates of breast cancer are low.

In the absence of evidence to the contrary, we do not deter women with estrogen receptor positive breast cancer from eating phytoestrogen-rich foods such as soy, as in a varied diet, there are likely to be benefits. We do, however, caution against the use of large doses of phytoestrogen supplements because these do not have the same long-term history of safe use.

Q: Should breast cancer patients treated with anti-estrogens such as Tamoxifen avoid taking phytoestrogens?
A: There are no human data to answer this question, but it is possible that interactions between phytoestrogens and Tamoxifen occur. Two studies with rats found that the anti-cancer effect of Tamoxifen was even greater when miso, or soy protein was also consumed. If this were to apply to humans, phytoestrogen-rich foods may provide an added benefit for women who are using Tamoxifen to prevent or treat breast cancer.

part III

Your phytoestrogen eating plan

chapter 12

Where to find phytoestrogens and how much to eat

*'And God said, "Look! I have given you the
seed-bearing plants throughout the earth and
all the fruit trees for your food"'*
GENESIS 1:29

Phytoestrogens are found in a wide range of plants and plant foods, but not in significant amounts in any animal products. More than 300 plants have been shown to contain substances that are similar to the estrogens in the body. There are probably more that are yet to be discovered. We don't consume all of these plants, though, as many are inedible. Pharmaceutical companies use some of them as starting material to make drugs and medicinal products.

The best way to protect against a phytoestrogen deficiency is to eat a variety of plant foods each day. We give you guidelines in this chapter on how much you should eat and which of the many foods you can choose from. You will find phytoestrogens in legumes, particularly soybeans, linseeds, other seeds and nuts, wholegrains, vegetables and fruits, although the levels vary considerably. You can also obtain them from supplements and plant extracts.

Intakes that promote good health

Based on the amount of soy foods eaten, the Japanese consume 15–30 mg of isoflavones each day. Intakes do vary in Asia, however, from 10 to 250 mg daily. There are regional differences and variations in intake due to age and socioeconomic status. The highest intakes seem to be in Indonesia where half of the population consumes more than 125 g of tempeh and tofu each day. This would provide around 60 to 250 mg of isoflavones, depending on the type of tofu and tempeh consumed, as levels differ markedly between brands.

In stark contrast, most people living in Western countries such as Australia, New Zealand, the US and the UK consume fewer than 1 mg of isoflavones daily. This is about 10 to 250 times less than Asians eat. Vegetarian and macrobiotic diets, where plant foods feature prominently on the menu, provide very high levels of phytoestrogens. But, if you are a carnivore and mostly just eat meats and other animal products, you will not be getting these phytoprotectants. Including only limited amounts of legumes, wholegrains, nuts, seeds, vegetables and fruits in your diet will not leave you highly protected against disease. Are you getting enough phytoestrogens? If you are unsure, do the quiz in Chapter 1 (pages 11–12) to find out.

Sadly, even Asian countries are undergoing dramatic changes as their traditional diet becomes 'Westernised'. In urban cities such as Seoul, South Korea, fast-food chains have proliferated and interest in traditional phytoestrogen-rich soy foods is declining, particularly among young people.

How much should you eat?

Based on the Asian experience, we recommend that you aim for a daily intake of a wide variety of plant foods, including phytoestrogen-rich foods, such as soy products. This applies whether you consume meat, poultry, fish, or you are a vegetarian.

As little as one food type a day providing a 'rich source' of phytoestrogens is likely to deliver health benefits, especially if consumed over a lifetime. More may be required to assist in managing certain conditions such as an elevated blood cholesterol level.

If you are to be optimally 'phytoprotected', we recommend you consume 20 to 50 mg of isoflavones in your daily diet. This can be achieved by choosing two foods from the 'rich source' group in the Phytoestrogen Food Guide (Table 12.1). Some clinical studies suggest higher amounts, 60 to 90 mg, are necessary to manage a condition or disease. But eating very large amounts isn't necessarily better. Studies at the Universities of Cincinnati in the US and Surrey in the UK, found that the law of diminishing returns applies when phytoestrogens are taken in foods. As you continue to increase your intake from foods, the proportion absorbed into the body declines. So there is no real advantage in eating huge amounts of phytoestrogen-rich foods. For phytoestrogen supplements, however, taking very large doses could be harmful because the body may not have the same inbuilt safety mechanism to limit their uptake. Some side-effects have been noted in people taking high doses (150–1000mg) of purified isoflavone extracts.

Refer to the composition tables in Appendix I for a comprehensive listing of the amounts of isoflavones in various foods and add up the number of milligrams in your daily diet.

To make it really easy, we have developed a seven-step daily phytoestrogen food guide. This is your blueprint to achieve a phytoestrogen-rich diet that is also high in other phytoprotectants. Foods not listed, such as fish, poultry, and meat—because they don't provide phytoestrogens—can be used at your discretion. Keep meat portions modest so you have plenty of room on your plate for the protective foods. Choose low fat varieties of dairy products and limit your intake of fast foods, sweets, unhealthy snack foods, oils and fat spreads. This approach ensures a well-balanced intake of nutrients.

CASE STUDY   DUNCAN'S STORY

Duncan, a 22-year-old university student is virtually a carnivore. For most of his life a fruit or vegetable never passed his lips. His usual diet is high in animal protein and saturated fat, biscuits, chocolate and at times junk food. He does, however, consume about a litre of orange juice each day. During the writing of this book, Duncan read a number of chapters and was persuaded to try eating a more protective diet. For three days he followed closely the *Eat to Live* guidelines and included foods such as a variety of fruits, vegetables, nuts and a little soy protein. After this time—and to his great surprise—the level of phyto-estrogens in his urine increased by more than 100 times compared to when he was on his phytoestrogen-deficient diet. The levels were 10 000 times higher than estrogen levels. This was now at the level we find in Japanese people and vegetarians, who have excellent health statistics. This demonstrates that it is possible within just three days of following the *Eat to Live* diet to achieve high levels of phytoestrogens in your body improving your level of phyto-protection.

Seven-step daily phytoestrogen food guide

Step 1

Soy and linseed foods Include two soy or linseed foods every day from Table 12.1, choosing at least one from the 'rich source' group. For example, pour soy milk over your breakfast cereal and make a tofu burger for dinner, or, have plain or flavoured soy milk as one choice and any of the following as another choice:

- Edamame, boiled and eaten as a delicious fresh snack
- Textured vegetable protein in spaghetti bolognaise or lasagne
- Soy flour in baking or making crepes
- Soy grits, softened and added to salads or casseroles
- Canned soybeans, mashed and used to make a dip or vegetable burgers
- Soy nuts, eaten as a crunchy snack
- Tofu yoghurt
- Soy protein shake, for extra nutrition between meals when needed
- Linseed meal (ground linseeds), sprinkled over breakfast cereal
- Linseeds, added to dough when baking bread

Variety is important. While we suggest using soy milk daily as it is an easy way to obtain phytoestrogens, always try to vary the second choice.

Step 2

Legumes Include legumes three or more times each week. See Table 12.1 for different varieties. Here are some ways in which you can incorporate legumes into your diet.

- A main dish, such as Chickpea Curry with Pumpkin and Baby Spinach (page 242)
- Soup such as Brown Lentil Soup with Dill (page 212)
- A side dish to main meals, e.g. Three-Bean Dhal (page 222) or dhal takeaway from Indian restaurants
- A quick lunch using canned pinto beans, e.g. Bean Burritos with Avocado, Tomato and Coriander (page 231)
- A spread for bread or sandwiches, e.g. hommus
- Convenience products that you can buy ready-made and simply warm at home, e.g. soy or lentil burgers, falafel balls, soy hot dogs and soy schnitzels

Step 3

Fruit Choose at least two types of fruit daily, mostly fresh. The majority of fruits provide a source of phytoestrogens. If they are not listed in Table 12.1 it means they probably haven't yet been analysed for phytoestrogen content. Dried fruits can provide more concentrated sources of phytoprotectants.

Step 4

Vegetables Choose a minimum of five different types of vegetables each day—as many colours as possible. For example, for lunch you might have a salad with mixed green leaves, cubed avocado and cherry tomatoes. For dinner, include broccoli, carrots and cauliflower in a stir-fry. Add sprouts such as alfalfa, which are a particularly 'rich source' of phytoestrogens, to sandwiches.

Step 5

Wholegrains Include plenty of grain foods each day according to your requirements but ensure that at least three are made from wholegrains. For example, one wholegrain cereal for breakfast and two slices of wholegrain bread with seeds, particularly linseeds, to make a sandwich for lunch.

Step 6

Nuts and seeds Include these at least three times per week. For example, snack on a handful of raw almonds, walnuts or macadamias or enjoy a heaped tablespoon of peanut butter, tahini or hazelnut butter on bread, preferably of the natural and unsalted variety.

Step 7

Drinks Include a minimum of eight glasses of water each day. Even though it does not provide phytoestrogens, adequate water is important for good health. Use fruit or vegetable juices and black, green or herbal teas instead of carbonated beverages.

Factors affecting phytoestrogen levels in foods

Just like nutrients such as vitamins and minerals, the levels of phytoestrogens vary in foods. There are differences in brands and even between batches of the same brand. But this is a natural phenomenon and is not a serious concern. We base our

TABLE 12.1
PHYTOESTROGEN FOOD GUIDE

RICH SOURCE: more than 15 mg per serving

Breads & grain products	Soy bread; Soy cereal, with or without linseeds; Soy pita bread
Dairy alternatives	Soy cheese; Soy dip; Soy infant formula; Soy milk, whole bean, many brands; Tofu yoghurt
Drinks	Soy-based meal replacement, most brands; Soy protein shake, most brands
Legumes & related products	Black beans; Canned soybeans; Dried soybeans; Soy flakes; Soy flour; Soy germ; Soy grits; Soy protein concentrate, water washed; Soy protein isolate
Meat alternatives	Tempeh burger; Textured vegetable protein (TVP)
Nuts & seeds	Linseed flour & meal; Linseeds
Snack foods	Green soybeans (Edamame); Soy nuts; Soy protein bars, most brands
Traditional Asian foods	Miso; Natto; Tempeh; Tofu
Vegetables & fruits	Alfalfa sprouts

GOOD SOURCE: 5–15 mg per serving	
Breads & grain products	Soy and linseed bread; Soy pasta, some brands
Dairy alternatives	Soy custard; Soy milk, entire bean, all brands; Soy milk, fat-free, all brands; Soy milk, soy protein-based, all brands; Soy milk, whole bean, low-fat; Soy milk, whole bean, some brands; Soy yoghurt
Legumes & related products	Broad beans, dry
Meat alternatives	Soy bacon; Soy burger; Soy hot dogs; Soy based deli slices; Soy sausages; Soy schnitzels
Vegetables & fruit	Soybean sprouts

SOURCE: up to 5 mg per serving	
Breads & grain products	Barley & barley bran; Bread with linseed; Bread with mixed grain; Bread with rye; Bread with wholewheat; Breakfast cereal with barley bran; Breakfast cereal with corn; Breakfast cereal with cornbran; Breakfast cereal with linseed; Breakfast cereal with oat bran; Breakfast cereal with rice bran; Breakfast cereal with rye; Breakfast cereal with wheat bran; Breakfast cereal with wholewheat; Brown rice; Hops; Muffin with linseed; Oats & oat bran; Pancakes with linseed; Pizza dough with linseed; Rye & rye bran; Triticale; Wheat & wheat bran; Wheat flakes
Dairy alternatives	Soy ice-cream
Drinks	Beer; Black tea; Bourbon; Coffee; Cow's milk; Green tea; Jasmine tea; Orange Juice; Red wine; White wine
Legumes & related products	Baked beans; Blackeyed beans; Broad beans, fresh; Chickpeas; Haricot beans; Lentils; Lima beans; Mung beans; Navy beans; Pinto beans; Red kidney beans; Soy protein concentrate, alcohol washed; Split peas, green; Split peas, yellow

Nuts & seeds	Caraway seeds; Cashew nuts; Hazelnuts; Peanuts; Rapeseed or canola; Sesame seeds; Sunflower seeds; Walnuts
Oils	Olive oil, extra virgin
Snack foods	Licorice; Soy chips
Traditional Asian foods	Chinese blackbean sauce; Miso soup; Soy sauce
Vegetables & fruits	Alfalfa; Apples; Asparagus; Avocado; Bananas; Beetroot; Blackberries; Blackcurrants; Bok choy; Boston lettuce; Broad beans; Broccoli; Brussels sprouts; Butter beans; Cabbage; Capsicum; Carrots; Cauliflower; Celery; Chives; Cranberries; Cucumber; Dried Apricots; French beans; Garlic; Gooseberries; Grapefruit; Green peas; Guava; Hijki seaweed; Iceberg lettuce; Leeks; Lemons; Lychees; Mekuba seaweed; Mung bean sprouts; Mushrooms; Onions; Oranges; Papaya; Peaches; Pears; Plums; Prunes; Potatoes; Radishes; Raspberries; Redcurrants; Rockmelon; Runner beans; Snow peas; Spinach; Squash; Strawberries; Sweet potatoes; Tomatoes; Turnips; Watercress

values on averages from various analyses conducted in laboratories around the world.

Natural variation

For most plants, the seed variety, the soil, the season, weather conditions and the timing of planting or harvesting will all influence the level of phytoestrogens.

Food processing

Some types of food processing can reduce the natural levels of phytoestrogens. Alcohol extraction, which is used for making many, but not all, types of concentrated soy protein, strips the protein of most of its phytoestrogens. Water extraction used to produce soy protein isolate does not lead to significant losses of phytoestrogens. Extrusion of soy causes a loss of phytoestrogens but the levels remaining are still sufficiently high to provide health benefits. The level of isoflavones in processed soy products can vary by more than ten-fold compared with whole soybeans.

Cooking

Unless you absolutely char or blacken food to a point beyond which you would not eat it, cooking, even at high temperatures, will not destroy phytoestrogens. You can also chill and/or freeze and reheat your food. However, there is some loss of phytoestrogens into water if you boil vegetables or green soybeans. Use the water to make soups or gravy to retain the phytoestrogens, or steam, stir-fry or microwave your vegetables instead.

PHYTOFOODS:
MORE NUTRITIONAL BONUSES

You may be surprised to learn that when you eat phyto-estrogen-rich foods, you also get more nutritional and health benefits in the same package.

Fibre Important for loosening the bowels and the control of blood sugar and blood fat levels; many phytoestrogen-rich foods supply fibre to the diet—linseeds are particularly effective in helping to keep the bowels regular.

No cholesterol Excess dietary cholesterol is undesirable for the heart; plant foods don't contain cholesterol, but rather 'phytosterols' that actually reduce the absorption of cho-lesterol from your diet. Soybeans are rich in phytoestrogens and phytosterols.

Low saturated fat In their natural state, phytoestrogen-rich foods are low in saturated fat; dietary guidelines advise us to eat less saturated fats to reduce the risk of heart dis-ease. These fats have also been linked to a higher risk of lung, bowel, breast, endometrial and prostate cancer.

Omega-3 fats Linseed, a 'rich source' of phytoestrogens, is also the best plant food source of alpha linolenic acid; this is converted in the body to the same omega-3 fats found in fish and fish oils.

Prebiotics Some phytoestrogen-containing foods such as legumes and wholegrains supply prebiotics. Dubbed 'colonic foods', these are vital for keeping the intestines healthy.

No lactose Plant foods are naturally free of lactose, the sugar found in milk. Phytoestrogen-rich foods such as calcium-fortified soy milks are a good alternative for people with lactose intolerance who cannot tolerate large amounts of dairy milk.

Plant protein In contrast to animal proteins, plant proteins such as soy protein do not cause hardening of the arteries; in fact, they help lower cholesterol levels to reduce the risk of heart disease. Plant proteins are also less demanding than animal proteins on the kidneys.

Phytochemicals Phytoestrogen-rich foods are bursting with many types of phytochemicals which, it has been suggested, help protect us from disease.

chapter 13

Boosting your phytoestrogen intake

'Soybean is the meat from the soil'
KOREAN FOLKLORE

This chapter contains all the practical information to help you plan, shop and cook phytoestrogen-rich meals and snacks. Once you familiarise yourself with the basics, boosting your phytoestrogen intake will become easy and a routine part of your diet.

Three key shopping tips

1. *Choose plenty of products made from plant foods.* Look for phytoestrogen-rich products on the shelves of your bakery, greengrocer and supermarket. See the following shopping list for suggestions. Phytoestrogen supplements and extracts can be found in the pharmacy section of many supermarkets, pharmacies, health food stores and are also available via the Internet.

2. *Look for an isoflavone claim on packaging* Many products are now alerting buyers to their isoflavone content, so you know exactly how much you're getting. The new joint Australia New Zealand Food Standards Code, for example, requires that if a manufacturer makes a phytoestrogen nutrient content claim on packaging they need to state the actual amount in the product. We are unaware of similar legislation in other countries.

3. *Check out the ingredient list* This will give you a clue as to whether a product is likely to contain phytoestrogens, since not all products will make an isoflavone claim. Look for ingredients such as soybeans, tofu, soy protein, soy grits, textured vegetable protein, soy nuts, linseed, wholegrains; products that contain these ingredients will likely be a 'good source' or 'rich source' of phytoestrogens.

The Lifefibre Company

A tasty way to keep you looking good and feel great.

HIFIBRE SEED BREAD

This bread is laden with goodness. Containing 5 fabulous seeds which keep you regular. Sesame seeds which are a rich source of calcium and linseeds have numerous attributes. Make delicious sandwiches everytime.

* Suitable for Freezing
* Suitable for Vegetarians
* Dairy Free

Ingredients: Wheatmeal flour, water, sesame seeds, linseeds, sunflower seed, poppy seeds, pinhead oatmeal, caramel, yeast, sea salt, oil dough conditioner, E282.

550g ℮   Store in a cool, dry place.

Baked by Kiely's Cameo, Castleisland, (066 - 7142944) for The Lifefibre Company: 087 665 7088.

Sliced
BEST BEFORE
23.12.02

5 098973 011012 >

A typical food label

Phytoestrogen shopping list

Bakery section
Dark rye bread
Mixed grain bread
Muffins, wholemeal
Muffins, with grains and seeds

Seeded bread, particularly with linseeds
Soy & linseed bread
Soy bread
Wholegrain bread

Fruit and vegetable section

A variety of seasonal fruits and vegetables is best

Apples	Leeks
Asparagus	Lemons
Bananas	Lychees
Beetroot	Mekuba seaweed
Blackberries	Mungbean sprouts
Blackcurrants	Mushrooms
Bok choy	Onions
Boston lettuce	Oranges
Broad beans	Papaya
Broccoli	Peaches
Brussels sprouts	Pears
Cabbage	Plums
Capsicum	Potatoes
Carrots	Radishes
Cauliflower	Raspberries
Celery	Redcurrants
Chives	Rockmelon
Cranberries	Runner beans
Cucumber	Snow beans
French beans	Spinach
Garlic	Squash
Gooseberries	Strawberries
Grapefruit	Sweet potatoes
Green peas	Tomatoes
Guava	Turnip
Hijki seaweed	Watercress
Iceberg lettuce	

Freezer section

Frozen fruit, such as berries

Frozen green soybeans
(Edamame)

Frozen vegetables

Soy ice-cream

Soy schnitzels

Refrigerated section

Alfalfa sprouts

Chilled soy milk, calcium
fortified

Natto

Orange juice

Soy bacon

Soy burger

Soy cheese

Soy custard

Soy hot dogs

Soy based deli slices

Soy sausages

Soy yoghurt

Soybean sprouts

Tempeh

Tempeh burger

Tofu

Tofu yoghurt

On shelf

Baked beans

Barley bran

Black beans, dry or canned

Blackeyed beans, dry or
canned

Broad beans, dry

Brown rice

Caraway seeds

Cashew nuts

Chickpeas, dry or canned

Chinese blackbean sauce

Dried apricots

Haricot beans, dry or canned

Hazelnuts

Lentils, dry or canned

Licorice

Lima beans, dry or canned

Linseeds

Long-life soy milk, calcium
fortified

Miso
Mung beans, dry or canned
Navy beans, dry or canned
Nut butters
Oat bran
Olive oil, extra virgin
Peanut butter
Peanuts
Pinto beans, dry or canned
Prunes
Red kidney beans, dry or canned
Rye bran
Sesame seeds
Soy flakes
Soy flour
Soy grits
Soy nuts, plain or flavoured
Soy pasta

Soy protein bars
Soy protein shakes
Soy-based breakfast cereals
Soybeans, dry or canned
Split peas, dry or canned
Stoneground wholemeal or rye flour
Sunflower seeds
Tea, black
Tea, green
Tea, jasmine
Triticale
Textured vegetable protein (TVP)
Walnuts
Wheat bran
Wholemeal products
Wholegrain breakfast cereals

Modifying recipes

You can modify many of your own recipes to boost their phyto-estrogen content. Often, it's simply a matter of replacing one ingredient with another, and there may be little change in flavour or texture. For example, use soy milk in place of dairy on cereal and in cooking. This is a simple way to increase the phytoestrogen content on a daily basis, easily supplying 20 mg of isoflavones (a 'rich source'), depending on the brand used. Here are some suggestions.

Common ingredient	Phytoestrogen-rich ingredient
Dairy milk	Soy milk
Dairy fruit yoghurt	Soy fruit yoghurt
Cream cheese	Silken tofu
Custard	Soy custard
Sour cream	Plain soy yoghurt
Ricotta cheese	Firm tofu, mashed
Smoked cheese	Smoked tofu
Wheat flour*	Soy flour
Stock cube	Miso
Chicken fillet	Slice of firm tofu or ready-made soy fillet/schnitzel
Mincemeat	Rehydrated textured vegetable protein (TVP)
Bulgur wheat	Soy grits

*You can only replace up to ¼ cup of the wheat flour in self-rising baked goods such as muffins and cakes, because soy flour does not contain gluten.

Snack foods

Many people enjoy snack foods. Now you can include snacks that not only taste good, but provide you with phytoprotectants.

Remember, lifestyle habits are set in childhood and adolescence. What you buy for kids today will impact their future choices. Here are some snack ideas to add to your shopping list that are suitable for children and grown-ups alike.

- *Green soybeans (Edamame)* Sweet tasting and absolutely delicious; fashionable at sushi bars and chic restaurants in the US.
- *Soy nuts* Crunchy, and high on the list of 'rich source' of phytoestrogens that would appeal to women. Less expensive than other nut varieties.

- *Soy fruit yoghurts* Smooth and easy to digest; great for kids.
- *Flavoured soy drinks* Flavours such as chocolate and strawberry usually appeal to children, but cappuccino flavours attract the more sophisticated adult palate. Choose calcium-fortified brands.
- *Soy ice-cream* Cool and refreshing; works well as a treat for people of any age, particularly in summer.
- *Soy protein bars* Various brands available targeting women and 'active' people. Sometimes called 'power bars'.
- *Fresh fruit* The original 'fast food'; everyone should be encouraged to eat more, especially children and men whose diets might be lacking in this respect. Choose a variety of fruits—berries are a great source of the lignan phyto-estrogens, for example. Also try dried fruit.
- *Nuts and seeds* A satisfying, healthy snack; choose from natural and unsalted varieties. Try peanuts or nut butters or buy mixed nuts; use a handful in place of other rich snacks if you are watching your weight.
- *Grainy, seeded bread or muffins* Particularly with linseeds. Fresh or toasted, spread with a nut butter for example.

Seven-day phytoestrogen eating plans

To get you started, we have designed two eating plans demonstrating what a phytoestrogen-rich diet might look like over seven days. The Food Lover's Plan is for those who really enjoy cooking and have more time to spend preparing their own food. The Busy Person's Guide shows how to eat a phytoestrogen-rich diet with less emphasis on preparing food from scratch and a greater use of convenience products. However,

---

CASE STUDY JOHN'S STORY

John, a 52-year-old university lecturer, felt that he could not manage to eat all the soy and linseed foods recommended every day, but was unsure of whether his preference for fruits, vegetables and wholegrain foods would give him a healthy level of phytoestrogens. Over a three day period John followed his usual diet. Breakfast included a glass of fruit juice and a bowl of museli containing lots of nuts and dried fruit. To this, he usually added low fat dairy milk, but on one day he tried soy milk. Lunch consisted of a wholegrain roll with fried eggplant slices and a variety of salad ingredients or grilled mushrooms and tabouli in a wholemeal roll. In the evenings he generally ate fish with a good helping of stir-fried vegetables (broccoli, cauliflower, carrots, bean sprouts, garlic and onions), jasmine rice or pasta, followed by fruit for dessert. At least four types of fruits in season—peaches, mango, strawberries and fresh lychees were consumed between meals whenever he felt peckish. When we analysed John's urine, we found that he managed to achieve a high and protective level of the lignan family of phytoestrogens— comparable to what we find in vegetarians. This was possible because he ate so many plant-based foods where lignans are naturally found.

---

even for the busy person we include one meal suggestion daily, based on a recipe. There is no substitute for home-cooked food.

These eating plans are rich in dietary fibre providing, on average, over 35 g daily. For most people this will improve bowel function. The plans are also an excellent source of calcium, supplying around 900 mg per day. The fat content is moderate at 60–70 g per day and this mainly comes from nuts, seeds, fish and extra virgin olive oil—foods that are known to promote good health. Only a relatively small proportion (14–17 per cent) of the fat in the eating plans is saturated fat. If you wish to further reduce the fat content you can for example substitute low fat or fat free soy products for their regular counterparts.

You will notice that meat and poultry are not emphasised in these eating plans. This doesn't mean you have to become vegetarian. If you wish, you can include modest amounts of lean red meat—about the size of a pack of cards—or poultry a few times per week. Just remember that animal products generally don't provide any phytoestrogens, so fill most of your plate with foods made from vegetables, legumes and wholegrains to achieve a phytoestrogen-rich diet. Variety is the spice of life, so once you get the hang of it, use these eating plans as guides and continue to design your own menus.

Food lover's seven-day phytoestrogen eating plan

	SUNDAY	MONDAY	TUESDAY	WEDNESDAY	THURSDAY	FRIDAY	SATURDAY
Breakfast	*Breakfast*	*Breakfast*	*Breakfast*	*Breakfast*	*Breakfast*	*Breakfast*	*Breakfast*
	• Spicy tomato juice • Egg-free scramble with capers & shallots* • Sourdough dark rye bread	• Peach nectar • Swiss muesli with mixed berries* and soy milk	• Fresh grapefruit • Soft polenta* with ground linseeds • Soy milk	• Banana & blueberry muffin* • Mango lassi*	• Fresh apple & carrot juice • Toasted five-grain muesli* with soy milk	• Crunchy wheat with tropical fruits* • Soy latte	• Orange juice • Golden waffles* with walnuts and maple syrup
Lunch	*Lunch*	*Lunch*	*Lunch*	*Lunch*	*Lunch*	*Lunch*	*Lunch*
	• Cashew fried rice* • Mandarins	• Brown lentil soup with dill* • Soy and linseed bread • Fresh pear	• Wholemeal pita bread with smoked soy slices & tabouli salad* • Fruit salad	• Niçoise salad with smoked tofu* • Wholegrain roll • Melon wedge	• Wok-fried rice noodles with bean curd, sprouts & crushed peanuts* • Bunch of grapes	• Tofu burger with ginger, chilli & garlic* • Banana	• Mini Mediterranean pizzas* • Fresh pineapple • Strawberry soy milk

* These meals are included in the recipe section.

Note: Select fruit and vegetables in season—buy local and regional produce where possible.

	SUNDAY	MONDAY	TUESDAY	WEDNESDAY	THURSDAY	FRIDAY	SATURDAY
Dinner	*Dinner*	*Dinner*	*Dinner*	*Dinner*	*Dinner*	*Dinner*	*Dinner*
	• Creamy leek & potato soup*	• Grilled fish fillets topped with fresh salsa*	• Chilli green pea soup with coriander*	• Spaghetti bolognaise with red wine*	• Chickpea curry with pumpkin & baby spinach*	• Pan-tossed perch with Mediterranean vegetables*	• Indian potato, cauliflower & tofu curry* or Lamb Korma curry
	• Pasta sauce with eggplant, red capsicum & currants*	• Steamed new potatoes	• Risotto with mushrooms & Edamame* or Risotto with chicken and Edamame	• Mixed salad with raspberry & pistachio vinaigrette*	• Steamed brown rice	• Sweet potato, pumpkin & potato mash*	• Three-bean dhal* with basmati rice
	• Soy fruit yoghurt	• Baby spinach, Roma tomato & red onion salad*	• Fresh apple		• Stewed pears with thick custard*	• Kiwi fruit	• Fresh raspberries
		• Soy fruit yoghurt					
Snack	*Snack*	*Snack*	*Snack*	*Snack*	*Snack*	*Snack*	*Snack*
	• Strawberry & banana smoothie*	• Roasted soy nuts*	• Chocolate soy milk	• European-style crepes* with fresh strawberry sauce*	• Dried fruit & nuts	• Peach & passionfruit shake*	• Edamame

* These meals are included in the recipe section.

Note: Select fruit and vegetables in season—buy local and regional produce where possible.

Busy person's seven-day phytoestrogen eating plan

SUNDAY	MONDAY	TUESDAY	WEDNESDAY	THURSDAY	FRIDAY	SATURDAY
Breakfast	*Breakfast*	*Breakfast*	*Breakfast*	*Breakfast*	*Breakfast*	*Breakfast*
• Grapefruit juice • Grilled soy sausages, tomato & mushrooms • Toasted wholegrain & seed bread	• Pineapple juice • Soy cereal with dried fruit & Soy milk	• Orange juice • Wholegrain flakes with Phytosprinkle* & Soy milk	• Fresh fruit salad • Wholemeal raisin toast with raspberry jam	• Apricot nectar • Wholegrain breakfast biscuits with sliced banana & pecans & Soy milk	• Fresh figs • Toasted 9 grain English muffins with scrape of margarine & Vegemite/ Marmite • Glass soy milk	• Dark grape juice • Hot oatmeal & honey with Phytosprinkle* & Soy milk
Lunch	*Lunch*	*Lunch*	*Lunch*	*Lunch*	*Lunch*	*Lunch*
• Baked jacket potato with coleslaw & shredded cheese • Orange	• Baked beans & salad sandwich on wholemeal bread • Fresh strawberries	• Sardines, sliced tomato, baby spinach & sprouts on dark rye bread with hommus • Pitted prunes & dried pears	• Soy hot dog with lettuce, tomato & barbecue sauce in wholegrain seeded roll • Papaya	• Cheese & salad sandwich on wholegrain bread • Tropical fruit salad	• Falafel roll with wholemeal Lebanese bread • Nashi pear	• Red salmon, chives & cucumber sandwich on soy & linseed bread • Red apple • Sunflower seed bar

* These meals are included in the recipe section.

Note: Select fruit and vegetables in season—buy local and regional produce where possible.

SUNDAY	MONDAY	TUESDAY	WEDNESDAY	THURSDAY	FRIDAY	SATURDAY
Dinner	*Dinner*	*Dinner*	*Dinner*	*Dinner*	*Dinner*	*Dinner*
• Red Thai vegetable curry with tofu* • Steamed jasmine rice • Plum & almond parfait*	• Vibrant vege & tofu stir-fry* or braised beef with vegetables • Steamed brown rice • Cubed rockmelon with Soy ice-cream	• Kumara, red lentil & lemon soup* • Crusty wholegrain dinner roll • Fresh lychees	• Creamy mushroom pasta with peppercorns* • Salad of mixed green leaves with lemon juice and extra virgin olive oil • Blueberries	• Bean burritos with avocado, tomato & coriander* • Fresh mango	• Roasted vegetables on couscous with Moroccan dressing* • Baked green apples with cranberries*	• Soy schnitzel (ready to heat) or chicken schnitzel • Potato mash • Char-grilled balsamic vegetables* • Cherries
Snack	*Snack*	*Snack*	*Snack*	*Snack*	*Snack*	*Snack*
• Peach	• Mixed nuts	• Soy protein bar	• Chocolate soy drink	• Roasted soy nuts*	• Soya-ccino	• Soy fruit yoghurt

* These meals are included in the recipe section.

Note: Select fruit and vegetables in season—buy local and regional produce where possible.

chapter 14

A–Z guide to phytoestrogen foods

'Food is an important part of a balanced diet'
FRAN LEBOWITZ

This section is a guide to foods that contain phytoestrogens: what they are; where you can buy them; and how to use and store them.

Most phytoestrogen-rich foods are made from soybeans, soy proteins and linseed. But there are many other important foods, such as wholegrains, nuts, fruits and vegetables, that provide a 'source' of phytoestrogens—small but useful amounts that add up to boost your overall daily intake. Soy oils, soy lecithin and soy sauce contain very low levels of isoflavones, as do soy protein concentrates that have been alcohol-extracted.

Bran *('source')*

Brans provide a 'source' of phytoestrogens from the lignan family. This is because the phytoestrogens are located directly beneath the bran layer of a wholegrain kernel and tend to be removed with the bran portion.

You can buy many types of bran—barley, oat, wheat, rye and rice bran. Add them to recipes for making bread or muffins or even to casseroles as a thickener. Many breakfast cereals are fortified with bran to boost their fibre content.

Concentrated soy protein *('source' or 'rich source', depending on processing)*

Concentrated soy protein, also known as soy protein concentrate, is an ingredient used by the food industry to add to meat products and to manufacture many soy foods such as soy hot dogs—it is not usually available for use in the home kitchen. It is produced when protein is extracted from soybeans and contains around 70 per cent protein. Concentrated soy protein also provides dietary fibre. Many concentrates are low in phytoestrogens as alcohol is used in their manufacture, stripping the phytoestrogens. Some manufacturers have recently modified their processing steps to better preserve the phytoestrogens. Check food labels for the type of soy protein used. If unsure, contact the manufacturer to confirm whether the soy protein contains phytoestrogens.

Fruits *('source')*

Fruits provide a 'source'of the lignan family of phytoestrogens. While only certain fruits, such as pears, plums, strawberries, bananas and apples, appear in our Phytoestrogen Food Guide, other fruits certainly contain phytoestrogens, but many have not yet been tested. Oranges have a flavone called *naringenin*, which also behaves like a phytoestrogen.

Our advice is to eat a variety of fresh fruits—at least two pieces each day. In general, those fruits that are good sources of fibre will have the highest lignan level.

Green soybeans *('rich source')*

Green soybeans, also called Edamame (pronounced ed-ah-MAH-may), are the fresh bright green soybeans in their pod. They are an excellent source of isoflavones.

Unlike dried soybeans, green soybeans are sweet tasting. They can be purchased fresh or frozen, in their pod or shelled, from Asian supermarkets and some gourmet supermarkets. They are very fashionable in the US where they are served in their pods in sushi bars and restaurants. You simply suck the beans out and discard the pod—even though the latter is also a considerable source of isoflavones. At home, you can boil them and serve them out of their pods as a side dish or toss into pasta, risotto or stir-fries.

Hops *('source')*

Hops are used to make beer. They contain a substance that is a stronger phytoestrogen than the types found in soy. However, it occurs in fairly low levels, so you would have to consume almost 100 litres of beer a day to expect 'estrogenic' effects!

Kudzu *('rich source')*

Kudzu is an edible vine indigenous to the People's Republic of China. The root of this plant has been traditionally used as a flour for baking. It is an uncommon food ingredient in the Western world but is a component of many phytoestrogen supplements. It has a high content of isoflavones, particularly peurarin and daidzin.

Legumes *('source', 'good source' or 'rich source')*

Legumes include dried beans such as lentils, black beans, kidney beans, navy beans, lima beans, blackeyed beans and pinto beans.

They provide both lignans and isoflavones. South Africa is leading the way in publicly recognising the important role of legumes in the diet. 'Eat dry beans, peas, lentils and soy regularly' is a newly released, unique Food-Based Dietary Guideline.

Soybeans have the highest amounts of phytoestrogens by far. The concentration of isoflavones in soybeans is almost 100–1000 times higher than in most other legumes. Peanuts are technically also a legume, but they supply only a 'source' of phytoestrogens. Legumes are found in health food stores and supermarkets either dried, or cooked in the can. We provide many delicious recipes using legumes in soups, sauces and curries.

Linseeds *('rich source')*

Linseeds, also known as flaxseeds, are very small, flattish dark-brown seeds probably best known for their super levels of Omega-3 fats. Linseeds are grown largely because they provide a valuable source of oil used in the manufacture of paints and other industrial products. Even clothes such as linen shirts are made from linseed! Linseeds are high in dietary fibre: one study found a 30 per cent improvement in bowel movements in just four weeks of taking 50 g linseeds daily. However, the recent nutritional interest in linseeds is because they provide a 'rich source' of the family of phytoestrogens called lignans, a scientific discovery first made by the co-author (KS) of this book. These are not typically found in linseed oil, unless they have been added.

You can add whole linseeds when making breads and muffins, or sprinkle them on your breakfast cereal. To grind linseed, use an electric coffee grinder. You can also mix ground linseeds into yoghurt, oatmeal and smoothies.

Linseeds are sold in health food stores and some supermarkets. Store whole seeds for up to one year in a dry, airtight container in a cool place such as your pantry or in the refrigerator if you live in a very hot and humid region. If you grind them, use immediately or place them in the freezer, otherwise the beneficial fatty acids are prone to turning rancid.

Miscellaneous soy foods *(variable)*

The range of products now available that contain soy is ever expanding. Products include pasta, pancake mixes, cake mixes, health bars, chocolate bars, mayonnaise and even soy coffee! You can find these in health food stores or supermarkets.

The phytoestrogen content of such products varies greatly because of the different ingredients used. If soybeans, soy flour, soy protein isolate, TVP or soy grits are used to make the product, it will probably be a 'good source' or 'rich source' of phytoestrogens. If the major ingredients are soybean oil or soy lecithin, the product will be lacking in phytoestrogens. Check the food packaging for the isoflavone level, or contact the manufacturer to see if this information is available.

Miso or soybean paste *('good source')*

Miso is a rich and salty fermented soybean paste made from cooked soybeans mixed with salt, a mould culture and usually a grain such as wheat, barley or rice, and then aged in vats for one to three years. Countries such as Japan, Korea, Taiwan, China and Indonesia use it as a flavouring agent in soups and other foods. Even though miso provides a 'good source' of phytoestrogens, use it sparingly because it is also high in salt. You can use miso instead of stock cubes to enhance the flavour of soups, sauces, dips, spreads, marinades or salad dressings.

Miso is usually found in the refrigerated section of Asian supermarkets or health food stores. It will last for several months provided you also store it in the fridge at home. If you see a white mould build up on top, just scrape it off—miso is made with a mould culture.

Natto *('rich source')*

Natto is a fermented soy food that originated in northern Japan, but similar products are now also found in some other Asian countries. It is made from whole soybeans that are fermented with bacteria to create a slimy appearance, sweet taste and characteristic aroma. The Japanese usually eat it at meals with boiled rice. Natto is not commonly found in general supermarkets but you can find it in the refrigerated section of Asian supermarkets.

Nuts and seeds *('source')*

Nuts and seeds—such as sunflower seeds—generally provide a 'source' of phytoestrogens. Linseeds and linseed meal, as mentioned, contain the highest levels of lignans of any food, supplying a 'rich source' to the diet. Although nuts are high in fat, nut consumption is not linked to obesity. People who consumed nuts five times or more per week were found to be no fatter than people who rarely ate nuts. You can buy nuts and seeds in all supermarkets and health food stores. They are wonderful as a snack food, but can also be tossed into salads and stir-fries or used in baking and desserts. Choose raw nuts in preference to salted or those roasted in oil.

Phytoestrogen extracts and raw materials *('rich source')*

A number of international companies specialise in extracting and processing phytoestrogens from plants. Many food, pharmaceutical and nutriceutical companies use these as starting materials to manufacture soy protein or phytoestrogen-rich foods, drinks and supplements. Soybean extracts are the most common and these are indicated on the labels of food packaging. The most widely used phytoestrogen-rich extracts include products such as the SUPRO® or Solae™ brands produced by Protein Technologies International (St Louis, Missouri, USA; www.proteintechnologies.com), Soyarich I® from The Central Soya Company, Inc. (Fort Wayne, Indiana, USA; www.centralsoya.com), Novasoy® made by the Archer Daniel Midland Company (Decatur, Illinois, USA; www.adm .archerdanielmidland.com), and the identity preserved non-GMO extracts, Solgen and Nutragen made by Solbar Plant Extracts (Ashdod, Israel; www.solbar.com) and Advatasoy™ from the Cargill Company (Minneapolis, Minnesota, USA; www.cargill.com). The most concentrated phytoestrogen plant extract available comes from the soybean germ and is marketed as SoyLife™ from SoyLife Nederland BV (Giessen, The Netherlands; www.soylife.com). Purified lignan extracts are now becoming available and these have so far been made from processing linseeds.

Phytoestrogen supplements *('rich source')*

There is a large number of phytoestrogen supplements on the market in the UK. Also, many can be purchased via the Internet. Most are based on isoflavones from either the soybean germ or extracted from the whole soybean. A few originate from clover, and some are mixtures that also contain kudzu root extract. To a lesser extent you can find lignan extracts made from linseed.

Phytoestrogen supplements are available in capsules, tablets or powders that are dissolved in water or taken with some other kind of drink. Those made from the soy germ are very high in isoflavones because the germ is part of the bean where isoflavones are naturally concentrated.

Recent research from the University of Cincinnati has found that many of the phytoestrogen supplements do not contain what they claim on packaging. This is often the case with supplements. While it may be impossible for you to know which are the best to purchase, as a rule of thumb choose those made by the more reputable pharmaceutical manufacturers rather than purchase through mail order or the Internet.

Red clover supplements *('rich source')*

Red clover is rich in two isoflavones called biochanin A and formononetin. These are much weaker in estrogenic activity than soy isoflavones—but when eaten, they are converted by the bacteria in the intestines to the same two isoflavones that are found in soy. Red clover phytoestrogens are being marketed to promote women's and men's health, despite limited evidence as to their effectiveness. These products are mostly sold in pharmacies and health food stores.

Soy and linseed breads *('good source')*

Soy and linseed breads have become increasingly popular in many Western countries. They are sometimes sold as three-grain, five-grain, seven-grain or nine-grain breads made with the addition of soy grits and whole linseeds. The fat-reduced varieties of bread use de-fatted soy grits. Soy and linseed breads provide a 'good source' of lignans and isoflavones—although this is not always evident from the packaging—and they are high in fibre. You can find soy and linseed breads, muffins or crispbreads at supermarkets, health food stores and bakeries.

Soy burgers, schnitzels, slices and hot dogs ('source' or 'good source')

Soy meat alternatives can be made from textured vegetable protein, soy protein isolate or soy protein concentrate. The phytoestrogen content varies according to the starting soy ingredient. Those made from alcohol-washed soy protein concentrate lack significant amounts of phytoestrogens.

Some soy meat alternatives are fortified with nutrients such as iron and vitamin B12, which is particularly useful for vegetarians. Many contain significantly less fat than meat and are low in saturated fat and free from cholesterol.

Look for soy meat alternatives in the freezer and refrigerator sections of supermarkets and health food stores.

Soy cereals ('good source' or 'rich source')

Many varieties of soy breakfast cereals are now available in supermarkets and health food stores. These contain soy flour, TVP, soy grits, soy nuts, soy flakes or soy extracts. They are mostly low in fat and good sources of dietary fibre and contain certain added vitamins and minerals. To start the day with a good dose of phytoestrogens, serve the cereal with soy milk.

Soy cheese ('source' or 'good source')

Soy cheese is made by combining soy extracts, soy milk or tofu with a vegetable oil, usually soybean oil or canola oil. Other ingredients can include casein—the protein found in milk. Some soy cheeses are therefore not dairy free, though dairy-free soy cheese is available.

You can use soy cheese in the same way you use regular cheese. Grate it and sprinkle onto pizzas, or slice it and add it to sandwiches. Soy cheese is available from supermarkets and health food stores.

Most soy cheese usually contains a level of fat similar to dairy milk cheese. However, the fat is mostly polyunsaturated or monounsaturated and there is no cholesterol. Fat-free soy cheese is available in some countries. Be aware that, in common with other processed cheeses, the salt content of soy cheese is usually high.

Soy flour *('rich source')*

Soy flour is made by pulverising roasted soybeans into a fine powder. It is available from supermarkets and health food stores as natural soy flour—which includes the fat from the soybeans. Sometimes it comes in a de-fatted version, where the fat has been removed. Soy flour is about 50 per cent protein.

Because of its naturally high phytoestrogen content, you can use soy flour to boost the phytoestrogen levels in many recipes. When making muffins, cakes, biscuits or pancakes try replacing one-quarter of the regular flour with soy flour. When making breads, add two tablespoons of soy flour to the bottom of every cup measure before filling it with wheat flour. Using these amounts generally doesn't affect the taste. Soy flour is gluten free and, as such, will not provide the elasticity of gluten-containing flours. This means you can't use it as a complete replacement for wheat and other flours containing gluten.

Store soy flour in dry, cool, odour-free and vermin-free conditions. It usually has a shelf life of 12 months, but is best used quickly.

Soy grits *('rich source')*

Soy grits are soybeans that have been cracked into small pieces to provide a coarse mix. They are then cooked and dehydrated. Add soy grits to bread-making dough, stews and casseroles or even use them in tabouli in place of cracked wheat. You just need to rehydrate them with water. Soy grits are available from supermarkets or health food stores. Store them in an airtight container in the cupboard/pantry.

Soy ice-cream *('source')*

Soy ice-cream is a blend of soybean extract or soy protein with vegetable oil, sugars, gums and flavours. It may also contain fruit. It is cholesterol free, low in saturated fat and usually dairy free. Soy ice-cream is available from supermarkets and health food stores.

Soy infant formula *('rich source')*

Soy infant formula is specially formulated to meet the nutritional requirements of term infants and to support normal growth and development. It is used as an alternative to breast milk or cow's milk formula. In Western countries, soy infant formula is made from isolated soy protein. Wholebean soy infant formula is available in South Korea. You can obtain soy infant formula from pharmacies and supermarkets.

Soy milk *('source' or 'good source')*

Soy milk is one of the most convenient means of obtaining a substantial daily intake of phytoestrogens. Some brands now display the isoflavone content on their labels.

Soy milk can be made from scratch by starting with soybeans—with or without their outer fibre layer—or by blending soy protein isolate with other ingredients. The taste, colour and nutritional quality will vary according to the recipe and process used. Some soy milks are fortified with a range of vitamins and minerals, such as calcium and vitamin B12—to make them a suitable replacement for dairy milk. Wholebean varieties provide dietary fibre.

Use soy milk exactly as you would use dairy milk—in cooking and baking, over your cereal, in mashed potato, or in hot or cold drinks. It is available in supermarkets and health food stores and comes fresh and in long-life or powdered form. You can choose from flavoured or plain, fat-free, low-fat and regular varieties. We recommend a calcium-fortified brand. As it is lactose free, soy milk is an excellent choice for people with lactose intolerance.

Soy nuts ('rich source')

Soy nuts are a great snack food made by soaking soybeans, then roasting them. They contain 60 per cent less fat than peanuts and they are much cheaper. You can make your own or buy them ready-to-eat from health food stores. They come in a variety of flavours. Store them in your pantry in a container with a lid and they will last for up to a year, if they don't get eaten!

Soy protein isolate ('good source')

Soy protein isolate, also known as isolated soy protein, is obtained when protein is extracted from soybeans. It is over 90 per cent pure protein, the highest level of any single soy food ingredient. It is rich in phytoestrogens and contains various other nutrients and phytochemicals, but has very little fat.

Soy protein isolate is used by the food industry to manufacture a variety of products ranging from soy milks to soy schnitzels. It is also used to produce soy infant formula and enteral feeds—the latter most commonly used in hospitals and nursing homes.

Soy protein isolate is available in health food stores and some supermarkets under the guise of 'soy protein powder' or similar. Try sprinkling it onto your cereal, mixing it into fruit juice or yoghurt or adding it to recipes for foods such as muffins.

Soy sauce ('source')

Soy sauce is a dark brown, salty liquid made from fermented soybeans. It is widely used in Asian cooking, but it is not a 'rich source' of phytoestrogens. There are different types of soy sauce—according to what is added to the soybeans. Shoyu is a blend of soybeans and wheat; tamari is a by-product from the process used to make miso and is made only from fermented soybeans. Teriyaki is usually slightly thickened and contains sugar, vinegar and other spices.

You can use soy sauce to season many foods from vegetables to rice, meat and fish. But beware! It is high in salt and therefore best diluted with water before use. You can buy soy sauce in general supermarkets, Asian supermarkets and health food stores.

Soy snack foods ('variable')

Soy bars, soy chocolates and soy chips contain variable amounts of phytoestrogens. Some soy snack foods may contain high levels of fat: soy crisps, for example, have a similar level of fat to ordinary potato crisps. Just because a product has 'soy' in its name, there is no guarantee that, overall, it is a healthy food choice. It may contain excessive amounts of fat, sugar and salt. Check food labels.

Soy yoghurt ('good source')

Soy yoghurt is different from dairy yoghurt in that it is made either from soybeans or soy protein rather than dairy milk.

Otherwise, the manufacturing process is the same. You can buy it in supermarkets or health food stores fruit flavoured. Alternatively, you can make unflavoured soy yoghurt yourself by using soy milk and a starter culture from any dairy yoghurt. Flavoured soy yoghurt makes a great snack and can be added to smoothies and lassis. Some soy yoghurts are fortified with calcium and may contain fibre. Check food labels.

Soybean sprouts *('good source')*

These are the sprouts of dried soybeans. Commonly used in Asian countries such as Korea—and becoming increasingly popular in Western countries—soy sprouts should be lightly cooked before eating. Add them to stir-fries, soups and salads.

Look for soybean sprouts at your greengrocers.

Soybeans *('rich source')*

There are more than 300 varieties of soybeans. They come in various shapes, sizes and colours and are used to make different traditional Asian soy foods such as miso, tofu, soy drinks, soy sprouts and tempeh. Soybeans are so prized in Asian countries that in Korea they say the soybean is 'the meat from the soil'. The most common variety you will find in supermarkets and health food stores are the small, round, yellow beans.

Soak dry soybeans overnight in plenty of water and use them to make soups, stews and casseroles, or mash them when cooked and use in burgers or as a base for dips. To save time, buy canned soybeans—these have already been cooked, or precook a batch of your own and freeze them. Store dry soybeans in a jar in your cupboard or pantry. They have a very long shelf life.

Sprouts ('source', 'good source' or 'rich source')

There are many varieties of sprouts. The US FDA has recently warned against potential *Salmonella* and *E.coli* 0157 infection through consuming raw sprouts. We recommend that you lightly cook sprouts and, at the very least, wash them thoroughly before eating. Add lightly cooked soy sprouts to salads, soups and stir fries. Alfalfa and mung bean sprouts can be used fresh in sandwiches and salads.

Tempeh ('rich source')

Tempeh is a traditional Indonesian food. It is probably the least appreciated Asian food as it can take some time to get used to its unique flavour. This is best described as smoky and nutty, while the texture is chewy. Whole soybeans, sometimes mixed with another grain such as rice, are fermented into a rich savoury cake to make tempeh.

You can slice, marinate and barbecue tempeh, or cut it into small cubes and lightly fry it. It works well skewered for making kebabs, crumbled to form burgers or balls. Store unused tempeh in the fridge until the use-by date. Don't worry if a white-coloured area starts to appear on the surface, it has not gone off. Tempeh is a fermented food and, just like Camembert cheese, it is normal for it to be covered with a white mould. You will find tempeh refrigerated in general and Asian supermarkets or health food stores.

Textured vegetable protein ('rich source')

Textured vegetable protein (TVP) is a 'soy mince' made from soy flour. It is made by compressing de-fatted soy flour under

pressure until the protein fibres change structure. The protein
is then extruded in special machines to produce a variety of
shapes and textures. You will find TVP in the form of dehydrated mince and dehydrated chunks. These are rehydrated
by simply adding water and allowing them to swell, which
usually takes around 15 minutes.

Use rehydrated TVP exactly how you would use minced
or diced meat. It is wonderful for making cholesterol-free
spaghetti bolognaise or lasagne. As TVP has a long shelf life,
keeping a packet in the cupboard makes a lot of sense—it is
very useful if you want to prepare a quick nutritious meal but
don't have too many fresh ingredients in the fridge. You will
find TVP in most supermarkets and health food stores.

Tofu *('rich source')*

Tofu (also called bean curd) is a soft, cheese-like curd made by
setting soy milk with a coagulant. Bland in flavour unless it is
smoked, tofu comes in firm and soft varieties. This is an advantage because it absorbs other flavours well. For example, you
can marinate the firm variety in soy sauce with crushed garlic,
ginger and chilli and then use it in stir-fries to add a contrast
in texture. Firm tofu can also be cubed or sliced and added to
soups, or grilled and made into a tofu burger. Smoked tofu is
wonderful in sandwiches and salads and soft tofu makes a good
substitute for cream cheese in cheesecakes. Silken tofu, which
has an even smoother texture, is excellent for dips, sauces or
mayonnaise.

Tofu set with calcium sulphate provides a good source of
calcium; tofu set with nigari or magnesium chloride usually
has a low calcium content. Compared with an equivalent

serving of lean red meat, tofu is lower in saturated fat and cholesterol free.

You can buy tofu in supermarkets, Asian shops and health food stores. Once opened, it should be stored in a container covered with plenty of water and refrigerated. Change the water daily to keep the tofu fresh.

Vegetables ('source')

Vegetables supply a 'source' of phytoestrogens but, unlike legumes and linseed, they are not rich sources of these phytoprotectants. They do provide many other valuable nutrients, though. Vegetables contain higher levels of the lignan family of phytoestrogens than fruits. One study found that the urine levels of lignans were higher when people ate a diet rich in carrots and spinach, or broccoli and cauliflower, than during a vegetable-free diet. Include at least five differently coloured vegetables each day—either cooked or raw in salads.

Wholegrains ('source')

There are many different types of grains—such as wheat, rye, corn, barley and products made from these. Only wholegrains and brans, however, supply the lignan family of phytoestrogens. When grains are refined and have their bran layer removed, most of the phytoestrogens are lost.

For good health, try to eat at least three foods made from wholegrains each day. For example, one serving of a wholegrain breakfast cereal, a slice of wholegrain bread and half a cup of cooked brown rice.

chapter 15

Eat to Live recipes

The following recipes are full of flavour, colour and aroma, which we hope will inspire you to want to cook! Many of our friends and family now use them regularly. But healthy recipes without taste don't work. Once you've tried them, you'll probably never make them again. So we believe that it's vital that food also tastes great, so you will keep coming back for more.

The best way to approach these recipes is to try a variety. Don't feel that you should only choose those that supply a 'rich source' of phytoestrogens. As long as you include at least two foods that provide a 'rich source' of phytoestrogens (as shown in the Phytoestrogen Food Guide on pages 148–151) each day, you will be taking in healthy levels of these phytoprotectants. The recipes can help you do this, but they are not the only way. Remember, individual foods and drinks such as soy milk or soy burgers are another easy way to boost your intake of phytoestrogens.

You will notice that we don't provide any recipes for meat dishes—this doesn't mean you have to become vegetarian. You can include modest amounts of lean red meat—about the size of a pack of cards—or poultry. However, animal products don't supply phytoestrogens and most people are already familiar with cooking meat and poultry. Our focus is, therefore, to help you broaden your diet by cooking more meals containing phytoestrogens.

Our recipes are not all low in fat. The craze for everything to be low-fat seems to have overtaken common sense, and is not the healthiest way to eat. The most recent research indicates that it is the type of fat that is most important and not just the total amount you consume; some fats should actually be included in the diet for good health. What we give you are recipes that are low in saturates (the unhealthy type) and cholesterol, while providing unsaturates from extra virgin olive oil, avocadoes, nuts and seeds and some fish. The nutritional analysis attached to each recipe shows just how low in saturated fat and cholesterol our recipes are, and the valuable contribution they make to your intake of dietary fibre and calcium. Note that the analyses do not include optional ingredients. The tablespoon measure used in the recipes is equivalent to 15 mL. This measure is commonly available in kitchenware shops. Check your spoon, however, as some standard measures for a tablespoon are 25 mL.

Breakfasts

CRUNCHY WHEAT WITH TROPICAL FRUITS

This dish makes a super breakfast and has real crunch to give your jaw a healthy workout. You can also serve it for dessert with a dollop of vanilla or fruity soy yoghurt, or as a snack. Instead of wholewheat, you can use other wholegrains, such as spelt or triticale.

    1 cup uncooked wholewheat
    1/4 cup pecans, chopped
    2 tablespoons pine nuts
    1/2 cup currants
    1/4 cup dried mango, diced
    1/4 cup dried paw paw, diced
    2 tablespoons honey

1   Rinse the wholewheat and cook, covered, with 5 cups of water until tender. This will take approximately 1 hour on a conventional stove, or 15 minutes in a pressure cooker.
2   Drain most of the water from the cooked wheat using a sieve— leave it a little moist and place into a large mixing bowl.
3   Add the remaining ingredients and mix well so that the honey is distributed and coats all the ingredients.
4   Serve in a breakfast bowl and enjoy! Keeps well in the fridge for up to a week.

Serves 5
Per serve: calories 291; fat 7 g (21 per cent of calories from fat); saturated fat 0.9 g; carbohydrate 55 g; fibre 3 g; cholesterol 0 mg; calcium 38 mg.
Phytoestrogens: 'source'

SWISS MUESLI WITH MIXED BERRIES

Inspired by the famous Swiss nutritionist Dr Bircher, this is no ordinary muesli. Its soft, thick creamy texture interspersed with bits of crunchy nuts will have you coming back for more—and not just at breakfast time. It's even served as a dessert in Switzerland and sold as a snack in street food stalls in Zurich. If you prefer it thinner, just add more soy milk. You can also serve it with sliced banana, mango or stone fruits.

2 cups rolled oats
$\frac{1}{2}$ cup mixed dried fruit such as dates, peaches and apricots, chopped
$\frac{1}{2}$ cup nuts such as hazelnuts, brazil nuts and almonds, smashed
3 cups soy milk
2 tablespoons honey
1 medium green apple, unpeeled
$2\frac{1}{2}$ cups mixed fresh berries such as raspberries, blueberries and boysenberries

1   Place the rolled oats, dried fruit and smashed nuts in a bowl. (Wrap the nuts in a tea towel and smash them against a bench so you get various textures—some ground, others in small pieces.)
2   Add the soy milk and mix together. Cover with a lid and leave in the fridge for about 8 hours, or overnight, until the mixture becomes soft and sticky.
3   Remove from fridge. Add the honey and grate in the apple. Mix well.
4   Serve the muesli in bowls topped with fresh berries. Canned berries in syrup also make a delicious topping.

Serves 6
Per serve: calories 340; fat 12 g (31 per cent of calories from fat); saturated fat 1 g; carbohydrate 50 g; fibre 8 g; cholesterol 0 mg; calcium 200 mg.
Phytoestrogens: 'rich source'

GOLDEN WAFFLES

By replacing cow's milk with soy milk, this recipe shows how you can enrich almost anything with phytoestrogens. It's delicious, too!

2 large eggs, separated

1½ cups plain white flour

½ cup wholemeal flour

2 teaspoons baking powder

pinch of salt

4 tablespoons sugar

2 tablespoons margarine, melted

2 cups soy milk

maple syrup or canned fruit in syrup, to serve, optional

1   Retaining the yolks, beat the egg whites in a bowl until soft peaks form. Set aside.

2   Place the white and wholemeal flours, baking powder, salt, sugar, margarine, egg yolks and soy milk in another mixing bowl and whisk until the batter mixture is smooth.

3   Fold in the egg whites using a large spoon.

4   Place about ¾ cup of batter mixture into a hot waffle-iron and cook according to the manufacturer's instructions.

5   Serve the waffles immediately with maple syrup or canned fruit in syrup such as whole black cherries. Waffles are also suitable for freezing.

Makes 12

Per serve (two waffles): calories 264; fat 7 g (23 per cent of calories from fat); saturated fat 1 g; carbohydrate 43 g; fibre 2 g; cholesterol 99 mg; calcium 31 mg.

Phytoestrogens: 'good source'

SOFT POLENTA

Soft polenta makes a great Sunday breakfast. Alternatively, use it as a base and stack it with roasted vegetables—to make a main meal. When making polenta, it is best to use a large rectangular wooden spoon. This acts like a paddle or a cricket bat to help mix the polenta so lumps don't form. Soak the pot in which you have cooked the polenta overnight with water, and it will be easy to wash the next day. Serving the polenta with soy milk turns this recipe into a 'rich source' of phytoestrogens.

1 teaspoon salt
2 cups polenta (corn meal)
800 ml soy milk, to serve

1   Place 6 cups of water and the salt into a saucepan. Cover with a lid and bring to the boil.
2   Gradually stir in the polenta, mixing vigorously with a wooden spoon so no lumps form. Be careful when you have nearly added all the polenta, as the mixture will become very hot and may start to splurt. If the polenta develops lumps, you can always blend it with a hand-held blender to make it smooth.
3   Cover the saucepan with a lid, reduce the heat and simmer for 20 minutes, stirring every 5 minutes.
4   Serve the polenta in bowls with soy milk.

Serves 4
Per serve: calories 350; fat 8 g (20 per cent of calories from fat); saturated fat 0.9 g; carbohydrate 57 g; fibre 4 g; cholesterol 0 mg; calcium 250 mg.
Phytoestrogens: 'rich source'

TOASTED FIVE-GRAIN MUESLI

This no-added-fat oven-toasted muesli is crunchy and also makes a delicious snack food. The wholegrains and dried fruits have a high antioxidant value.

1 cup rolled oats
½ cup triticale flakes
½ cup barley flakes
½ cup soy wholegrain flakes
½ cup wheat germ
¼ cup shredded coconut
¼ cup sesame seeds
¼ cup sunflower kernels
2 tablespoons honey
¾ cup apricot nectar
½ cup dried currants
½ cup dried pineapple, diced

1 Preheat oven to 100°C (210°F).
2 Blend the rolled oats and triticale, barley and soy flakes in a food processor for 30 seconds.
3 Combine the blended flakes, wheat germ, coconut, sesame seeds and sunflower kernels in a large mixing bowl.
4 Mix together the honey and apricot nectar and pour over the dry ingredients. Combine well.
5 Spread the mixture onto two oven trays lined with non-stick baking paper.
6 Bake for about 45 minutes, stirring every 15 minutes to break up any clusters.

7   Cool completely and mix in the dried currants and dried
     pineapple.

8   Serve topped with sliced banana and soy milk. Store in an airtight
     container.

Makes 5 cups/serves 10

Per serve: calories 212; fat 7 g (27 per cent of calories from fat); saturated
fat 2 g; carbohydrate 35 g; fibre 5 g; cholesterol 0 mg; calcium 60 mg.

Phytoestrogens: 'good source'

APPLE, QUINCE & PRUNE COMPOTE

Compote is delicious eaten for breakfast or as a snack. It is high in fibre and will help keep you regular.

1 small quince, peeled and cored
2 medium apples, peeled and cored
12 prunes, pitted
1 tablespoon sugar
1 small cinnamon stick

1   Cut the quince and the apples into small squares, about 2 cm in size.
2   Place the fruit, prunes, sugar, cinnamon stick and 6 cups of water into a saucepan and bring to the boil.
3   Allow the compote to simmer for about 25 minutes on medium heat—until the fruit is soft. Remove the cinnamon stick and serve the compote warm in a mug or soup bowl with a spoon.

Serves 4

Per serve: calories 153; fat 0.4 g (2 per cent of calories from fat); saturated fat 0.05 g; carbohydrate 40 g; fibre 5 g; cholesterol 0 mg; calcium 25 mg.

Phytoestrogens: 'source'

BANANA & BLUEBERRY MUFFINS

These phytoestrogen-enriched muffins are very easy and quick to make. You can eat them for breakfast and kids will love them as a tasty snack.

1 cup self-raising wholemeal flour
1 cup self-raising white flour
2 medium-sized ripe bananas, mashed
1 cup blueberries, fresh or frozen
½ cup sugar
1 egg
3 tablespoons vegetable oil
1 cup soy milk

1   Preheat oven to 180°C (350°F). Grease a non-stick muffin tray suitable for 12 muffins.
2   Sift the wholemeal and plain flours into a large bowl. Add the mashed banana, blueberries and sugar.
3   Whisk the egg in a small jug and blend in the oil and soy milk. Gently fold this liquid into the flour mixture, until all ingredients are just combined.
4   Spoon the mixture into the muffin tray indentations.
5   Bake the muffins for about 30 minutes, or until they are golden brown.

Makes 12 medium-sized muffins
Per muffin: calories 175; fat 5 g (27 per cent of calories from fat); saturated fat 0.8 g; carbohydrate 29 g; fibre 2 g; cholesterol 19 mg; calcium 67 mg.
Phytoestrogens: 'source'

EGG-FREE SCRAMBLE WITH CAPERS & SHALLOTS

This phytoestrogen-rich recipe only takes a few minutes to cook and is a great replacement for scrambled eggs. The capers and shallots work well together to enhance the flavour. The most delicious tofu comes from an Asian shop. It's stored in a container, covered with water. You can also use this recipe as a sandwich filling.

200 g firm tofu
1 tablespoon extra virgin olive oil
$\frac{1}{2}$ teaspoon ground turmeric
4 shallots, finely sliced
2 teaspoons capers, drained
pinch ground hot paprika
pinch salt, optional

1   Drain the tofu and cover with absorbent paper. Press the paper down to remove as much moisture as possible. When dry, mash with a fork.

2   Heat the oil in a frypan and add the mashed tofu. Cook for a few minutes.

3   Mix in the ground turmeric. The tofu will turn yellow.

4   Add the shallots, capers, paprika and salt (if desired) and continue frying for another few minutes.

5   Serve with toasted wholegrain bread, freshly sliced tomato and kalamata olives.

Serves 2

Per serve: calories 172; fat 12 g (60 per cent of calories from fat); saturated fat 2 g; carbohydrate 9 g; fibre 1 g; cholesterol 0 mg; calcium 179 mg.

Phytoestrogens: 'rich source'

PHYTOSPRINKLE

This crunchy sprinkle is an easy way to boost the phytoestrogen content of your meals and recipes. It also adds fibre, which is great to promote healthy bowels. It will last you about a month if you use a spoonful daily.

$1/2$ cup linseeds, whole
$1/2$ cup sesame seeds, whole
$1/2$ cup sunflower kernels, whole
$1/2$ cup almonds, coarsely chopped

1   Mix all the ingredients together. Store in an airtight glass jar in a dark cupboard or pantry.
2   Use daily on your breakfast cereal, add it to the topping for fruit crumble or use in bread or muffins.

Makes around 2 cups or 25 level tablespoons

Per tablespoon: calories 60; fat 5 g (70 per cent of calories from fat); saturated fat 0.5 g; carbohydrate 2 g; fibre 2 g; cholesterol 0 mg; calcium 43 mg.

Phytoestrogens: 'rich source'

Soups

CHILLI GREEN PEA SOUP WITH CORIANDER

If you want to impress your guests, serve them this bright-green soup, which takes very little time to make. It will tantalise their tastebuds and they will think you spent hours over a hot stove!

> 1 tablespoon extra virgin olive oil
>
> 1 medium onion, finely chopped
>
> 1 very small red chilli, deseeded and finely chopped
>
> 500 g frozen green peas
>
> 1 large (10 g) chicken-style vegetable stock cube
>
> ½ small bunch coriander, finely chopped

1. Heat the oil in a soup pot and add the onion and chilli. Sauté until very soft.
2. Add the frozen peas, crumble in the stock cube and add 1 litre of water.
3. Boil for approximately 15 minutes until the peas are cooked.
4. Add the chopped coriander leaves and transfer the mixture to a blender.
5. Purée the mixture until very smooth. Adjust the flavour with extra salt or pepper if required.

Serves 4

Per serve: calories 110; fat 4 g (35 per cent of calories from fat); saturated fat 0.7 g; carbohydrate 14 g; fibre 5 g; cholesterol 0.2 mg; calcium 82 mg.

Phytoestrogens: 'source'

SWEET POTATO, RED LENTIL & LEMON SOUP

This soup makes a perfect meal with grainy or rye bread and is also an excellent source of vitamin C.

200 g red lentils, picked over for stones and rinsed

1 large (10 g) chicken-style vegetable stock cube, crumbled

1 large onion, peeled and roughly chopped

1 small sweet potato, peeled and roughly chopped

2 cloves garlic, peeled

2 tablespoons extra virgin olive oil

1 teaspoon ground cumin

$\frac{1}{2}$ cup tomato pasta sauce

2 tablespoons chopped fresh dill

3 tablespoons lemon juice

1   Place the washed lentils in a large saucepan together with $1\frac{1}{4}$ litres of water and the stock cube and bring to the boil. Skim the white foam that appears on the surface of the soup and simmer, half-covered, for about 15 minutes, or until you prepare the other ingredients.

2   Blend the onion, sweet potato and garlic in a food processor until the vegetables are finely chopped, but not puréed.

3   Heat the oil in a large frypan and add the chopped vegetables, cumin and tomato pasta sauce. Sauté for about 5 minutes.

4   Add the sautéed vegetables to the pot of boiling lentils and simmer for a further 15 minutes.

5   Mix in the dill and lemon juice and serve.

Serves 4

Per serve: calories 342; fat 9 g (24 per cent of calories from fat); saturated fat 1 g; carbohydrate 52 g; fibre 9 g; cholesterol 0.2 mg; calcium 69 mg.

Phytoestrogens: 'source'

CREAMY LEEK & POTATO SOUP

This is a wonderfully warming soup to serve on a cold evening. Using soy milk boosts the phytoestrogen content but does not alter the mouth-watering flavour.

2 tablespoons extra virgin olive oil

1 large leek with outside leaves removed, sliced

2 cloves garlic, crushed

2 large potatoes, peeled and cut into small chunks

1 large (10 g) chicken-style vegetable stock cube

pinch cracked black pepper

1 bay leaf

1 cup soy milk

2 tablespoons parsley, finely chopped

1   Heat the oil in a deep soup pot and sauté the leek until very soft.

2   Add the garlic, potato chunks, stock cube, pepper, bay leaf and $3\frac{1}{2}$ cups of water. Cover with a lid and bring to the boil.

3   Boil the soup for about 15 minutes or until the potatoes are cooked—this will depend on the size of the chunks. Test with a fork.

4   Remove the bay leaf and purée the soup in a blender until it is creamy and smooth.

5   Return the soup to the pot and gradually stir in the soy milk and parsley.

6 Warm gently to heat through, but do not boil or soy milk may curdle.

7 Serve in soup bowls with crusty bread.

Serves 5

Per serve: calories 190; fat 8 g (38 per cent of calories from fat); saturated fat 1 g; carbohydrate 26 g; fibre 2 g; cholesterol 0.2 mg; calcium 99 mg.

Phytoestrogens: 'good source'

CANNELINI BEAN & CARROT SOUP
WITH PARSLEY

This traditional Croatian dish is particularly satisfying in winter, but you can cook it all year round and the leftovers make for a hearty meal. You can also use other dry beans such as borlotti, red kidney or small lima beans.

$1\frac{1}{2}$ cups dry cannelini beans

1 tablespoon extra virgin olive oil

1 large onion, finely chopped

2 cloves garlic, crushed

2 medium carrots, peeled and chopped into small pieces

1 large very soft tomato, coarsely chopped

$1\frac{1}{2}$ teaspoons salt

cracked black pepper to taste

1 tablespoon imitation bacon chips

2 tablespoons ground sweet paprika

2 tablespoons plain white flour

3 tablespoons parsley, finely chopped

Easy preparation the night before: Pick over the beans to remove any stones and place them in a large bowl. Cover with plenty of water, allowing the beans to soak overnight so they will take less time to cook.

What you need: The quickest way to cook beans is to use a pressure cooker, which takes around 20 minutes. Alternatively, you can cook the beans on a conventional stove, which will take around 50 minutes or more depending on the bean.

1   Heat the oil in a pressure cooker, uncovered, or a soup pot and
    sauté the onion and garlic.

2   Add the carrots, tomato, cannelini beans, salt, pepper, bacon
    chips and 6 cups of water. Mix well.

3   Cover the pressure cooker with the lid and turn up the heat. Once
    the pressure has built up, turn down the heat and cook for 20
    minutes. If you are cooking the beans on a conventional stove,
    cover the soup pot with a lid until the soup comes to the boil, then
    turn down the heat and simmer for about 50 minutes, or until the
    beans are soft, stirring frequently.

4   Add the ground paprika to the flour, and gradually stir in $1/2$ cup of
    water until a smooth, thin paste forms. Make sure there are no
    lumps. Mix the paste into the bean soup and bring to the boil.

5   Boil the soup for a few minutes until it thickens slightly.

6   Mix in the parsley and serve the soup hot as a main course with
    crusty wholegrain bread. A fresh salad made from tomato and
    onion or coleslaw makes a nice accompaniment.

Serves 6

Per serve: calories 243; fat 4 g (14 per cent of calories from fat); saturated
fat 0.6 g; carbohydrate 43 g; fibre 14 g; cholesterol 0 mg; calcium 113 mg.

Phytoestrogens: 'source'

SPICY HUNGARIAN POTATO PAPRIKASH

Paprikash is a hearty soup served as a main meal. Don't confuse it with goulash—a thick stew. To remove the skin from the tomato, place in a bowl and pour over boiling water until covered. Keep the tomato submerged for one minute, then remove it from the water—the skin will peel off easily.

1 tablespoon extra virgin olive oil

1 large onion, finely chopped

3 soy sausages sliced into 2-cm pieces

2 large potatoes, peeled and diced into small cubes

2 large (20 g) chicken-style vegetable stock cubes, crumbled

2 tablespoons plain white flour

3 tablespoons sweet paprika

pinch hot paprika, optional

1 teaspoon sugar

1 large ripe tomato, peeled and chopped into small pieces

2 cloves garlic, crushed

2 tablespoons parsley, finely chopped

½ cup red wine

1   Heat the oil in a deep soup pot and sauté the onion until translucent.

2   Add the soy sausage pieces, diced potatoes and stock cubes and cover with 5 cups of water.

3   Combine the flour, paprika and sugar and gradually mix into the soup so there are no lumps.

4   Cover with a lid and bring to the boil. Turn down the heat and simmer, half-covered, for 10 minutes, stirring occasionally.

5   Add the tomato and continue to cook for another 10 minutes, stirring occasionally.

6   Add the garlic, parsley and red wine and cook uncovered for another 5 minutes until the alcohol has evaporated. Serve as a main meal with crusty wholegrain bread.

Serves 4

Per serve: calories 324; fat 8 g (23 per cent of calories from fat); saturated fat 1 g; carbohydrate 48 g; fibre 6 g; cholesterol 0.5 mg; calcium 47 mg.

Phytoestrogens: 'good source'

BROWN LENTIL SOUP WITH DILL

This tasty and filling soup is perfect as a main meal.

1 tablespoon extra virgin olive oil

1 medium onion, finely chopped

2 cloves garlic, crushed

1 large carrot, scrubbed and diced into small cubes

1 large potato, peeled and diced into small cubes

1 cup dry brown lentils, picked over for stones and rinsed

3 tablespoons tomato paste

dried Italian herbs

1 large (10 g) chicken-style vegetable stock cube, crumbled

3 tablespoons fresh dill, chopped

salt, optional

1 Heat the oil in a soup pot and sauté the onion and garlic until soft.

2 Add the carrot, potato, lentils, tomato paste, Italian herbs, stock cube and $5\frac{1}{2}$ cups of water. Stir, cover with a lid and bring to the boil.

3 Reduce the heat and simmer with the lid on for 20 minutes. Add the dill and adjust to taste with salt if desired. Continue cooking for a further 10 minutes or until the lentils are tender. Serve with grainy bread.

Serves 4

Per serve: calories 313; fat 5 g (13 per cent of calories from fat); saturated fat 0.7 g; carbohydrate 54 g; fibre 19 g; cholesterol 0.2 mg; calcium 69 mg.

Phytoestrogens: 'source'

Salads, sides & snacks

TABOULI SALAD

This is a terrific salad full of flavour. The soy grits replace the traditional bulgur wheat, increasing the phytoestrogen content.

1 cup soy grits
1 large bunch parsley, chopped
2 medium firm tomatoes, finely diced
1 small cucumber, finely diced
3 shallots, finely sliced
10 mint leaves, finely chopped
$\frac{1}{2}$ cup lemon juice (approx. 2 lemons)
2 tablespoons extra virgin olive oil
freshly ground black pepper
salt, optional

1   Pour 2 cups of boiling water over the soy grits and let stand for 15 minutes. Drain well and mop up the excess moisture with absorbent paper.

2   Place the parsley in large salad bowl. Add the tomato, cucumber, shallots, mint leaves and the drained soy grits.

3   Pour the lemon juice and olive oil over the salad ingredients and sprinkle with pepper and a little salt if desired. Mix well. Serve with a main course or in sandwiches. This salad will last several days if kept refrigerated—the lemon juice is a natural preservative.

Serves 8

Per serve: calories 153; fat 9 g (50 per cent of calories from fat); saturated fat 1.3 g; carbohydrate 12 g; fibre 5 g; cholesterol 0 mg; calcium 70 mg.

Phytoestrogens: 'rich source'

SOYBEAN & BLACK OLIVE PASTE

This lightly sweetened chilli paste is perfect as a spread on bread. It is healthier than butter, margarine or cream cheese and is loaded with phytoestrogens. To make a dip consistency, add an extra $1/2$ cup soy milk and blend.

$1^3/_4$ cup canned soybeans with Thai Sweet Chilli sauce

2 cloves garlic, crushed

2 tablespoons soy milk

1 tablespoon extra virgin olive oil

2 tablespoons parsley, finely chopped

10 pitted black olives, coarsely chopped

1   Drain the soybeans and place in a food processor.

2   Add the remaining ingredients and blend for a couple of minutes until the mixture is smooth and forms a paste. Serve with crispbread, pumpernickel bread or wholegrain pita bread. Store in an airtight container in the fridge. Makes approximately 20 tablespoons.

Serves 4 as appetiser.

Per serve: calories 169; fat 11 g (55 per cent of calories from fat); saturated fat 1 g; carbohydrate 9 g; fibre 4 g; cholesterol 0 mg; calcium 94 mg.

Phytoestrogens: 'rich source'

MIXED SALAD WITH RASPBERRY AND PISTACHIO VINAIGRETTE

This salad is a feast for the eyes with its bright colours. The aroma and crunch of toasted pistachios is delicious and the sprouts give it a phytoestrogen boost.

100 g mixed lettuce leaves (radicchio, rocket, cos, butter, mesclun etc.)

2 small Lebanese cucumbers

1 large ripe tomato

$\frac{1}{2}$ small red onion, thinly sliced

4 tablespoons mung bean sprouts

handful snow pea sprouts

2 tablespoons extra virgin olive oil

2 tablespoons raspberry-flavoured wine vinegar

pinch salt

3 tablespoons pistachios, shelled

1   Wash the lettuce leaves and drain well. Place in a glass salad bowl.
2   Wash the cucumbers and tomato. If the cucumber skin is fresh, you don't need to peel it. Slice the cucumbers and cut the tomato into small chunks. Add to the lettuce.
3   Add the onion and mung bean and snow pea sprouts to the salad.
4   Drizzle the salad with olive oil and raspberry vinegar and add a pinch of salt. Toss well until all ingredients are coated with the dressing.

5 Dry-roast the pistachios in a small frypan for a few minutes, until they start to brown and release their aroma. Sprinkle on top of salad and serve immediately.

Serves 4

Per serve: calories 146; fat 11 g (65 per cent of calories from fat); saturated fat 1 g; carbohydrate 10 g; fibre 3 g; cholesterol 0 mg; calcium 33 mg.

Phytoestrogens: 'source'

NIÇOISE SALAD WITH SMOKED TOFU

This colourful salad, inspired by the traditional Niçoise salad from France, is a wonderful centrepiece for a buffet. It also makes for a delicious phytoestrogen-enriched summer lunch.

800 g small new potatoes

240 g mixed yellow and green French beans

1 soft lettuce, e.g. mignonette

4 roma tomatoes, quartered

10 large basil leaves, chopped

1 clove garlic, crushed

4 tablespoons extra virgin olive oil

4 tablespoons lemon juice

freshly ground black pepper, optional

pinch salt, optional

1 teaspoon olive oil, extra

100 g smoked tofu set with calcium sulphate, cubed

12 marinated black olives

1 Scrub the potatoes well and boil in their skins for about 15 minutes, until just cooked.

2 Top and tail the beans and boil in a separate saucepan for about 10 minutes, until just tender.

3 Wash the lettuce leaves, drain well and spread over a serving platter.

4 Place the whole potatoes, whole beans, tomato quarters, basil leaves, garlic, olive oil, lemon juice, pepper and salt, and toss gently until the dressing coats all ingredients. Pile the salad on top of the prepared serving platter.

5   Heat the extra teaspoon of oil in a frypan and fry the smoked tofu
    pieces until just crispy. Remove from the heat and drain.
6   Sprinkle the marinated black olives and fried smoked tofu pieces
    over the salad. Serve while the tofu is still warm.

Serves 4

Per serve: calories 439; fat 22 g (43 per cent of calories from fat); saturated
fat 3 g; carbohydrate 56 g; fibre 9 g; cholesterol 0 mg; calcium 275 mg.

Phytoestrogens: 'good source'

FOUR-BEAN SUMMER SALAD

This hearty salad is full of flavour and quick to make if you're in a hurry for lunch. Double the quantities if you want to serve it to more people at a barbecue.

1 can (420 g) four bean mix, drained and rinsed

1 large tomato, cut into small wedges

2 shallots or 1/4 very small Spanish onion, finely chopped

1 tablespoon basil, chopped

1 tablespoon apple cider vinegar

1 tablespoon extra virgin olive oil

10 whole kalamata olives

coarsely ground black pepper to taste

1 small clove garlic, crushed, optional

1   Toss all the ingredients together in a bowl. Adjust the seasonings to taste. If you would like a tangier flavour, add a little more apple cider vinegar. Serve as a light summer lunch accompanied by wholegrain or dark rye bread with smooth ricotta cheese.

Serves 2

Per serve: calories 432; fat 14 g (28 per cent of calories from fat); saturated fat 2 g; carbohydrate 61 g; fibre 18 g; cholesterol 0 mg; calcium 126 mg.

Phytoestrogens: 'source'

ROASTED RED CAPSICUMS WITH GARLIC

Roasted red capsicums are succulent and sweet. Serve them as a side salad, with antipasto, on top of soft polenta together with char-grilled vegetables, or add them to sandwich fillings or pizzas.

8 large red capsicums
2 cloves garlic, thinly sliced
$1/4$ cup extra virgin olive oil

1 Preheat oven to 180°C (350°F).
2 Wash the capsicums and place them on an oven tray that has been lined with non-stick baking paper. Put into the hot oven.
3 Roast for about 1 hour until the skins blacken and the capsicums have softened.
4 Remove from the oven and transfer into a deep bowl. Cover with a wet tea towel and allow to cool down for a few hours or overnight. Peel off the skins, starting at the stalk, and remove seeds. Gently tear the capsicums into thick pieces with your hands. They will be soft and supple.
5 Place the capsicum strips into a glass jar, interspersing with the garlic slices.
6 Pour over the extra virgin olive oil. Keep refrigerated until ready to use.

Serves 8

Per serve: calories 156; fat 8 g (43 per cent of calories from fat); saturated fat 1 g; carbohydrate 21 g; fibre 6 g; cholesterol 0 mg; calcium 31 mg.

Phytoestrogens: 'source'

THREE-BEAN DHAL

What makes this dhal special is that it combines the flavours and textures of three types of beans. It's not as thick as some lentil purées and works well drizzled over rice. You can omit the chilli if you prefer a less spicy flavour.

$\frac{1}{2}$ cup red lentils

$\frac{1}{2}$ cup channa dhal (split yellow peas)

$\frac{1}{2}$ cup moong dhal (split and skinned mung beans)

1 large onion, finely chopped

1 teaspoon salt

$\frac{1}{2}$ teaspoon turmeric

3 tablespoons canola oil

1 teaspoon cumin seeds

1 teaspoon dried chilli

3 cloves garlic, crushed

3 tablespoons fresh coriander, chopped

1   Pick over and rinse the beans and place in a large pot together with the onion, salt, turmeric and 5 cups of water. Cover with a lid and bring to the boil.

2   Reduce the heat and simmer, half-covered, for about 15–20 minutes until soft, stirring frequently so that the beans don't stick to the bottom of the pot.

3   Heat the oil in a frypan. Add the cumin seeds and fry for about 1 minute until they start to pop. Add the dried chilli and continue frying for another 5 seconds. Add the garlic, removing pan from the heat as soon as the garlic begins to turn golden. Don't allow the garlic to burn.

4   Add the hot oil mixture to the beans and mix through. Place in a serving dish and garnish with chopped coriander.

Serves 6

Per serve: calories 236; fat 8 g (30 per cent of calories from fat); saturated fat 0.6 g; carbohydrate 31 g; fibre 11 g; cholesterol 0 mg; calcium 53 mg.

Phytoestrogens: 'source'

SWEET POTATO, PUMPKIN & POTATO MASH

This is no ordinary mash—it is sweeter, more colourful and attention-grabbing. Kids and adults alike will love it.

500 g yellow sweet potato, peeled and cut into small pieces
500 g butternut pumpkin, peeled and cut into small pieces
500 g potato, peeled and cut into small pieces
½ cup soy milk
½ teaspoon salt
½ teaspoon ground cumin

1   Place the sweet potato, pumpkin and potato in a large pot and add plenty of water until covered.

2   Cover with a lid and bring to the boil. Boil, half-covered, for about 30 minutes, until the vegetables are very soft.

3   Drain the water and add the soy milk, salt and ground cumin, and mash well until the consistency is smooth. Serve the mash in a large bowl or on dinner plates as a base for other main dishes— such as fish, curries and casseroles.

Serves 6
Per serve: calories 190; fat 1 g (5 per cent of calories from fat); saturated fat 0.2 g; carbohydrate 42 g; fibre 4 g; cholesterol 0 mg; calcium 70 mg.
Phytoestrogens: 'source'

BABY SPINACH, ROMA TOMATO & RED ONION SALAD

This is a simple, delicious salad that's quick to make.

180 g baby spinach leaves

2 large Roma tomatoes, quartered lengthwise

$1/2$ small red onion, sliced into rings

2 tablespoons balsamic vinegar

1 tablespoon extra virgin olive oil

pinch salt, optional

2 tablespoons pine nuts

1 Wash the spinach leaves and drain and place them, along with the tomatoes and onion, into a salad bowl.

2 Mix the vinegar, oil and salt well and pour over the salad.

3 Toss the salad until all the ingredients are well coated with the dressing.

4 Dry-roast the pine nuts in a hot pan and sprinkle over the salad just prior to serving. Serve as an entrée or a side dish to a main meal.

Serves 4

Per serve: calories 94; fat 7 g (62 per cent of calories from fat); saturated fat 1 g; carbohydrate 7 g; fibre 3 g; cholesterol 0 mg; calcium 51 mg.

Phytoestrogens: 'source'

ROASTED SOY NUTS

Roasted soy nuts are tasty and one of the richest sources of phytoestrogens. They make an ideal snack, and are the perfect addition to salads. To make a mixed snack food, add some small pretzels and breakfast cereal shapes of your choice.

2 cups soybeans
1 teaspoon soybean or canola oil
1 teaspoon ground sweet paprika
$\frac{1}{2}$ teaspoon ground cumin
$\frac{1}{2}$ teaspoon ground coriander
pinch salt, optional
pinch ground hot chilli, optional

1 Cover the soybeans with plenty of water (at least 1.5 litres) and soak overnight.
2 Preheat oven to 180°C (350°F).
3 Drain the soybeans and spread on two non-stick oven trays.
4 Roast in the oven for about 45 minutes, stirring occasionally, until the soybeans are golden brown. Remove from the oven and place in a mixing bowl.
5 Heat the oil and drizzle it over the roasted soybeans. Mix well so that each soybean is coated.
6 Sprinkle the soybeans with the ground spices, mixing well. Adjust to taste with salt and ground hot chilli. Serve immediately or store in an airtight container for later use. Makes 3 cups.

Serves 12

Per serve: calories 128; fat 6 g (42 per cent of calories from fat); saturated fat 0.9 g; carbohydrate 9 g; fibre 3 g; cholesterol 0 mg; calcium 85 mg.

Phytoestrogens: 'rich source'

Light meals

WOK-FRIED RICE NOODLES WITH BEAN CURD, SPROUTS & CRUSHED PEANUTS

This Thai-inspired noodle dish is easy and makes a tasty lunch or light evening meal. Using bean curd and sprouts boosts the phytoestrogen content.

200 g dried rice noodles

2 tablespoons peanut oil

80 g bean curd (tofu), diced into small cubes

2 cloves garlic, crushed

1 red chilli, deseeded and finely chopped

150 g bean sprouts

3 shallots, sliced diagonally

1 tablespoon lemon juice

2 tablespoons salt-reduced soy sauce

2 tablespoons fresh coriander, finely chopped

$1/4$ cup crushed peanuts

lime wedges to serve, optional

1   Pour boiling water over the rice noodles in a large bowl and allow to rehydrate for about 5 minutes. Don't allow to hydrate for too long as the noodles will become mushy.

2   Heat the oil in a wok and fry the tofu cubes until they are golden brown. Add the garlic, chilli and bean sprouts and stir-fry for about 10 seconds, until fragrant.

3   Add the rice noodles and shallots and toss for 1 minute.

4   Add the lemon juice and soy sauce and mix through.

5   Toss in the coriander and peanuts. Serve with lime wedges on the side.

Serves 2

Per serve: calories 734; fat 31 g (36 per cent of calories from fat); saturated fat 5 g; carbohydrate 104 g; fibre 4 g; cholesterol 0 mg; calcium 183 mg.

Phytoestrogens: 'good source'

MINI MEDITERRANEAN PIZZAS

Mini pizzas make a speedy lunch for adults, and a great snack for kids. The smoked soy adds flavour and extra phytoestrogens.

4 wholemeal pita pocket breads or Egyptian-style pita
4 tablespoons tomato pasta sauce
1 teaspoon mixed Italian herbs
1 garlic, crushed
$\frac{1}{2}$ cup shredded fat-reduced cheese
4 large button mushrooms, wiped and sliced
$\frac{1}{2}$ medium red capsicum, sliced
4 smoked soy slices, cut into small pieces
1 small onion, sliced
8 marinated kalamata olives

1   Preheat the oven to 200°C (400°F) while preparing the pizzas.
2   Place the pocket breads on a large oven tray. Spoon over the tomato pasta sauce and sprinkle with mixed herbs and garlic.
3   Pile on the other ingredients—sprinkle with cheese, mushrooms, capsicum, smoked soy pieces, onion and olives.
4   Place the pizzas in the oven and bake for about 10 minutes, or until the topping begins to brown. Makes 4 mini pizzas.

Serves 2
Per serve: calories 602; fat 12 g (17 per cent of calories from fat); saturated fat 2 g; carbohydrate 102 g; fibre 17 g; cholesterol 6 mg; calcium 221 mg.
Phytoestrogens: 'good source'

BEAN BURRITOS WITH AVOCADO, TOMATO & CORIANDER

These yummy burritos make a quick lunch or snack. Because
you are using beans, the burritos are cholesterol free, low in
saturated fat, high in fibre and provide a 'source' of
phytoestrogens.

6 burrito tortillas
2 medium tomatoes, diced into small pieces
3 tablespoons fresh coriander, chopped
425 g can Mexican chilli beans
6 iceberg lettuce leaves, shredded
$\frac{1}{2}$ avocado, peeled and sliced
salsa, optional

1   Preheat the oven to 180°C (350°F).
2   Wrap the tortillas in aluminium foil and warm in the oven for 10
    minutes.
3   Mix the tomatoes with the coriander.
4   Empty the beans from the can into a small saucepan and heat.
5   Divide the ingredients into 6 portions and assemble the burritos:
    spread each burrito with shredded lettuce; top with tomato and
    coriander mixture; add sliced avocado and spoonfuls of chilli beans
    in chilli sauce. Roll up the burrito and place the join face-down on
    a serving platter. Serve with salsa if desired. Makes 6 burritos.

Serves 3
Per serve: calories 455; fat 12 g (23 per cent of calories from fat); saturated
fat 2 g; carbohydrate 74 g; fibre 12 g; cholesterol 0 mg; calcium 108 mg.
Phytoestrogens: 'source'

TOFU BURGERS WITH GINGER, CHILLI & GARLIC

Store any unused tofu submerged in cold water in a container in the fridge. Change the water daily and the tofu will stay fresh for about a week. Tofu burgers make an excellent instant lunch or quick snack.

200 g firm tofu prepared with calcium sulphate
2 teaspoons peanut oil
1 teaspoon ginger, minced
1 small clove garlic, crushed
$\frac{1}{2}$ red chilli, deseeded and finely chopped
1 tablespoon light soy sauce

1   Cut the tofu into 4 slices, approximately 1 cm thick. (Each slice should cover a small burger bun.) Place the tofu on absorbent kitchen paper to mop up excess moisture.

2   Heat 1 teaspoon of the oil in a non-stick frypan and brown the tofu slices for a few minutes, turning so both sides are golden brown. Remove and place on absorbent kitchen paper to mop up excess oil.

3   Place the remaining teaspoon of oil in the pan and add the ginger, garlic and chilli and fry for about 10 seconds.

4   Dilute the soy sauce with 4 tablespoons of water and pour over the ginger, garlic and chilli in the pan. You will hear a hissing sound. Keep the windows open as the chilli will release some chemicals that may make you cough.

5   Toss the tofu slices back into the pan for 1 minute, allowing them to absorb some of the juices.

6   Serve the burgers on a wholemeal bun with your favourite
    vegetables such as salad greens, sliced tomatoes, sliced beetroot
    and fresh onions. Drizzle the remaining sauce from the pan on top
    of the burgers. Makes 4 delicious burgers.

Serves 2

Per serve: calories 129; fat 9 g (62 per cent of calories from fat); saturated
fat 1 g; carbohydrate 4 g; fibre 0.5 g; cholesterol 0 mg; calcium 165 mg.
Phytoestrogens: 'rich source'

CASHEW FRIED RICE

Brown rice is ideal for making fried rice because the grains don't cling together. It has a nutty flavour and is more nutritious, being a wholegrain food. Quick-cook brown rice is also available in some supermarkets. The Edamame are sweet and bring contrast to the slight chilli flavour.

1 cup brown rice

1 egg

1 tablespoon peanut oil

1 small onion, finely chopped

1 clove garlic, crushed

$\frac{1}{2}$ small red chilli, deseeded and finely chopped, optional

4 rashers imitation bacon (made from soy), chopped into small
    pieces

1 medium carrot, peeled and grated

$\frac{1}{2}$ cup frozen Edamame (green soybeans)

$\frac{1}{4}$ cup cashews

2 teaspoons salt-reduced soy sauce

2 teaspoons sesame oil

1   Cook the brown rice and spread on a tray to cool. (Brown rice is
     best cooked the day before.) In a pressure cooker, cook the rice
     with 3 cups of water for 9 minutes. For conventional cooking, add
     $2\frac{1}{2}$ cups of water to the rice and simmer it in a pot with the lid on
     for about 45 minutes—adding extra water if required.

2   Make an omelette by whisking the egg with a fork and pouring
     into a hot non-stick pan. Cook on both sides. Remove from the pan
     and slice into thin strips. Set aside.

3   Heat the peanut oil in a large non-stick frypan and sauté the onion and garlic (and chopped chilli if desired). Add the imitation bacon and cook until bacon becomes slightly crispy. Add the carrot and Edamame and cook for a further few minutes.

4   Toss in the cooked brown rice, cashews, soy sauce, sesame oil and strips of egg omelette. Lightly fry until the flavours mix in. Serve with a green salad.

Serves 3

Per serve: calories 502; fat 23 g (41 per cent of calories from fat); saturated fat 4 g; carbohydrate 62 g; fibre 6 g; cholesterol 0 mg; calcium 89 mg.

Phytoestrogens: 'good source'

CHAR-GRILLED BALSAMIC VEGETABLES

Char-grilled balsamic vegetables are also delicious when cooked on a barbecue. You can serve them as a side dish to accompany fish, chicken or meat. The Mediterranean-style dressing brings out the flavour of the vegetables.

4 medium zucchinis, chopped into 2-cm pieces
4 large field or flat mushrooms, quartered
2 Spanish onions, peeled and quartered
8 yellow baby squash, quartered
1/8 cup extra virgin olive oil
1 sprig fresh rosemary, leaves stripped, very finely chopped
1 clove garlic, crushed
2 tablespoons balsamic vinegar
1 tablespoon extra virgin olive oil
pinch sea salt, optional

1   Preheat the oven to 200°C (400°F). Line a large oven tray with non-stick baking paper or foil.

2   Place the vegetables on the lined tray. Brush the pieces with 1/8 cup olive oil and sprinkle with the rosemary.

3   Place in the oven for about 25 minutes, until vegetables are golden brown.

4   Transfer the vegetables to a large bowl and add the crushed garlic, balsamic vinegar, extra tablespoon of olive oil and pinch of sea salt (if desired). Toss gently until all the pieces are coated with dressing. Pile on top of cooked pasta, Soft Polenta (see page 195) or couscous and serve.

Serves 4

Per serve: calories 225; fat 15 g (54 per cent of calories from fat); saturated fat 2 g; carbohydrate 21 g; fibre 6 g; cholesterol 0 mg; calcium 75 mg.
Phytoestrogens: 'source'

BRUSCHETTA WITH TOMATO & BASIL ON RYE

This is very simple to make for a quick snack or a light meal.
Dark rye bread is particularly rich in the lignan family of
phytoestrogens.

2 firm, ripe tomatoes, cut into very small pieces

handful basil leaves, finely chopped

$\frac{1}{2}$ small clove garlic, crushed

$\frac{1}{8}$ small Spanish onion, finely chopped

1 tablespoon extra virgin olive oil

pinch sea salt

pinch crushed black pepper

4 thick slices rye bread

1   Combine the tomatoes, basil, garlic, onion, olive oil, salt and
     pepper in a mixing bowl.

2   Place the rye slices on an oven tray and toast lightly on both sides
     under the griller for a few minutes. Serve the toasted rye bread
     piled high with the tomato mixture. Serves two people as a snack,
     or four if offered as an appetiser.

Serves 2

Per serve: calories 209; fat 9 g (39 per cent of calories from fat); saturated
fat 1 g; carbohydrate 28 g; fibre 4 g; cholesterol 0 mg; calcium 50 mg.

Phytoestrogens: 'source'

TASTY TEMPEH FINGERS

A traditional Indonesian soy food, tempeh has a light, nutty flavour and chewy texture. It is rich in phytoestrogens. Add Tasty Tempeh Fingers to kids' sandwiches or stuff in a pita pocket bread with salad.

300 g tempeh
2 tablespoons soy sauce
1 teaspoon ground cumin
$\frac{1}{2}$ teaspoon ground coriander
$\frac{1}{2}$ teaspoon ground turmeric
pinch ground hot chilli
4 tablespoons peanut oil

1　Slice the tempeh thinly and then cut into finger-sized pieces.
2　To prepare the marinade, combine the soy sauce with 1 tablespoon of water in a marinating dish and blend in the cumin, coriander, turmeric and chilli.
3　Add the tempeh fingers to the marinade and coat well.
4　Heat the oil in a frypan and, when hot, add the tempeh fingers, frying until golden brown and crisp.
5　Remove from the pan and drain on absorbent paper. Serve with rice and stir-fried vegetables or mashed potato, or add to kebabs.

Serves 6
Per serve: calories 193; fat 16 g (69 per cent of calories from fat); saturated fat 2.8 g; carbohydrate 6 g; fibre 0.4 g; cholesterol 0 mg; calcium 67 mg.
Phytoestrogens: 'rich source'

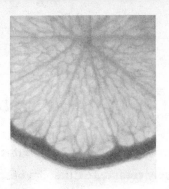

Main courses

RISOTTO WITH MUSHROOMS & EDAMAME

Risotto takes about 30 minutes to cook, but it is well worth the effort. With its lovely creamy texture, it's best served right away. You can use green peas instead of Edamame, but Edamame does have a much higher content of phytoestrogens.

$\frac{1}{2}$ teaspoon saffron threads, optional

1.25 litres chicken or vegetable stock—you can use stock cubes to make this

2 tablespoons butter

2 tablespoons extra virgin olive oil

2 cloves garlic, crushed

2 cups Arborio rice

2 heaped cups (200 g) mixed fresh mushrooms (e.g. oyster, Swiss brown, porcini), stems removed and sliced

1 cup frozen Edamame (green soybeans)

1 cup dry white wine

$\frac{1}{2}$ cup freshly grated parmesan cheese, optional

coarsely ground black pepper

1   Soak the saffron threads in 1 tablespoon warm water and set aside.

2   Heat the stock in a medium-sized saucepan and keep hot over a low heat.

3   Melt the butter in a large saucepan and add the olive oil. Stir in the mushrooms and crushed garlic and sauté for a few minutes until mushrooms start to soften. Mix in the Edamame.

4   Turn up the heat and gradually stir in the rice, cooking for about 3 minutes until all grains are well coated with the butter/oil mixture.

5   Reduce the heat and pour in the wine. Cook, stirring constantly until the liquid has been absorbed.

6   Add a ladle-full of hot stock. Cook, stirring constantly until the stock has been absorbed.

7   Add the remaining stock, one ladle-full at a time, stirring constantly until the liquid has been absorbed.

8   Remove the risotto from the heat and mix in the soaked saffron (optional) to give the risotto a lovely yellow colour.

9   Stir in the grated cheese (optional as it adds extra saturated fat) and season with black pepper. Serve immediately. Risotto can be eaten as a main meal with a tossed green salad, or as an entrée.

Serves 4

Per serve: calories 571; fat 15 g (24 per cent of calories from fat); saturated fat 4 g; carbohydrate 84 g; fibre 5 g; cholesterol 11 mg; calcium 99 mg.

Phytoestrogens: 'good source'

CHICKPEA CURRY WITH PUMPKIN & BABY SPINACH

You will love making this easy curry with its slightly sweet and spicy flavour.

1 tablespoon extra virgin olive oil

1 medium onion, finely chopped

2 cloves garlic, crushed

1 teaspoon chilli powder

1 teaspoon ground coriander

2 teaspoons ground cumin

2 tablespoons tomato paste

415 g canned peeled tomatoes, puréed

$1\frac{1}{2}$ cups cooked or canned chickpeas, drained

320 g pumpkin, peeled and chopped into small pieces

salt, optional

2 tablespoons fresh coriander, chopped

100 g baby spinach leaves

1   Heat the oil and sauté the onion and garlic until soft. Mix in the chilli powder, coriander, cumin, tomato paste, puréed tomatoes and 1 cup of water. Stir well.

2   Add the chickpeas and pumpkin pieces and bring to the boil. Adjust the flavour with a little salt if desired. Reduce the heat and simmer for around 15 minutes, or until the pumpkin is just tender.

3 Add the coriander and baby spinach leaves and simmer for a few minutes until the leaves just start to wilt. Serve the curry on top of steamed basmati rice and garnish with extra coriander leaves, and a pappadum. If you find this curry a little hot, try some yoghurt on the side.

Serves 4

Per serve: calories 197; fat 6 g (24 per cent of calories from fat); saturated fat 0.7 g; carbohydrate 33 g; fibre 7 g; cholesterol 0 mg; calcium 154 mg.

Phytoestrogens: 'source'

VIBRANT VEGE & TOFU STIR-FRY

For the perfect stir-fry, you will need a gas stove with a wok burner and a good Chinese wok. Make sure the vegetables are well drained after you wash them, otherwise they will start to stew. Use fresh mushrooms or rehydrated shiitake mushrooms if oyster mushrooms are unavailable.

2 tablespoons peanut oil

400 g marinated tofu (available in many supermarkets), drained and sliced into small cubes or strips

2 medium carrots, peeled and sliced thinly on the diagonal

1 bunch baby bok choy, leaves separated from stems, stems diagonally cut into 2-cm pieces

180 g snow peas, washed, ends trimmed

150 g oyster mushrooms

3 cups bean sprouts

2 cloves garlic, crushed

nob of ginger, peeled and grated

1 tablespoon cornflour

⅛ cup soy sauce

1   Prepare all the ingredients according to order listed above. This will make stir-frying quick and easy.

2   Heat 1 tablespoon of the oil in a wok and stir-fry the tofu until golden brown. Remove from the wok and set aside.

3   Heat the second tablespoon of the oil in the wok and stir-fry the vegetables, adding them in the following order (from the most firm to soft): carrot and bok choy stems; snow peas and oyster mushrooms; bok choy leaves and bean sprouts; garlic and ginger. Stir-fry for a few minutes after each addition. Vegetables should just start to soften but remain crisp and brightly coloured.

4   Return the fried tofu pieces to the wok.

5   Blend the cornflour in $3/4$ cup of water until smooth. Add the soy sauce.

6   Pour the soy sauce/cornflour mixture into the wok over the vegetables and tofu and continue to stir-fry for a few more minutes. The wok contents should start to sizzle and vegetables will become glossy as the sauce thickens slightly. Serve on top of steamed jasmine rice.

Serves 4

Per serve: calories 284; fat 16 g (46 per cent of calories from fat); saturated fat 2 g; carbohydrate 23 g; fibre 5 g; cholesterol 0 mg; calcium 335 mg.

Phytoestrogens: 'rich source'

LASAGNE WITH FETTA, ROCKET AND CHAMPIGNONS

This meal is a 'rich source' of phytoestrogens because it contains TVP—a versatile ingredient that you can use in many recipes instead of mincemeat. Lasagne is best made the day before because it's easier to handle without falling apart. Slice while cold and then reheat.

$1\frac{1}{2}$ cups dehydrated textured vegetable protein (TVP)

820 g canned whole peeled tomatoes

$\frac{1}{2}$ tablespoon dried sweet basil

1 tablespoon extra virgin olive oil

1 medium onion, finely chopped

1 clove garlic, crushed

$\frac{1}{2}$ cup champignons, sliced

6 large instant lasagne sheets

80 g rocket (arugula) or baby spinach leaves, washed and drained well

100 g fetta cheese, crumbled

500 g creamed cottage cheese

2 teaspoons parmesan cheese

1   Rehydrate the TVP by covering it with 1 cup hot water and letting it stand for about 15 minutes—while you prepare the other ingredients.

2   Purée the tomatoes in a blender for 1 minute and mix in the sweet basil. Set aside.

3   Preheat the oven to 200°C (400°F).

4   Heat the oil and sauté the onion and garlic until soft. Add the rehydrated TVP and champignons and continue frying for a few minutes. Set aside.

5   Spread a few spoonfuls of the tomato and basil sauce onto the bottom of a lasagne dish. Line the dish with two large lasagne sheets to cover the bottom.

6   Spread half of the TVP mixture evenly over the lasagne sheets. Cover with half of the rocket leaves and half of the creamed cottage cheese. Sprinkle with half of the crumbled fetta cheese and pour over a third of the remaining tomato and basil sauce.

7   Cover with another layer of lasagne sheets. Repeat step six, using the remaining half of the ingredients.

8   Cover with the last two lasagne sheets and pour over the remaining tomato and basil sauce. Sprinkle with the parmesan cheese and bake for 30 minutes at 200°C (400°F). Reduce the heat to 150°C (300°F), and bake for another 10 minutes, or until golden brown. Serve as a main meal with a tossed green salad. Lasagne cuts best the next day when cold.

Serves 6

Per serve: calories 377; fat 12 g (28 per cent of calories from fat); saturated fat 6 g; carbohydrate 41 g; fibre 6 g; cholesterol 28 mg; calcium 232 mg.

Phytoestrogens: 'rich source'

ROASTED VEGETABLES ON COUSCOUS WITH MOROCCAN DRESSING

This Moroccan-style dish will impress with its vibrant colours and spicy, fragrant dressing.

ROASTED VEGETABLES

2 small Spanish onions, peeled and quartered

2 medium waxy potatoes, scrubbed well and quartered

500 g pumpkin, peeled and cut into 3-cm chunks

1 small sweet potato, peeled and cut into 3-cm chunks

1 tablespoon extra virgin olive oil

COUSCOUS

250 g instant couscous

DRESSING

$\frac{1}{2}$ cup extra virgin olive oil

$\frac{1}{2}$ teaspoon hot paprika

1 tablespoon ground cumin

1 tablespoon ground coriander

2 tablespoons coriander leaves, chopped

2 tablespoons tomato purée

5 tablespoons lemon juice

SALAD TOPPING

80 g mixed green salad leaves, washed and drained

100 g fetta cheese, crumbled

2 tablespoons pepitas

1   Preheat the oven to 200°C (400°F).

2   Prepare the vegetables and spread onto two oven trays lined with non-stick paper. Brush with extra virgin olive oil.

3   Place the trays in the hot oven and roast the vegetables at 200°C (400°F) for 45 minutes, removing the onions after about 30 minutes when they are browned.

4   Place the couscous in a pot and pour over 2$\frac{1}{2}$ cups of boiling water. Cover with a lid and let stand for 45 minutes while the vegetables are roasting. Work through the couscous with a fork until the granules separate and it is fluffy.

5   Prepare the dressing by combining all the ingredients and mixing well. Set aside.

6   Pile up the ingredients on a platter in the following order: couscous, roasted vegetables, lettuce leaves, crumbled fetta, pepitas. Pour over the salad dressing. Serve and enjoy!

Serves 6

Per serve: calories 598; fat 29 g (43 per cent of calories from fat); saturated fat 6 g; carbohydrate 74 g; fibre 7 g; cholesterol 15 mg; calcium 179 mg.

Phytoestrogens: 'source'

PASTA SAUCE WITH EGGPLANT, RED CAPSICUM & CURRANTS

This sauce is stunningly different but very easy to make. It is reminiscent of exotic Persian flavours combining eggplant, currants and cumin.

2 tablespoons extra virgin olive oil

$1/2$ medium red capsicum, cut into small pieces

1 medium eggplant, cut into strips

$1/2$ tablespoon ground cumin

2 cloves garlic, crushed

500 g bottled tomato pasta sauce

$1/4$ cup currants

pinch salt, optional

pinch hot paprika, optional

12 pitted kalamata olives

2 tablespoons coriander, finely chopped

1   Heat the olive oil in a pan and sauté the capsicum until it softens.

2   Add the eggplant strips to the pan and mix with the capsicum. Cover the pan and sauté for about 10 minutes, or until the eggplant strips soften and start turning golden brown.

3   Add the cumin and garlic and fry for 1 minute. Mix in the tomato pasta sauce, currants, pinch of salt, pinch of hot paprika and an extra $1/2$ cup of water. Allow the sauce to simmer, half-covered, for another 10 minutes, until flavours cook through.

4   Toss in the olives and coriander and serve the sauce piping hot on top of cooked pasta. Both spirali and penne pasta work well.

Serves 4

Per serve: calories 182; fat 9 g (41 per cent of calories from fat); saturated fat 1 g; carbohydrate 25 g; fibre 6 g; cholesterol 0 mg; calcium 60 mg.

Phytoestrogens: 'source'

OVEN-BAKED WHOLE FISH WITH GREMOLATA & WHITE WINE

This fantastic recipe works especially well if you can get really fresh deep-sea fish.

3 tablespoons extra virgin olive oil

3 medium carrots, finely diced

6 sticks celery, finely diced

4 tablespoons lemon zest, finely grated

2 large cloves garlic, crushed

1 cup parsley, finely chopped

4 x 300 g snapper or bream, scaled and gutted

1 teaspoon salt, optional

$1\frac{1}{2}$ cups dry white wine

1 Preheat the oven to 250°C (480°F).

2 Heat the oil in a large, deep oven dish, big enough to fit the four fish side by side. Sauté the carrots and celery for about 10 minutes, until soft. Set aside.

3 To make the gremolata, mix together the lemon zest, garlic and parsley.

4 Cut criss-cross slits, 3 cm apart, on both sides of each fish.

5 Rub the fish with salt and stuff the slits with the gremolata.

6 Place the stuffed fish on top of the vegetables in the oven dish and pour over the white wine.

7 Bake for about 30 minutes, occasionally basting the fish with its juices. Serve with steamed brown rice.

Serves 4

Per serve: calories 442; fat 14 g (29 per cent of calories from fat); saturated fat 2 g; carbohydrate 19 g; fibre 6 g; cholesterol 74 mg; calcium 164 mg.

Phytoestrogens: 'source'

LENTIL, OLIVE & SEMI-DRIED TOMATO PASTA SAUCE

This great-tasting sauce with Mediterranean flavours is perfect for pasta or rice.

1 tablespoon extra virgin olive oil

1 large onion, finely chopped

2 cloves garlic, crushed

1/2 teaspoon ground coriander

1/2 teaspoon ground cumin

400 g cooked or canned brown lentils

500 g bottled tomato pasta sauce

12 small pieces semi-dried tomatoes

12 pitted kalamata olives

2 tablespoons fresh dill, chopped

1   Heat the oil in a pan and sauté the onion and garlic until soft. Mix in the coriander and cumin.

2   Add the lentils, tomato pasta sauce, semi-dried tomato pieces, olives and dill and bring to the boil. Adjust the flavour if desired with a little salt and simmer for around 10 minutes. Serve on top of freshly cooked pasta such as fettuccine, spaghetti or spirali with a sprinkle of parmesan.

Serves 4

Per serve: calories 262; fat 6 g (19 per cent of calories from fat); saturated fat 0.7 g; carbohydrate 44 g; fibre 13 g; cholesterol 0 mg; calcium 87 mg.

Phytoestrogens: 'source'

RED THAI VEGETABLE CURRY WITH TOFU

**This curry is so quick to make and has a stimulating bite. Add
extra fresh red chilli if you prefer a hotter flavour.**

1 tablespoon peanut oil

1 medium Spanish onion, cut into $1/8$ wedges

1 small eggplant, cut into 2-cm cubes

120 g green beans, topped and tailed, cut into 2.5-cm pieces

$1/2$ cup bamboo shoots

$1/2$ cup baby corn

2 tablespoons red curry paste

200 g firm tofu, cut into 2-cm cubes

400 ml light coconut milk

pinch salt, optional

sprigs fresh coriander or Thai basil

1   Heat the oil in a deep pan and sauté the onion wedges for a few
    minutes.

2   Add the eggplant cubes and continue to sauté for a few minutes,
    until they start turning a golden colour.

3   Mix in the green beans, bamboo shoots, baby corn, curry paste,
    tofu, 1 cup of water and the coconut milk and simmer for 5–10
    minutes. Adjust the flavour with salt if desired. Serve on steamed
    jasmine rice, garnished with the coriander or Thai basil.

Serves 5

Per serve: calories 252; fat 18 g (60 per cent of calories from fat); saturated
fat 1 g; carbohydrate 17 g; fibre 4 g; cholesterol 0 mg; calcium 322 mg.

Phytoestrogens: 'good source'

CREAMY MUSHROOM PASTA WITH PEPPERCORNS

This tastes so good, you would never tell it is low in saturated fat. It's also a breeze to make. You can use any type of pasta, but for this recipe we recommend using one that contains phytoestrogens—such as soy pasta.

375 g soy pasta twists

2 tablespoons extra virgin olive oil

400 g mixed mushrooms (e.g. Swiss brown, button), wiped and sliced

2 cloves garlic, crushed

$\frac{1}{2}$ teaspoon salt

1 teaspoon green peppercorns

$\frac{1}{2}$ cup white wine

1 teaspoon cornflour

1 cup low-fat evaporated milk

2 tablespoons parsley, finely chopped

1 Bring 2.5 litres water to a rolling boil in a deep pot. Add the soy pasta and cook until al dente. Drain and set aside in a low temperature oven to keep warm while preparing the sauce.

2 Heat the oil in a non-stick frypan. Add the mushrooms and sauté for about 5 minutes, until soft. By briefly covering the frypan with a lid, the mushrooms will soften and release their juice.

3 Mix in the garlic, salt and peppercorns and sauté for a few minutes without the lid.

4 Add the white wine and cook for a further few minutes, allowing the alcohol to evaporate.

5   Mix the cornflour into the evaporated milk and add this mixture
     to the mushroom sauce. Bring to the boil and boil for 1 minute.
     Toss in the parsley. Serve the mushroom sauce on top of the
     cooked pasta. Sprinkle with parmesan cheese if desired. This dish
     tastes great with a green salad drizzled with balsamic vinegar and
     extra virgin olive oil.

Serves 4

Per serve: calories 518; fat 9 g (16 per cent of calories from fat); saturated
fat 1 g; carbohydrate 83 g; fibre 4 g; cholesterol 2 mg; calcium 217 mg.

Phytoestrogens: 'good source'

GRILLED FISH FILLETS TOPPED WITH FRESH SALSA

The fresh salsa in this recipe is juicy and gives the fillets a tangy flavour. While the fish itself does not provide phytoestrogens, combining it with phytoestrogen-containing foods may offer additional benefits.

FISH
pinch salt, optional
pinch ground sweet paprika
4 × 225 g snapper fillets, or other white-fleshed fish
1 tablespoon extra virgin olive oil

SALSA
2 medium, firm tomatoes, finely diced
1 medium cucumber, peeled and finely diced
$\frac{1}{2}$ red Spanish onion, peeled and finely diced
$\frac{1}{2}$ firm, ripe avocado, peeled and finely diced
3 tablespoons fresh coriander, chopped
1 small red chilli, deseeded and finely chopped
3 tablespoons lemon juice, or juice from 1 lemon
2 tablespoons extra virgin olive oil
pinch salt, optional

1   Rub the salt and ground paprika over the fish fillets.
2   Place the fillets on foil-lined and greased oven tray.
3   Brush the fillets with olive oil and place under a hot griller for about 5 minutes on each side, or until golden brown.

4   To prepare the salsa, toss the tomatoes, cucumber, Spanish onion and avocado with the coriander, chilli, lemon juice, olive oil and salt.

5   Serve the grilled fillets on a large plate topped with the fresh salsa. Potato mash with garlic and crushed olives makes a great accompaniment to this dish.

Serves 4

Per serve: calories 231; fat 16 g (60 per cent of calories from fat); saturated fat 2 g; carbohydrate 10 g; fibre 3 g; cholesterol 20 mg; calcium 47 mg.

Phytoestrogens: 'source'

SUE'S PESTO PASTA

This is an all-time favourite recipe. It is simple and quick to make and incredibly tasty. It contains a fair amount of fat, but this is a healthy fat coming mainly from the extra virgin olive oil and nuts, which are heart protective and rich in anti-oxidants. Pesto is delicious with a mixed salad.

600 g farfalle (bow-tie pasta)
$1/4$ cup pine nuts
1 large bunch fresh basil
2 cloves garlic, crushed
pinch cracked black pepper
pinch salt, optional
$1/2$ cup Italian parmesan, grated
$1/3$ cup extra virgin olive oil

1   Boil plenty of water in a large pot and cook the pasta for about 15 minutes, or until al dente. Rinse with cold water to stop the cooking process and set aside.
2   Grind the pine nuts in a food processor for about 30 seconds.
3   Wash the basil and remove the leaves from the stalks.
4   Add the basil leaves, garlic, black pepper, salt, parmesan and olive oil to the ground pine nuts in the food processor. Purée for 3 minutes, or until a smooth green paste forms.
5   Remove the pesto paste from the processor and place in a small container with a tight-fitting lid. This reduces exposure to air and helps maintain a bright green colour. Pesto paste can be stored in the fridge for several days, or frozen for later use.

6   Divide the farfalle into 6 servings. Allow each person to mix in their desired amount of pesto paste. This recipe makes around 15 tablespoons of pesto paste.

Serves 6

Per serve: calories 560; fat 20 g (32 per cent of calories from fat); saturated fat 4 g; carbohydrate 78 g; fibre 4 g; cholesterol 5 mg; calcium 162 mg.

Phytoestrogens: 'source'

INDIAN POTATO, CAULIFLOWER & TOFU CURRY

Who would have thought this mouth-watering dish was so healthy! Frying the tofu first makes it crispy and gives it a chewier texture.

600 g new potatoes

3 tablespoons peanut oil

200 g firm tofu, cut into small cubes

2 onions, coarsely chopped

small bunch fresh coriander, chopped

2 tablespoons Korma curry paste (mild or medium hot)

280 g fresh cauliflower, cut into small pieces

1   Boil the new potatoes in their skins for about 15 minutes. Drain and allow to cool. If the new potatoes are a little large, halve them after they are cooked and cooled.

2   Heat the oil in a deep non-stick pot and fry the tofu cubes until golden brown. Drain and place on absorbent paper.

3   Reduce the heat and add the onions to the remaining oil and sauté until translucent.

4   Dissolve the curry paste with $1/2$ cup of water and add to the onions.

5   Stir in the cauliflower and 1 cup of water. Cover with a lid and simmer for about 15 minutes until the cauliflower becomes tender.

6   Mix in the coriander, fried tofu cubes, potatoes and stir until all
the flavours have combined. You can add an additional $1/2$ cup of
water if you want more sauce. Heat through and serve. Serve with
steamed basmati rice and Three-Bean Dhal (see page 222) on the
side.

Serves 5

Per serve: calories 274; fat 14 g (43 per cent of calories from fat); saturated
fat 2 g; carbohydrate 33 g; fibre 6 g; cholesterol 0 mg; calcium 125 mg.

Phytoestrogens: 'good source'

PAN-TOSSED PERCH WITH
MEDITERRANEAN VEGETABLES

If you can't buy sea perch, use cod. While fish does not contain phytoestrogens, eating it with vegetables enables you to get a 'source' of phytoestrogens.

MARINADE

4 cloves garlic, crushed

3 tablespoons soy sauce

1 tablespoon extra virgin olive oil

MAIN RECIPE

500 g sea perch fillets, cut into 3-cm cubes

2 red Spanish onions

1 medium red capsicum

2 medium zucchinis

400 g small button mushrooms

3 tablespoons extra virgin olive oil

$1/3$ cup cornflour

pinch cracked black pepper

salt, optional

$1/2$ bunch fresh chives, finely chopped

1   To prepare the marinade, combine the garlic, soy sauce and olive oil and mix well.

2   Add the fish pieces to the marinade. Mix well and leave them to marinate for about 20 minutes.

3   Cut the vegetables into similar-sized small pieces as the fish and set aside.

4   Heat the oil in a large non-stick pan and add the onions and
     capsicum. Sauté for about 5 minutes until they begin to soften.
     Add the zucchinis and mushrooms and briefly cover with a lid
     until the mushrooms release their juice. Continue cooking for a
     further 10 minutes, until the vegetables begin to brown slightly.

5   Add the marinated fish pieces. Cook for a further 5 minutes, until
     the fish is cooked through. Toss gently as perch is soft fleshed and
     will otherwise fall apart.

6   Dissolve the cornflour in 3 cups of cold water to form a smooth
     paste. Pour into the pan and stir through until sauce begins to
     thicken.

7   Season with black pepper and adjust flavour with salt if desired.
     Serve piled on top of Sweet Potato, Pumpkin & Potato Mash (see
     page 224) and sprinkle with chives. Steamed brown rice also
     makes a great accompaniment.

Serves 6

Per serve: calories 243; fat 11 g (41 per cent of calories from fat); saturated
fat 2 g; carbohydrate 17 g; fibre 3 g; cholesterol 75 mg; calcium 99 mg.

Phytoestrogens: 'source'

SPAGHETTI BOLOGNAISE WITH RED WINE

This is a really easy low-fat and cholesterol-free spaghetti bolognaise recipe to replace the traditional fatty meat sauce. And it is packed with flavour and phytoestrogens!

1 cup dehydrated textured vegetable protein (TVP)

1 tablespoon extra virgin olive oil

1 medium onion, peeled and finely chopped

2 cloves garlic, crushed

2 teaspoons dried sweet basil

pinch ground hot paprika

500 g tomato pasta sauce

$\frac{1}{2}$ cup red wine

1   Place the TVP in a small bowl and cover with $\frac{2}{3}$ cup hot water. Set aside and allow to rehydrate for about 10 minutes.

2   Heat the oil in a saucepan and sauté the onion and garlic until soft and translucent.

3   Add the basil, paprika, hydrated TVP, 1 cup of water and tomato pasta sauce and mix well. Cover the sauce with a lid and bring to the boil.

4   Mix in the red wine and simmer for 15 minutes, half-covered, stirring occasionally. Serve on top of the spaghetti with a sprinkle of parmesan cheese. Wholemeal spaghetti is available and will further boost the fibre content of this meal. Makes around 4 cups of bolognaise sauce.

Serves 6

Per serve: calories 128; fat 3 g (22 per cent of calories from fat); saturated fat 0.4 g; carbohydrate 16 g; fibre 4 g; cholesterol 0 mg; calcium 40 mg.

Phytoestrogens: 'rich source'

Desserts

EUROPEAN-STYLE CREPES

These thin European-style crepes are delectable. You can fill them with virtually any sweet or savoury filling. Crepes can be made up to several days before you serve them—they keep well in the fridge. Simply reheat in the microwave.

1 egg
$\frac{1}{2}$ teaspoon canola or sunflower oil
2 cups plain white flour
$\frac{1}{2}$ cup soy flour
$\frac{1}{4}$ teaspoon salt
1 litre low-fat soy milk
$\frac{1}{8}$ cup extra canola or sunflower oil

1   Whisk the egg and the oil with an electric beater for about 5 seconds, until combined. Gradually blend in the dry ingredients with the soy milk and an extra $\frac{1}{3}$ cup water. Whisk with the electric beater until the batter is smooth and lump free.

2   Cover the batter mixture and allow to stand for 30 minutes.

3   Heat a 25-cm crepe pan and drizzle in about 2 ml of oil from the extra amount of oil. Add 1 soup ladleful (about $\frac{1}{2}$ cup) of the batter mixture to the centre of the hot pan, swirling so that a crepe forms on the entire surface of the pan. Flip the crepe over when you notice the sides have turned golden brown. You will know the crepe is ready to flip if it moves when you gently shake the pan forwards and backwards.

4   Repeat with the remaining batter mixture until all the crepes are
cooked. Place crepes on a plate and cover with foil to keep warm
before serving. The batter mixture makes 14 crepes. Serve with
Fresh Strawberry Sauce (see page 270), gourmet jams such as
apricot, dark plum or quince jam or canned berries. Add the filling
to one side of a crepe and roll or fold it into quarters. To garnish
stuffed crepes, drizzle with extra filling of your choice.

Serves 7

Per serve: calories 284; fat 6 g (19 per cent of calories from fat); saturated
fat 0.6 g; carbohydrate 43 g; fibre 2 g; cholesterol 34 mg; calcium 198 mg.
Phytoestrogens: 'rich source'

FRESH STRAWBERRY SAUCE

This is an all-time favourite sauce to serve with European-Style Crepes (see page 268). It is delicious, super-quick to make and looks spectacular if you want to impress guests. You can also serve this sauce on scoops of soy ice-cream.

750 g fresh, ripe strawberries, hulled and thinly sliced
$\frac{1}{4}$ cup caster sugar

1 Place the strawberries in a pan and sprinkle with the caster sugar. Heat on a moderate flame until the sugar begins to melt and caramelise and the strawberries begin to soften and release their juice.

2 Add $\frac{1}{4}$ cup of water to the strawberries and continue cooking for a further few minutes until the strawberries are soft and a sauce has formed.

Makes sauce for 8 crepes

Per serve: calories 52; fat 0.4 g (6 per cent of calories from fat); saturated fat 0.01 g; carbohydrate 13 g; fibre 2 g; cholesterol 0 mg; calcium 13 mg.

Phytoestrogens: 'source'

THICK CUSTARD

This custard is quick and easy to make and tastes delicious with canned pears or any other fruit you like. Using soy milk gives you the benefit of extra phytoestrogens.

4 tablespoons custard powder
2 cups soy milk
1 teaspoon vanilla essence
$2\frac{1}{2}$ tablespoons sugar

1   Place the custard powder in a saucepan and stir in 1 cup of the soy milk. Place on the stove on low heat. Add the vanilla essence and sugar and blend well until smooth.

2   Mix in the remaining soy milk and bring to the boil, stirring constantly. Boil for a few minutes until the custard thickens. Serve hot over stewed fruit or pieces of fresh fruit.

Serves 4

Per serve: calories 123; fat 4 g (31 per cent of calories from fat); saturated fat 0.5 g; carbohydrate 17 g; fibre 0 g; cholesterol 0 mg; calcium 150 mg.

Phytoestrogens: 'good source'

BAKED GREEN APPLES WITH CRANBERRIES

This is a much-loved, simple, classic recipe. Using Phytosprinkle in the stuffing means it's rich in phytoestrogens.

4 large green apples
2 tablespoons Phytosprinkle (see page 201)
2 tablespoons sweetened dried cranberries
1 tablespoon honey

1   Preheat the oven to 190°C (375°F).

2   Wash and core the apples. Cut a slit around the middle of each apple to prevent it from exploding into an undesirable shape. The peel will also lift off easily when the apples are baked.

3   Combine the dried cranberries (reserve 4 berries for garnishing), Phytosprinkle and honey.

4   Fill the hollowed centre of each apple with the stuffing mixture, pressing down firmly and finishing off with a berry.

5   Place the apples in a baking dish and add approximately $\frac{1}{2}$ cm of water to the bottom of the dish.

6   Bake uncovered for approximately 45 minutes, until the apples are browned. Serve piping hot, or refrigerate and serve the next day as a cold dessert.

Serves 4

Per serve: calories 190; fat 3 g (15 per cent of calories from fat); saturated fat 0.4 g; carbohydrate 42 g; fibre 7 g; cholesterol 0 mg; calcium 39 mg.

Phytoestrogens: 'rich source'

PLUM & ALMOND PARFAIT

This recipe is big on the delectable factor, visually appealing
and so easy to make. The trick is to assemble the parfait quickly
while the custard is still hot and before it starts setting. You
can also use commercially prepared ready-to-use soy custard,
but make sure you choose a thick, rather than runny, brand.

> 12 canned dark plums, drained
> ½ cup slivered almonds
> 500 ml Thick Custard

1   Halve each plum, gently removing the stone. Set aside.
2   Toast the slivered almonds in a hot pan for about 1 minute, until
    they begin to turn golden. Remove from the heat.
3   Make the custard, according to the recipe on page 271.
4   Assemble the parfaits immediately using parfait glasses or tall
    dessert glasses. For each glass, place 2 plum halves on the bottom,
    drizzle with a spoonful of custard and sprinkle with toasted
    slivered almonds. Repeat the process twice, finishing off with the
    slivered almonds. You should achieve a two-colour rainbow effect.
    Serve, or refrigerate and enjoy the following day.

Serves 4

Per serve: calories 247; fat 11 g (38 per cent of calories from fat); saturated
fat 0.98 g; carbohydrate 33 g; fibre 2.5 g; cholesterol 0 mg; calcium 179 mg.
Phytoestrogens: 'good source'

RHUBARB CRUMBLE

This variation on the traditional British fruit crumble is rich in phytoestrogens and fibre and has less fat and sugar! You can also use other fruit in season, such as blackberries or apples.

FRUIT BASE
1 large bunch of rhubarb (700 g)
300 ml water
$\frac{1}{3}$ cup sugar

1   Remove the leaves from the rhubarb, as they are toxic. Wash the stems and cut into 2-cm pieces. Place in a saucepan.
2   Add the water and sugar and bring to the boil.
3   Boil for approximately 5 minutes until the rhubarb has just softened. Note: rhubarb cooks very quickly.
4   Strain the juice, saving it to drizzle over the crumble when prepared. Place the stewed rhubarb on the bottom of an oven dish.

CRUMBLE TOPPING
1 cup wholemeal flour
1 level tablespoon linseeds, ground
$\frac{1}{2}$ cup brown sugar
$\frac{2}{3}$ cup rolled oats
2 tablespoons unsalted soy nuts, crushed
6 level tablespoons soy margarine

1   Preheat oven to 200°C (400°F).

2   Combine all of the ingredients in a large bowl and rub them together with your fingers until the mixture reaches an even consistency.

3   Cover the stewed rhubarb with the crumble and place the dish in the oven for approximately 20 minutes, until the top has crusted. Serve while still warm, drizzled with the saved juice. Accompany with soy ice-cream or Thick Custard (see page 271) if desired.

Serves 6

Per serve: calories 358; fat 14 g (34 per cent of calories from fat); saturated fat 2 g; carbohydrate 55 g; fibre 6 g; cholesterol 0 mg; calcium 140 mg.

Phytoestrogens: 'rich source'

Drinks

MANGO LASSI

This Indian-inspired thick, creamy, cooling drink is super-easy to make. It requires no cooking and will only take you a few minutes with a good blender—and it provides a 'good source' of phytoestrogens.

6 large ice cubes
1 cup ripe mango flesh (fresh or canned)
200 g mango flavoured low-fat soy yoghurt
2 teaspoons honey

1   Crush the ice cubes in a blender.
2   Add the mango flesh, soy yoghurt and honey, and purée for about 1 minute, until smooth. Serve chilled. Makes 2 cups.

Serves 2
Per serve: calories 179; fat 3 g (14 per cent of calories from fat); saturated fat 0.05 g; carbohydrate 36 g; fibre 6 g; cholesterol 0 mg; calcium 132 mg.
Phytoestrogens: 'good source'

PEACH & PASSIONFRUIT SHAKE

This shake is a great way to have a nutritious, phytoestrogen-
rich liquid breakfast when you are in a hurry. It's also high in
fibre to help keep you regular.

2 cups canned, sliced peaches, drained
pulp from 2 large passionfruit
$1\frac{1}{2}$ cups low-fat soy milk
1 tablespoon honey
1 teaspoon linseed, ground
$\frac{1}{2}$ teaspoon vanilla essence

1   Purée all the ingredients in a blender until you have a smooth,
     thick shake.
2   Add slightly more honey for a sweeter taste, if desired.
3   Serve in tall glasses.

Serves 2
Per serve: calories 228; fat 2 g (7 per cent of calories from fat); saturated
fat 0.05 g; carbohydrate 47 g; fibre 7 g; cholesterol 0 mg; calcium 242 mg.
Phytoestrogens: 'rich source'

STRAWBERRY & BANANA SMOOTHIE

Smoothies take seconds to whip up and are a delicious way of drinking your phyto-nutrition. If you would like a sweeter taste, just add more honey.

1 banana

1½ cups strawberries

2 cups low-fat soy milk

1 tablespoon honey

2 tablespoons wheat germ

½ teaspoon cocoa or carob powder, optional

1   Purée all the ingredients in a blender until smooth and creamy.

2   Pour into two tall clear glasses and serve. Sprinkle with cocoa or carob powder if desired.

Serves 2

Per serve: calories 245; fat 3 g (9 per cent of calories from fat); saturated fat 0.2 g; carbohydrate 46 g; fibre 5 g; cholesterol 0 mg; calcium 323 mg.

Phytoestrogens: 'rich source'

Phytoestrogen composition tables

The following tables show the isoflavone levels in foods, drinks, infant formula and supplements. Isoflavones are the most researched family of phytoestrogens, because of the wealth of evidence supporting their potential health effects and the economic importance of the soybean. Fewer studies are available on the lignan content of foods, despite their ubiquitous occurrence in plants. Data on the levels of coumestans, a much more potent class of phytoestrogens, is sparse. The lignan and coumestan content of foods are also not currently listed on food labels. Here, we provide you with figures for isoflavones in a wide range of foods.

How to use these tables

The values given are for the maximum amount of isoflavones the body can absorb from foods. They do not include the weight of sugar molecules to which isoflavones are naturally linked in plants (see Chapter 2). The figures have been compiled from information contained in over 18 reputable scientific publications, from food companies and our own unpublished laboratory findings.

HINT

If you don't know the isoflavone content of a soy food, you can make a guess from the amount of soy protein it contains. Assume that for every 1 g of soy protein there are 1–2 mg of isoflavones. This rule does not apply to products made from soy protein that has been alcohol-washed—commonly referred to as 'concentrated soy protein'.

TABLE A
ISOFLAVONE CONTENT OF FOODS AND DRINKS

Food	Amount in 100 g edible portion	Amount per serving
Breads & grain products		
Bread, 9-grain	0.02 mg	0.015 mg/2 slices (76 g)
Soy & linseed bread	8.6–18.8 mg	5.1–11.3 mg/2 slices (60 g)
Soy cereal, with or without linseeds	22.5–101 mg	12.5–40 mg/$^1/_2$ –1 cup (40–50 g)
Soy pasta	9.3–18.5 mg	6.3–12.6 mg/68 g
Dairy		
Cow's milk, 76 samples from different states of Australia	0.003–0.04 mg	0.007–0.096 mg/1 cup (250 ml)
Dairy alternatives		
Soy cheese	78 mg	16.4 mg/slice (21 g)
Soy custard	3.2–6.4 mg	3.2–6.4 mg/100 ml
Soy dip	30–36 mg	23–27 mg/75 g
Soy ice-cream	4–5 mg	3–4 mg/$^1/_2$ cup (83 g)
Soy milk, entire bean, fat free	2.3–3.1 mg	5.7–7.8 mg/1 cup (250 ml)
Soy milk, entire bean, regular	4.4–4.8 mg	11–12 mg/1 cup (250 ml)
Soy milk, powdered	75–134 mg	19–34 mg/25 g
Soy milk, soy protein based, fat free	2.3–5.3 mg	5.7–13.3 mg/1 cup (250 ml)
Soy milk, soy protein based, low fat	2.3–3.9 mg	5.7–9.7 mg/1 cup (250 ml)
Soy milk, soy protein based, regular	2.4–4.6 mg	6.1–11.5 mg/1 cup (250 ml)
Soy milk, wholebean, low fat	1.9–9.2 mg	4.7–23 mg/1 cup (250 ml)
Soy milk, wholebean, regular	3.0–11.6 mg	7.4–29 mg/1 cup (250 ml)
Soy protein shake powder	246–364 mg	69–102 mg /1 level scoop (28 g)
Soy yoghurt	2.1–5.6 mg	4.2–11.2 mg/200 g tub
Tofu yoghurt	16 mg	32 mg/200 g carton

Drinks

Beer, 29 varieties	0.00002–0.0007 mg	0.000096mg–0.00336 mg/480 ml
Bourbon	Traces	Traces
Soy based meal replacement	15 mg	44 mg/296 ml
Tea, Japanese green	<1 mg (trace)	< 0.02 mg/tea bag
Tea, Jasmine	<1 mg (trace)	< 0.02 mg/tea bag

Legumes

Baked beans	0.007 mg	0.009 mg/½ cup (137 g)
Black beans, dry	131 mg	98 mg/½ cup (75 g)
Blackeyed beans, dry	0.05 mg	0.03 mg/½ cup (75 g)
Broad beans, dry	<10 mg	<7.5 mg/½ cup (75 g)
Chickpeas, dry	3.6 mg	2.8 mg/½ cup (80 g)
Green soybeans (Edamame)	36.6 mg	31.1 mg/⅔ cup (85 g)
Haricot beans, cooked	0.015 mg	0.01 mg/½ cup (88 g)
Lentils, dry	0.04 mg	0.03 mg/½ cup (80 g)
Lima beans, dry	0.04 mg	0.03 mg/½ cup (80 g)
Mung beans, cooked	0.01 mg	0.01 mg/½ cup (107 g)
Navy beans, dry	0.43 mg	0.34 mg/½ cup (80 g)
Red kidney beans, dry	0.07 mg	0.05 mg/½ cup (80 g)
Soybeans, boiled	55 mg	71.5 mg/½ cup (130 g)
Soybeans, canned	80 mg	80 mg/½ cup (100 g)
Soybeans, dry, American	183 mg	146 mg/½ cup (80 g)
Soybeans, dry, Brazilian	88 mg	70 mg/½ cup (80 g)
Soybeans, dry, Japanese	119 mg	95 mg/½ cup (80 g)
Soybeans, dry, Korean	145 mg	116 mg/½ cup (80 g)
Split peas, green, dry	0.02 mg	0.009 mg/¼ cup (45 g)
Split peas, yellow, dry	0.02 mg	0.009 mg/¼ cup (45 g)

Meat alternatives

Soy bacon	12 mg	6.8 mg/3 slices (57 g)
Soy burger, frozen	14.7 mg	9.3 mg/burger (63 g)

Soy hot dog	16 mg	7.4 mg/dog (46 g)
Soy based deli slices	12.6 mg	7.6 mg/3 slices (60 g)
Soy sausages	7.3 mg	14.6 mg/2 sausages (200 g)
Soy schnitzels	9.1 mg	10 mg/one schnitzel (110 g)
Textured vegetable protein (TVP), dry	114–245 mg	29–61mg/$\frac{1}{4}$ cup (25 g); (makes $\frac{1}{2}$ cup ready-to-use TVP)

Nuts & seeds

| Peanuts | 0.14 mg | 0.07 mg/(50 g) |

Snack foods

Soy chips	2–6 mg	1–3 mg /50 g
Soy nuts (roasted soybeans)	106–181 mg	29.7–50.6 mg/$\frac{1}{3}$ cup (28 g)
Soy protein bars	>33 mg	>20 mg/1 bar (61.5 g)

Soy ingredients

Soy flakes	50–176 mg	12–42 mg/$\frac{1}{4}$ cup (24 g)
Soy flour	188–276 mg	79–115 mg/$\frac{1}{2}$ cup (42 g)
Soy flours from Korea, various brands	69–231 mg	35–115 mg/$\frac{1}{2}$ cup (50 g)
Soy germ	2300 mg	115 mg/1 teaspoon (5 g)
Soy grits	60–166 mg	14–63 mg/$\frac{1}{4}$ cup (38 g)
Soy protein concentrate, aqueous washed	102 mg	29 mg/28 g
Soy protein concentrate, produced by alcohol extraction	5.6–13 mg	1.6–3.6 mg/28 g
Soy protein isolate	46–98 mg	13–27 mg/28 g

Traditional Asian foods

Miso, various types	43–153 mg	7.7–27.5 mg/1 tablespoon (18 g)
Natto	59 mg	47 mg/80 g serve
Soy sauce	0.2–1.2 mg	0.03–0.22 mg/1 tablespoon (18 g)
Tempeh	35–191 mg	29–158 mg/$\frac{1}{2}$ cup (83 g)
Tempeh burger	29 mg	19 mg/1 burger (67 g)
Tofu, firm and soft	11–32 mg	9.9–28.8 mg/$\frac{1}{2}$ cup (90 g)

Vegetables

Asparagus	0.0009 mg	0.0006 mg/5 spears (70 g)
Broad beans, fresh, raw	0.002 mg	0.0016 mg/$\frac{1}{2}$ cup (78 g)
Brussels sprouts, frozen	0.004 mg	0.0034 mg/8 small sprouts (85 g)
Butter beans, raw	0.115 mg	0.08 mg/$\frac{1}{2}$ cup (70 g)
Cabbage, Savoy, raw	0.002 mg	0.0009 mg/$\frac{1}{2}$ cup (43 g)
Celeriac, cooked	0.004 mg	0.003 mg/$\frac{1}{2}$ cup (70 g)
Eggplant, cooked	0.0008 mg	0.0008 mg/$\frac{1}{2}$ cup (98 g)
French beans, cooked	0.035 mg	0.029 mg/$\frac{2}{3}$ cup (85 g)
Green peas, frozen	0.004 mg	0.0034 mg/$\frac{2}{3}$ cup (85 g)
Mushrooms, common, raw	0.002 mg	0.0007 mg/$\frac{1}{2}$ cup (35 g)
Okra, raw	0.007 mg	0.002 mg/6 ladies fingers (30 g)
Potatoes, cooked	0.004 mg	0.004 mg/1 medium (100 g)
Pumpkin	0.001 mg	0.0009 mg/$\frac{1}{2}$ cup (85 g)
Radish, raw	0.002 mg	0.001 mg/4 radishes (60 g)
Runner beans, raw	0.393 mg	0.28 mg/$\frac{1}{2}$ cup (70 g)
Salad onions	0.0002 mg	0.0001 mg/$\frac{1}{2}$ cup (60 g)
Snow beans, frozen	0.006 mg	0.005 mg/$\frac{2}{3}$ cup (84 g)
Spinach leaf, frozen	0.001 mg	0.00085 mg/$\frac{1}{3}$ cup (85 g)
Sprouts, alfalfa	261 mg	26 mg/$\frac{1}{4}$ cup (10 g)
Sprouts, alfalfa mixed with clover sprouts	5173 mg	517 mg/$\frac{1}{4}$ cup (10 g)
Sprouts, mung bean	0.573 mg	0.15 mg/$\frac{1}{4}$ cup (26 g)
Sprouts, soybean	41 mg	10.2 mg/$\frac{1}{2}$ cup (25 g)
Sweetcorn, canned	0.003 mg	0.003 mg/$\frac{1}{2}$ cup (88 g)
Tomato, raw	0.003 mg	0.004 mg/1 tomato (129 g)
Turnip, raw	0.002 mg	0.002 mg/ $\frac{1}{2}$ cup (120 g)

TABLE B
ISOFLAVONE CONTENT OF INFANT FEEDS

Type of infant formula	Amount in 1 litre ready to feed
Cow's milk infant formula	Less than 0.005 mg
Human breast milk	0.005 mg
Infasoy	22 mg
Isomil powdered formula	29 mg
Karicare Soya Infant formula	17 mg

TABLE C

ISOFLAVONE CONTENT OF PHYTOESTROGEN SUPPLEMENTS, HERBALS AND POWDERS

Supplement	Main ingredient	Independently analysed isoflavone level (per capsule, tablet or serving)	Manufacturer claim of isoflavone content (per capsule, tablet or serving)
Basic Soy Isoflavones, Basic Drugs Inc.	Soybean extract	16.6 mg	25.0 mg
Carlson Easy Soy Gold, JR Carlson Laboratories Inc.	Soy germ extract	36.2 mg	50.0 mg
Carlson Easy Soy, JR Carlson Laboratories Inc.	Soy germ extract	10.2 mg	12.5 mg
Erdic, Cerdic B.V.	Extract of hops, barley, wheat & other grains	None	Level not stated
Estroven, Amerifit	Soybean & kudzu extract*	7.8 mg	50.0 mg
Flash Fighters, Nature's Bounty	Soybean extract	16.8 mg	21.7 mg
Genistein, Soy Isoflavone Extract, Solgar Laboratories.	Soybean extract	9.4 mg	15.0 mg
H &B Soya Isoflavones, Holland & Barrett	Soy germ extract	16.2 mg	16.7 mg
Healthy Woman, Personal Products Co.	Soybean extract	48.8 mg	55.0 mg
Herbal Blends Menopause Balance, Walgreens	Soybean & clover extract	2.3 mg	8.0 mg
Kudzu Root Extract, Solaray Inc.	Kudzu root extract	11.5 mg	3.0 mg
Naturally Preferred Soy Germ, Inter-American Products	Soy germ extract	12.3 mg	10.0 mg
Nature's Herbs Phytoestrogen Power, Alvita	Soy germ extract	7.3 mg	5.3 mg
New Phase, Sunsource, Chatham Inc.	Soy germ & kudzu extract	8.6 mg	80.0 mg
NovaSoy, Archer Daniel Midland	Soybean extract	40.8 mg	50.0 mg
One a Day, Bayer Corp. Consumer Care Division	Soybean extract	12.8 mg	42.0 mg

Phyto Estrin, *USANA Inc.*	Soybean extract	10.3 mg	14.0 mg
Phyto Soya, *Arkopharma*	Soy germ extract	12.5 mg	17.5 mg
Phytosoy, *Nature's Sunshine*	Soybean extract	3.4 mg	4.0 mg
Promensil, *Novogen Inc.*	Clover extract	41.7 mg	40.0 mg
Red Clover Tea Bags, Alvita	Clover leaf extract	1.1 mg	Level not stated
Revival-powder, *Physician's Laboratory*	Soybean extract	1.78 mg/g	2.78 mg/g
Solaray PhytoEstrogen, *Nutraceutical Corp. for Solaray Inc.*	Soy germ extract	10.6 mg	10.0 mg
Soy Care, *S.C.P.I.*	Soybean extract	23.2 mg	25.0 mg
Soy Choice, *Vitanica*	Soy germ extract	25.8 mg	56.0 mg
Soy Extract, *Enzymatic Therapy*	Soybean extract	11.3 mg	13.0 mg
Soy Isoflavones, *Nature's Resources*	Soybean extract	43.4 mg	50.0 mg
Soy Life 25, *Schouten USA Inc.*	Soy germ extract	20.2 mg	25.0 mg
Soy Plus, *Feeling Fine Co.*	Soybean extract	18.1 mg	20.0 mg
Soyamax-powder, *USANA Inc.*	Soybean extract	1.96 mg/g	2.06 mg/g
Spring Valley Phytoestrogen Complex, *NaturPharma*	Soy germ extract	12.7 mg	7.0 mg
Sundown-Soy Isoflavones, *Sundown Vitamins*	Soybean extract	39.2 mg	40.0 mg
Trinovin, *Novogen Inc.*	Clover extract	36.9 mg	40.0 mg

We have analysed the levels of isoflavones in many over-the-counter phytoestrogen supplements from Australia, the US and the UK and compared these with the claims on packaging. Surprisingly, a lot of products failed to deliver what they promised. Many can be bought through the Internet.

For more detailed information on these analyses refer to the Journal of Nutrition, Year 2001, Volume 131, pages 1362s–1375s. Note, periodically the formulations or the ingredients of supplements may change, for example, Estroven* no longer uses kudzu as an ingredient.

Glossary

Aberrant crypts. The microscopic changes in the lining of the bowel that provide an early warning signal for cancer.

Alzheimer's disease. A progressive brain disease resulting in confusion, memory failure and disorientation.

Androgens. Male hormones.

Antioxidants. Chemicals that protect the body by mopping up 'free radicals' which damage DNA, fats and proteins.

Aromatase. An enzyme responsible for changing testosterone into estrogen.

Benign prostatic hyperplasia (BHP). The pre-cancerous condition in which the prostate becomes larger and places pressure upon the urethra, making it difficult to pass urine.

Cognition. The brain's ability to remember, reason and process information.

Coumestans. One of the three main families of phytoestrogens, found in alfalfa and other sprouts.

Cystic fibrosis. A hereditary disease affecting many organs but mainly the pancreas and lungs manifesting in breathing difficulties and an inability to digest foods.

Endometriosis. The growth of migrated uterine cells in the abdomen, causing inflammation, severe abdominal pain, irregular periods, bleeding and sometimes infertility.

Enzyme. A protein, which is a biological catalyst controlling the rate at which reactions occur in the body.

Estrogen. A hormone essential for the development of the male and female reproductive systems.

Free radicals. Highly reactive molecules produced within the body or from the environment that damage our DNA, fats and proteins.

Hereditary haemorrhagic telangiectasia (nosebleed syndrome). This is a rare genetic disorder that causes chronic nosebleeds, severe headaches and intestinal bleeding.

Isoflavones. The most well-researched family of phytoestrogens, found in high levels in soybeans and most soy products.

Lignans. One of the three main families of phytoestrogens, found in all plants but particularly abundant in linseeds.

Lobules. Seen under the microscope, these are flower-like structures within the breast that are formed from the terminal end buds and ducts.

Metabolites. Substances formed in many cells of the body and also by bacteria within the large intestine; phytoestrogens are converted into many metabolites by the resident bacteria.

Neuroblastoma. A common childhood cancer of the autonomic nervous system.

Nipple aspirate fluid (NAF). Fluid obtained under suction from the breast nipple.

Osteoblasts. Cells that make new bone to replace depleted bone.

Osteoclasts. Cells that break down existing bone.

Osteoporosis. A condition in which bones are leached of calcium and become porous and prone to fracture.

Phytoestrogens. These estrogen-like substances come from plants and are natural plant protectants that have a range of positive effects on the body and offer protection against many diseases.

Phytoprotectants. Natural protective components found in plant foods. Phytoestrogens are an important class of phytoprotectants.

Plaque. Fatty deposits that accumulate in the inner lining of the blood vessels which cause atherosclerosis.

Prostate. A small gland positioned at the base of the penis that adds fluid to sperm.

Protein tyrosine kinases. Enzymes that regulate the way many growth factors work in cells.

Selective Estrogen Receptor Modulators (SERMs). Designer estrogen drugs that provide the positive effects of estrogens without the negative ones.

Terminal end buds (TEBs) and terminal ducts. Seen under the microscope, these are tiny, bud-like structures found in the breasts—they are very prone to develop into cancer and are the sites where most breast cancer begins.

Selected references

Chapter 1

Adlercreutz, H., Hämäläinen, E., Gorbach, S., & Goldin, B. (1992) 'Dietary phyto-oestrogens and the menopause in Japan,' *Lancet* 339: 1233.

Crouse, J. R., 3rd, Morgan, T., Terry, J. G., Ellis, J., Vitolins, M., & Burke, G. L. (1999) 'A randomized trial comparing the effect of casein with that of soy protein containing varying amounts of isoflavones on plasma concentrations of lipids and lipoproteins,' *Arch Intern Med* 159: 2070–2076.

de Lorgeril, M., Salen, P., Martin, J. L., Monjaud, I., Boucher, P., & Mamelle, N. (1998) 'Mediterranean dietary pattern in a randomized trial: prolonged survival and possible reduced cancer rate,' *Arch Intern Med* 158: 1181–1187.

Ho, S. C. (1996) 'Body measurements, bone mass and fractures—does the East differ from the West?' *Clin Orthop Relat Res* 323: 75–80.

Jacobsen, B. K., Knutsen, S. F., & Fraser, G. E. (1998) 'Does high soy milk intake reduce prostate cancer incidence? The Adventist Health Study (United States),' *Cancer Causes Control* 9: 553–557.

Key, T. (1998) 'Mortality in vegetarians and non-vegetarians: a collaborative analysis of 8300 deaths among 76 000 men and women in five prospective studies,' *Public Health Nutr* 1: 33–41.

Knight, D. C., & Eden, J. A. (1996) 'A review of the clinical effects of phyto-estrogens,' *Obstet Gynecol* 87: 897–904.

Lydeking-Olsen, E., Beck Jensen, J.-E., Setchell, K. D. R., Damhus, M., & Jensen, T. H. (2002) 'Isoflavone-rich soymilk prevents bone-loss in the lumbar spine of postmenopausal women. A two-year study'. *J Nutr* 132: 581S (abs).

Parkin, D. M. (1989) 'Cancers of the breast, endometrium and ovary: geographic correlations,' *Eur J Cancer Clin Oncol* 25: 1917–1925.

Phillips, R. L. (1975) 'Role of life-style and dietary habits in risk of cancer among Seventh-day Adventists,' *Cancer Res* 35: 3513–3522.

Potter, S. M., Baum, J. A., Teng, H., Stillman, R. J., Shay, N. F., & Erdman, J. W., Jr. (1998) 'Soy protein and isoflavones: their effects on blood lipids and bone density in postmenopausal women,' *Am J Clin Nutr* 68: 1375S–1379S.

Setchell, K. D. R., Borriello, S. P., Hulme, P., Kirk, D. N., & Axelson, M. (1984) 'Nonsteroidal estrogens of dietary origin: possible roles in hormone- dependent disease,' *Am J Clin Nutr* 40: 569–578.

Setchell, K. D. R., & Cassidy, A. (1999) 'Dietary isoflavones: biological effects and relevance to human health,' *J Nutr* 129: 758S-767S.

Taha, F. A. (1993) 'Japan adds Western flavor to its traditional diet,' *Food Rev* 16: 30–37.

Writing Group for the Women's Health Initiative Investigators (2002) 'Risks and benefits of estrogen plus progestin in healthy postmenopausal women,' *JAMA* 288: 321–333.

Chapter 2

Adlercreutz, H., Bannwart, C., Wähälä, K., Mäkelä, T., Brunow, G., Hase, T., Arosemena, P. J., Kellis, J. T., Jr., & Vickery, L. E. (1993) 'Inhibition of human aromatase by mammalian lignans and isoflavonoid phytoestrogens,' *J Steroid Biochem Mol Biol* 44: 147–153.

Akiyama, T., Ishida, J., Nakagawa, S., Ogawara, H., Watanabe, S., Itoh, N., Shibuya, M., & Fukami, Y. (1987) 'Genistein, a specific inhibitor of tyrosine-specific protein kinases,' *J Biol Chem* 262: 5592–5595.

Australian Institute of Health and Welfare. (2000) Australia's Health 2000, Canberra.

Axelson, M., Sjövall, J., Gustafsson, B. E., & Setchell, K. D. R. (1982) 'Origin of lignans in mammals and identification of a precursor from plants,' *Nature* 298: 659–660.

Bonneterre, J., Buzdar, A., Nabholtz, J. M., Robertson, J. F., Thurlimann, B., von Euler, M., Sahmoud, T., Webster, A., & Steinberg, M. (2001) 'Anastrozole is superior to tamoxifen as first-line therapy in hormone receptor positive advanced breast carcinoma,' *Cancer* 92: 2247–2258.

Colborn, T., Dummanoske, D., & Peterson, M. (1996) *Our Stolen Future*. Penguin Books, New York.

Coward, L., Barnes, N. C., Setchell, K. D. R., & Barnes, S. (1993) 'Genistein and daidzein, and their ß-glycosides conjugates: anti-tumor isoflavones in soybean foods from American and Asian diets,' *J Agric Food Chem* 41: 1961–1967.

Evans, B. A., Griffiths, K., & Morton, M. S. (1995) 'Inhibition of 5 alpha-reductase in genital skin fibroblasts and prostate tissue by dietary lignans and isoflavonoids,' *J Endocrinol* 147: 295–302.

Fotsis, T., Pepper, M., Adlercreutz, H., Fleischmann, G., Hase, T., Montesano, R., & Schweigerer, L. (1993) 'Genistein, a dietary-derived inhibitor of in vitro angiogenesis,' *Proc Natl Acad Sci USA* 90: 2690–2694.

Jacobsen, B. K., Knutsen, S. F., & Fraser, G. E. (1998) 'Does high soy milk intake reduce prostate cancer incidence?' The Adventist Health Study (United States). *Cancer Causes Control* 9: 553–557.

Jordan, V. C., & Morrow, M. (1999) 'Tamoxifen, raloxifene, and the prevention of breast cancer,' *Endocr Rev* 20: 253–278.

Knuckles, B. E., deFremery, D., & Kohler, G. O. (1976) 'Coumestrol content of fractions obtained during wet processing of alfalfa,' *J Agric Food Chem* 24: 1177–1180.

Mitchell, J. H., & Collins, A. R. (1999) 'Effects of a soy milk supplement on plasma cholesterol levels and oxidative DNA damage in men—a pilot study,' *Eur J Nutr* 38: 143–148.

Peterson, G., & Barnes, S. (1991) 'Genistein inhibition of the growth of human breast cancer cells: independence from estrogen receptors and the multi-drug resistance gene,' *Biochem Biophys Res Commun* 179: 661–667.

Sadowska-Krowicka, H., Mannick, E. E., Oliver, P. D., Sandoval, M., Zhang, X. J., Eloby-Childess, S., Clark, D. A., & Miller, M. J. (1998) 'Genistein and gut inflammation: role of nitric oxide,' *Proc Soc Exp Biol Med* 217: 351–357.

Salzman, A. L., Preiser, J.-C., Setchell, K. D. R., & Szabo, C. (1999) 'Isoflavone-mediated inhibition of tyrosine kinase: a novel anti-inflammatory approach,' *J Medicinal Food* 2: 179–181.

Schairer, C., Lubin, J., Troisi, R., Sturgeon, S., Brinton, L., & Hoover, R. (2000) 'Menopausal estrogen and estrogen-progestin replacement therapy and breast cancer risk,' *JAMA* 283: 485–491.

Setchell, K. D. R., Borriello, S. P., Hulme, P., Kirk, D. N., & Axelson, M. (1984) 'Nonsteroidal estrogens of dietary origin: possible roles in hormone-dependent disease,' *Am J Clin Nutr* 40: 569–578.

Setchell, K. D. R., Brown, N. M., Zimmer-Nechemias, L., Brashear, W. T., Wolfe, B., Kirschner, A. S., Cassidy, A., & Heubi, J. E. (2002) 'Evidence for lack of absorption of soy isoflavone glycosides in humans, supporting the crucial role of intestinal metabolism for bioavailability,' *Am J Clin Nutr* 76: 442–453.

Shertzer, H. G., Puga, A., Chang, C., Smith, P., Nebert, D. W., Setchell, K. D. R., & Dalton, T. P. (1999) 'Inhibition of CYP1A1 enzyme activity in mouse hepatoma cell culture by soybean isoflavones,' *Chem Biol Interact* 123: 31–49.

Verma, S. P., & Goldin, B. R. (1998) 'Effect of soy-derived isoflavonoids on the induced growth of MCF-7 cells by estrogenic environmental chemicals,' *Nutr Cancer 30*: 232–239.

Chapter 3

Adlercreutz, C. H., Goldin, B. R., Gorbach, S. L., Hockerstedt, K. A., Watanabe, S., Hämäläinen, E. K., Markkanen, M. H., Mäkelä, T. H., Wähälä, K. T., & Adlercreutz, T. (1995) 'Soybean phytoestrogen intake and cancer risk,' *J Nutr* 125: 757S-770S.

Bennetts, H. W., Underwood, E. J., & Shier, F. L. (1946) 'A specific breeding problem of sheep on subterranean clover pastures in Western Australia,' *Aust. J. Agric. Res.* 22: 131–138.

Bloedon, L. T., Jeffcoat, A.R., Lapaczynski, W., Schell, M. J., Black, T. M., Dix, K. J., Thomas, B. F., Albright, C., Busby, M. G., Crowell, J. A., & Zeisel, S. (2002) 'Safety and pharmacokinetics of purified soy isoflavones: single-dose administration to postmenopausal women,' *Am J Clin Nutr* 76: 1126–1137.

Coward, L., Barnes, N. C., Setchell, K. D. R., & Barnes, S. (1993) 'Genistein and daidzein, and their ß-glycosides conjugates: anti-tumor isoflavones in soybean foods from American and Asian diets,' *J Agric Food Chem* 41: 1961–1967.

de Kleijn, M. J. J., van der Schouw, Y. T., Wilson, P. W. F., Grobbee, D. E., & Jacques, P. F. (2001) 'Dietary intake of phytoestrogens is associated with a favorable metabolic cardiovascular risk profile in postmenopausal U. S. women': The Framingham Study. *J Nutr* 132: 276–282.

Ingram, D., Sanders, K., Kolybaba, M., & Lopez, D. (1997) 'Case-control study of phyto-oestrogens and breast cancer,' *Lancet* 350: 990–994.

Izumi, T., Piskula, M. K., Osawa, S., Obata, A., Tobe, K., Saito, M., Kataoka, S., Kubota, Y., & Kikuchi, M. (2000) 'Soy isoflavone aglycones are absorbed faster and in higher amounts than their glucosides in humans,' *J Nutr* 130: 1695–1699.

Knekt, P., Adlercreutz, H., Rissanen, H., Aromaa, A., Teppo, L., & Heliövaara, M. (2000) 'Does antibacterial treatment for urinary tract infection contribute to the risk of breast cancer?' *Br J Cancer* 82: 1107–1110.

McCann, S. E., Moysich, K. B., Freudenheim, J. L., Amborose, C. B., & Shields, P. G. (2002) 'The risk of breast cancer associated with dietary lignans differs by CYP17 genotype in women,' *J Nutr* 132: 3036–3041.

Rowland, I. R., Wiseman, H., Sanders, T. A., Adlercreutz, H., & Bowey, E. A. (2000) 'Interindividual variation in metabolism of soy isoflavones and lignans: influence of habitual diet on equol production by the gut flora,' *J Nutr* 36: 27–32.

Setchell, K. D. R., Borriello, S. P., Hulme, P., Kirk, D. N., & Axelson, M. (1984) 'Nonsteroidal estrogens of dietary origin: possible roles in hormone- dependent disease,' *Am J Clin Nutr* 40: 569–578.

Setchell, K. D. R., Brown, N. M., Desai, P., Zimmer-Nechemias, L., Wolfe, B. E., Brashear, W. T., Kirschner, A. S., Cassidy, A., & Heubi, J. E. (2001) 'Bioavailability of pure isoflavones in healthy humans and analysis of commercial soy isoflavone supplements,' *J Nutr* 131: 1362S-1375S.

Setchell, K. D. R., Gosselin, S. J., Welsh, M. B., Johnston, J. O., Balistreri, W. F., Kramer, L. W., Dresser, B. L., & Tarr, M. J. (1987) 'Dietary estrogens—a probable cause of infertility and liver disease in captive cheetahs,' *Gastroenterology* 93: 225–233.

Setchell, K. D. R., Lawson, A. M., Borriello, S. P., Harkness, R., Gordon, H., Morgan, D. M., Kirk, D. N., Adlercreatz, H., Anderson, L. C., & Axelson, M. (1981) 'Lignan formation in man—microbial involvement and possible roles in relation to cancer,' *Lancet* 2: 4–7.

Setchell, K. D. R., Lawson, A. M., Mitchell, F. L., Adlercreutz, H., Kirk, D. N., & Axelson, M. (1980) 'Lignans in man and in animal species,' *Nature* 287: 740–742.

Zheng, W., Dai, Q., Custer, L. J., Shu, X. O., Wen, W. Q., Jin, F., & Franke, A. A. (1999) 'Urinary excretion of isoflavonoids and the risk of breast cancer,' *Cancer Epidemiol Biomarkers Prev* 8: 35–40.

Chapter 4

Adlercreutz, C. H., Goldin, B. R., Gorbach, S. L., Hockerstedt, K. A., Watanabe, S., Hämäläinen, E. K., Markkanen, M. H., Mäkelä, T. H., Wähälä, K. T., & Adlercreutz, T. (1995) 'Soybean phytoestrogen intake and cancer risk,' *J Nutr* 125: 757S-770S.

Adlercreutz, H., Fotsis, T., Heikkinen, R., Dwyer, J. T., Woods, M., Goldin, B. R., & Gorbach, S. L. (1982) 'Excretion of the lignans enterolactone and enterodiol and of equol in omnivorous and vegetarian postmenopausal women and in women with breast cancer,' *Lancet* 2: 1295–1299.

Adlercreutz, H., Markkanen, H., & Watanabe, S. (1993) 'Plasma concentrations of phyto-oestrogens in Japanese men,' *Lancet* 342: 1209–1210.

Bennink, M., Thiagarajan, D., Bourquin, L., & Mayle, J. (1999) 'Dietary soy is associated with decreased cell proliferation rate and zone in colon mucosa of subjects at risk for colon cancer. Proceedings of the Third International Symposium on the Role of Soy in Preventing and Treating Chronic Disease,' *J Nutr* (abs).

Brown, A., Jolly, P., & Wei, H. (1998) 'Genistein modulates neuroblastoma cell proliferation and differentiation through induction of apoptosis and regulation of tyrosine kinase activity and N-myc expression,' *Carcinogenesis* 19: 991–997.

Cancer Research UK, Cancer Stats Incidence – UK, September 2002.

Cassidy, A., Bingham, S., & Setchell, K. D. R. (1994) 'Biological effects of a diet of soy protein rich in isoflavones on the menstrual cycle of premenopausal women,' *Am J Clin Nutr* 60: 333–340.

Constantinou, A. I., Mehta, R. G., & Vaughan, A. (1996) 'Inhibition of N-methyl-N-nitrosourea-induced mammary tumors in rats by the soybean isoflavones,' *Anticancer Res* 16: 3293–3298.

Constantinou, A. I., Xu, H., Morgan Lucas, L., & Lantvit, D. (2001) 'Soy enhances tamoxifen's cancer chemopreventive effects in female rats'. 4th International Symposium on the Role of Soy in Preventing and Treating Chronic Disease, San Diego, USA.

Cummings, S. R., Eckert, S., Krueger, K. A., Grady, D., Powles, T. J., Cauley, J. A., Norton, L., Nickelsen, T., Bjarnason, N. H., Morrow, M., Lippman, M. E., Black, D., Glusman, J. E., Costa, A., & Jordan, V. C. (1999) 'The effect of raloxifene on risk of breast cancer in postmenopausal women: results from the MORE randomized trial,' *Multiple Outcomes of Raloxifene Evaluation. JAMA* 281: 2189–2197.

Dalu, A., Haskell, J. F., Coward, L., & Lamartiniere, C. A. (1998) 'Genistein, a component of soy, inhibits the expression of the EGF and ErbB2/Neu receptors in the rat dorsolateral prostate,' *Prostate* 37: 36–43.

Evans, B. A., Griffiths, K., & Morton, M. S. (1995) 'Inhibition of 5 alpha-reductase in genital skin fibroblasts and prostate tissue by dietary lignans and isoflavonoids,' *J Endocrinol* 147: 295–302.

Ferlay, J., Parkin, D., & Pisani, D. (1998) 'Globocan 1, Cancer incidence, mortality and prevalence worldwide,' International Agency for Research on Cancer, World Health Organization. IARC Press.

Ferlay, J., Bray, F., Pisani, P., & Parkin, D. M. (2001) 'Globocan 2000: Cancer incidence, mortality and prevalence worldwide,' Version 1.0. IARC CancerBase No. 5 Lyon, IARC Press.

Fleming, R. (2001) 'Breast enhanced scintigraphy test (B.E.S.T.) demonstrates improvements in breast inflammation in women consuming soy protein.' 4th International Symposium on the Role of Soy in Preventing and Treating Chronic Disease, San Diego, USA.

Foth, D., & Cline, J. M. (1998) 'Effects of mammalian and plant estrogens on mammary glands and uteri of macaques,' *Am J Clin Nutr* 68: 1413S-1417S.

Fritz, W. A., Eltoum, I-E., Cotroneo, M. S., & Lamartiniere, C. A. (2002) 'Genistein alters growth but is not toxic to the rat prostate,' *J Nutr* 132: 3007–3111.

Geller, J., Sionit, L., Partido, C., Li, L., Tan, X., Youngkin, T., Nachtsheim, D., & Hoffman, R. M. (1998) 'Genistein inhibits the growth of human-patient BPH and prostate cancer in histoculture,' *Prostate* 34: 75–79.

Goodman, M. T., Wilkens, L. R., Hankin, J. H., Lyu, L. C., Wu, A. H., & Kolonel, L. N. (1997) 'Association of soy and fiber consumption with the risk of endometrial cancer,' *Am J Epidemiol* 146: 294–306.

Gotoh, T., Yamada, K., Yin, H., Ito, A., Kataoka, T., & Dohi, K. (1998) 'Chemoprevention of N-nitroso-N-methylurea-induced rat mammary carcinogenesis by soy foods or biochanin A,' *Jpn J Cancer Res* 89: 137–142.

Grodstein, F., Martinez, M. E., Platz, E. A., Giovannucci, E., Colditz, G. A., Kautzky, M., Fuchs, C., & Stampfer, M. J. (1998) 'Postmenopausal hormone use and risk for colorectal cancer and adenoma,' *Ann Intern Med* 128: 705–712.

Hale, G. E., Hughes, C. L., Robboy, S. J., Agarwal, S. K., & Bievre, M. (2001) 'A double-blind randomized study on the effects of red clover isoflavones on the endometrium,' *Menopause* 8: 338–346.

Hargreaves, D. F., Potten, C. S., Harding, C., Shaw, L. E., Morton, M. S., Roberts, S. A., Howell, A., & Bundred, N. J. (1999) 'Two-week dietary soy supplementation has an estrogenic effect on normal premenopausal breast,' *J Clin Endocrinol Metab* 84: 4017–4024.

Hirayama, T. (1984) 'Epidemiology of stomach cancer in Japan. With special reference to the strategy for the primary prevention,' *Jpn J Clin Oncol* 14: 159–168.

Horn-Ross, P. L., Hoggatt, K. J., & Lee, M. (2001) 'Phytoestrogens and thyroid cancer risk among women'. 4th International Symposium on the Role of Soy in Preventing and Treating Chronic Disease, San Diego, USA.

Ingram, D., Sanders, K., Kolybaba, M., & Lopez, D. (1997) 'Case-control study of phyto-oestrogens and breast cancer,' *Lancet* 350: 990–994.

Jacobsen, B. K., Knutsen, S. F., & Fraser, G. E. (1998) 'Does high soy milk intake reduce prostate cancer incidence? The Adventist Health Study (United States),' *Cancer Causes Control* 9: 553–557.

Jenab, M., & Thompson, L. U. (1996) 'The influence of flaxseed and lignans on colon carcinogenesis and beta- glucuronidase activity,' *Carcinogenesis* 17: 1343–1348.

Jordan, V. C., & Morrow, M. (1999) 'Tamoxifen, raloxifene, and the prevention of breast cancer,' *Endocr Rev* 20: 253–278.

Koo, L. C. (1988) 'Dietary habits and lung cancer risk among Chinese females in Hong Kong who never smoked,' *Nutr Cancer* 11: 155–172.

Kucuk, O. (2001) 'Soy isoflavones in the treatment of prostate cancer'. 4th International Symposium on the Role of Soy in Preventing and Treating Chronic Disease, San Diego, USA.

Lamartiniere, C. A., Cotroneo, M. S., Fritz, W. A., Wang, J., Mentor-Marcel, R., & Elgavish, A. (2001) 'Dietary genistein protects against mammary and prostate cancers'. 4th International Symposium on the Role of Soy in Preventing and Treating Chronic Disease, San Diego, USA.

Lamartiniere, C. A., Moore, J., Holland, M., & Barnes, S. (1995) 'Neonatal genistein chemoprevents mammary cancer,' *Proc Soc Exp Biol Med* 208: 120–123.

Lamartiniere, C. A., Moore, J. B., Brown, N. M., Thompson, R., Hardin, M. J., & Barnes, S. (1995) 'Genistein suppresses mammary cancer in rats,' *Carcinogenesis* 16: 2833–2840.

Laudauer, M. R., Seed, T. M., Srinivasan, S., Shapiro, A., Takimoto, C. H., Wang, P. S., & Smith, C. D. (2001) 'Genistein protects mice from ionizing radiation injury,' 4th International Symposium on the Role of Soy in Preventing and Treating Chronic Disease., San Diego.

Lee, H. P., Gourley, L., Duffy, S. W., Esteve, J., Lee, J., & Day, N. E. (1991) 'Dietary effects on breast-cancer risk in Singapore,' *Lancet* 337: 1197–1200.

Li, D., Yee, J. A., McGuire, M. H., Murphy, P. A., & Yan, L. (1999) 'Soybean isoflavones reduce experimental metastasis in mice,' *J Nutr* 129: 1075–1078.

Liu, J.-C., Seiberg, M., Miller, J., Wu, J., Shapiro, S., & Grossman, R. (2001) 'Applications of soy in skin care'. 4th International Symposium on the Role of Soy in Preventing and Treating Chronic Disease, San Diego, USA.

Lund, T. D., Rhees, R. W., Setchell, K. D. R., & Lephart, E. D. (2001) 'Altered sexually dimorphic nucleus of the preoptic area (SDN-POA) volumes in adult Long-Evans rats by dietary soy phytoestrogens,' *Brain Research* 914: 92–99.

McMichael-Phillips, D. F., Harding, C., Morton, M., Roberts, S. A., Howell, A., Potten, C. S., & Bundred, N. J. (1998) 'Effects of soy-protein supplementation on epithelial proliferation in the histologically normal human breast,' *Am J Clin Nutr* 68: 1431S-1435S.

Messina, M. J., & Loprinzi, C.L. (2001) 'Soy for breast cancer survivors: A critical review of the literature,' *J Nutr* 131: 3095S–3108S.

Morton, M. S., Matos-Ferreira, A., Abranches-Monteiro, L., Correia, R., Blacklock, N., Chan, P. S., Cheng, C., Lloyd, S., Chieh-ping, W., & Griffiths, K. (1997) 'Measurement and metabolism of isoflavonoids and lignans in the human male,' *Cancer Lett* 114: 145–151.

Murrill, W. B., Brown, N. M., Zhang, J. X., Manzolillo, P. A., Barnes, S., & Lamartiniere, C. A. (1996) 'Prepubertal genistein exposure suppresses mammary cancer and enhances gland differentiation in rats,' *Carcinogenesis* 17: 1451–1457.

Nagai, M., Hashimoto, T., Yanagawa, H., Yokoyama, H., & Minowa, M. (1982) 'Relationship of diet to the incidence of esophageal and gastric cancer in Japan,' *Nutr Cancer* 3: 257–268.

Nagata, C., Takatsuka, N., Inaba, S., Kawakami, N., & Shimizu, H. (1998) 'Effect of soymilk consumption on serum estrogen concentrations in premenopausal Japanese women,' *J Natl Cancer* Inst 90: 1830–1835.

Parkin, D. M. (1989) 'Cancers of the breast, endometrium and ovary: geographic correlations,' *Eur J Cancer Clin Oncol* 25: 1917–1925.

Peterson, G., & Barnes, S. (1996) 'Genistein inhibits both estrogen and growth factor-stimulated proliferation of human breast cancer cells,' *Cell Growth Differ* 7: 1345–1351.

Petrakis, N. L., Barnes, S., King, E. B., Lowenstein, J., Wiencke, J., Lee, M. M., Miike, R., Kirk, M., & Coward, L. (1996) 'Stimulatory influence of soy protein isolate on breast secretion in pre- and postmenopausal women,' *Cancer Epidemiol Biomarkers Prev* 5: 785–794.

Pietinen, P., Stumpf, K., Männistö, S., Kataja, V., Uusitupa, M., & Adlercreutz, H. (2001) 'Serum enterolactone and risk of breast cancer: A case-control study in Eastern Finland.' *Cancer Epidemiol Biomarkers Prevention* 10: 339–244.

Pollard, M., & Luckert, P. H. (1997) 'Influence of isoflavones in soy protein isolates on development of induced prostate-related cancers in L-W rats,' *Nutr Cancer* 28: 41–45.

Record, I. R., Broadbent, J. L., King, R. A., Dreosti, I. E., Head, R. J., & Tonkin, A. L. (1997) 'Genistein inhibits growth of B16 melanoma cells in vivo and in vitro and promotes differentiation in vitro,' *Int J Cancer* 72: 860–864.

Ross, R. K., Bernstein, L., Lobo, R. A., Shimizu, H., Stanczyk, F. Z., Pike, M. C., & Henderson, B. E. (1992) '5-alpha-reductase activity and risk of prostate cancer among Japanese and US white and black males,' *Lancet* 339: 887–889.

Serraino, M., & Thompson, L. U. (1991) 'The effect of flaxseed supplementation on early risk markers for mammary carcinogenesis,' *Cancer Lett* 60: 135–142.

Serraino, M., & Thompson, L. U. (1992) 'Flaxseed supplementation and early markers of colon carcinogenesis,' *Cancer Lett* 63: 159–165.

Setchell, K. D. R., Borriello, S. P., Hulme, P., Kirk, D. N., & Axelson, M. (1984) 'Nonsteroidal estrogens of dietary origin: possible roles in hormone- dependent disease,' *Am J Clin Nutr* 40: 569–578.

Setchell, K. D. R., Lawson, A. M., Borriello, S. P., Harkness, R., Gordon, H., Morgan, D. M., Kirk, D. N., Adlercreatz, H., Anderson, L. C., & Axelson, M. (1981) 'Lignan formation in man—microbial involvement and possible roles in relation to cancer,' *Lancet* 2: 4–7.

Severson, R. K., Nomura, A. M., Grove, J. S., & Stemmermann, G. N. (1989) 'A prospective study of demographics, diet, and prostate cancer among men of Japanese ancestry in Hawaii,' *Cancer Res* 49: 1857–1860.

Sharma, O. P., Adlercreutz, H., Strandberg, J. D., Zirkin, B. R., Coffey, D. S., & Ewing, L. L. (1992) 'Soy of dietary source plays a preventive role against the pathogenesis of prostatitis in rats,' *J Steroid Biochem Mol Biol* 43: 557–564.

Shu, X. O., Jin, F., Dai, Q., Wen, W., Potter, J. D., Kushi, L. H., Ruan, Z., Gao, Y. T., & Zheng, W. (2001) 'Soyfood intake during adolescence and subsequent risk of breast cancer among Chinese women,' *Cancer Epidemiol Biomarkers* Prev 10: 483–488.

Sung, M. K., Lautens, M., & Thompson, L. U. (1998) 'Mammalian lignans inhibit the growth of estrogen-independent human colon tumor cells,' *Anticancer Res* 18: 1405–1408.

Thiagarajan, D. G., Bennink, M. R., Bourquin, L. D., & Kavas, F. A. (1998) 'Prevention of precancerous colonic lesions in rats by soy flakes, soy flour, genistein, and calcium,' *Am J Clin Nutr* 68: 1394S-1399S.

Uckun, F. M., Evans, W. E., Forsyth, C. J., Waddick, K. G., Ahlgren, L. T., Chelstrom, L. M., Burkhardt, A., Bolen, J., & Myers, D. E. (1995) 'Biotherapy of B-cell precursor leukemia by targeting genistein to CD19-associated tyrosine kinases,' *Science* 267: 886–891.

Verma, S. P., & Goldin, B. R. (1998) 'Effect of soy-derived isoflavonoids on the induced growth of MCF-7 cells by estrogenic environmental chemicals,' *Nutr Cancer* 30: 232–239.

Watanabe, Y., Tada, M., Kawamoto, K., Uozumi, G., Kajiwara, Y., Hayashi, K., Yamaguchi, K., Murakami, K., Misaki, F., Akasaka, Y., & et al. (1984) 'A case-control study of cancer of the rectum and colon,' *Nippon Shokakibyo Gakkai Zasshi* 81: 185–193.

Weber, K. S., Jacobson, N. A., Setchell, K. D. R., & Lephart, E. D. (1999) 'Brain aromatase and 5alpha-reductase, regulatory behaviors and testosterone levels in adult rats on phytoestrogen diets,' *Proc Soc Exp Biol Med* 221: 131–135.

Witte, J. S., Longnecker, M. P., Bird, C. L., Lee, E. R., Frankl, H. D., & Haile, R. W. (1996) 'Relation of vegetable, fruit, and grain consumption to colorectal adenomatous polyps,' *Am J Epidemiol* 144: 1015–1025.

World Cancer Research Fund in Association with American Institute for Cancer Research (1997) Food, Nutrition and the Prevention of Cancer: A Global Perspective.

World Health Organization WHO/MONICA Project database.

Wu, A. H., Ziegler, R. G., Horn-Ross, P. L., Nomura, A. M., West, D. W., Kolonel, L. N., Rosenthal, J. F., Hoover, R. N., & Pike, M. C. (1996) 'Tofu and risk of breast cancer in Asian-Americans,' *Cancer Epidemiol Biomarkers Prev* 5: 901–906.

Xu, X., Duncan, A. M., Merz, B. E., & Kurzer, M. S. (1998) 'Effects of soy isoflavones on estrogen and phytoestrogen metabolism in premenopausal women,' *Cancer Epidemiol Biomarkers Prev* 7: 1101–1108.

Yan, L., Yee, J. A., Li, D., McGuire, M. H., & Thompson, L. U. (1998) 'Dietary flaxseed supplementation and experimental metastasis of melanoma cells in mice,' *Cancer Lett* 124: 181–186.

Yatani, R., Chigusa, I., Akazaki, K., Stemmermann, G. N., Welsh, R. A., & Correa, P. (1982) 'Geographic pathology of latent prostatic carcinoma,' *Int J Cancer* 29: 611–616.

Zava, D. T., & Duwe, G. (1997) 'Estrogenic and antiproliferative properties of genistein and other flavonoids in human breast cancer cells in vitro,' *Nutr Cancer* 27: 31–40.

Zheng, W., Dai, Q., Custer, L. J., Shu, X. O., Wen, W. Q., Jin, F., & Franke, A. A. (1999) 'Urinary excretion of isoflavonoids and the risk of breast cancer,' *Cancer Epidemiol Biomarkers Prev* 8: 35–40.

Zhou, J. R., Mukherjee, P., Gugger, E. T., Tanaka, T., Blackburn, G. L., & Clinton, S. K. (1998) 'Inhibition of murine bladder tumorigenesis by soy isoflavones via alterations in the cell cycle, apoptosis, and angiogenesis,' *Cancer Res* 58: 5231–5238.

Chapter 5

Abbey, M., Noakes, M., Belling, G. B., & Nestel, P. J. (1994) 'Partial replacement of saturated fatty acids with almonds or walnuts lowers total plasma cholesterol and low-density-lipoprotein cholesterol,' *Am J Clin Nutr* 59: 995–999.

American Heart Association (1999) Heart and Stroke Statistical Update.

Anderson, J. W. (1995) 'Dietary fibre, complex carbohydrate and coronary artery disease,' *Can J Cardiol* 11 Suppl G: 55G-62G.

Anderson, J. W., Johnstone, B. M., & Cook-Newell, M. E. (1995) 'Meta-analysis of the effects of soy protein intake on serum lipids,' *N Engl J Med* 333: 276–282.

Anthony, M. S., Clarkson, T. B., Bullock, B. C., & Wagner, J. D. (1997) 'Soy protein versus soy phytoestrogens in the prevention of diet-induced coronary artery atherosclerosis of male cynomolgus monkeys,' *Arterioscler Thromb Vasc Biol* 17: 2524–2531.

British Heart Foundation Health Promotion Research Group (2002) Coronary heart disease statistics 2002 edition.

Cassidy, A., Bingham, S., & Setchell, K. D. R. (1994) 'Biological effects of a diet of soy protein rich in isoflavones on the menstrual cycle of premenopausal women,' *Am J Clin Nutr* 60: 333–340.

Cassidy, A., Faughnan, M., Hughes, R., Fraser, C., Cathcart, A., Taylor, N., Setchell, K. D. R., & Bingham, S. A. (1998) 'Hormonal effects of phytoetrogens in post-menopausal women and middle-aged men,' *Am J Clin Nutr* 68S: 1531S (abs.).

Clackson, T. B. (2002) 'Soy, soy phytoestrogens and cardiovascular disease,' *J Nutr* 132: 566S–569S.

Crouse, J. R., 3rd, Morgan, T., Terry, J. G., Ellis, J., Vitolins, M., & Burke, G. L. (1999) 'A randomized trial comparing the effect of casein with that of soy protein containing varying amounts of isoflavones on plasma concentrations of lipids and lipoproteins,' *Arch Intern Med* 159: 2070–2076.

Cunnane, S. C., Hamadeh, M. J., Liede, A. C., Thompson, L. U., Wolever, M. S., & Jenkins, D. J. A. (1994) 'Nutritional attributes of traditional flaxseed in healthy young adults,' *Am J Clin* Nutr 61: 62–68.

De Kleijn, M. J. J., va der Schouw, Y. T., Wilson, P. W. F., Grobbee, D. E., & Jacques, P. F. (2002) 'Dietary intake of phytoestrogens is assocaited with a favorable metabolic cardiovascular risk profile in postmenopausal US women: The Framingham Study.' *J Nutr* 132: 276–282.

Dwyer, T., Iwane, H., Dean, K., Odagiri, Y., Shimomitsu, T., Blizzard, L., Srinivasan, S., Nicklas, T., Wattigney, W., Riley, M., & Berenson, G. (1997) 'Difference in HDL cholesterol concentrations in Japanese, American and Australian children,' *Circulation* 96: 2830–2836.

Erdman, J. W., Jr. (2000) AHA Science Advisory: 'Soy protein and cardiovascular disease: A statement for healthcare professionals from the Nutrition Committee of the AHA,' *Circulation* 102: 2555–2559.

Gooderham, M. H., Adlercreutz, H., Ojala, S. T., Wähälä, K., & Holub, B. J. (1996) 'A soy protein isolate rich in genistein and daidzein and its effects on plasma isoflavone concentrations, platelet aggregation, blood lipids and fatty acid composition of plasma phospholipid in normal men,' *J Nutr* 126: 2000–2006.

Hertog, M. G., Feskens, E. J., Hollman, P. C., Katan, M. B., & Kromhout, D. (1993) 'Dietary antioxidant flavonoids and risk of coronary heart disease: the Zutphen Elderly Study,' *Lancet* 342: 1007–1011.

Honore, E. K., Williams, J. K., Anthony, M. S., & Clarkson, T. B. (1997) 'Soy isoflavones enhance coronary vascular reactivity in atherosclerotic female macaques,' *Fertil Steril* 67: 148–154.

Jenkins, D. J. A., Kendall, C. W. C., Garsetti, M., Rosenberg-Zand, R. S., Jackson, C.-J., Agarwal, S., Rao, A. V., Diamandis, E. P., Parker, T., Faulkner, D., Vuksan, V., & Vidgen, E. (2000) 'Effect of soy protein foods on low-density lipoprotein oxidation and ex vivo sex hormone receptor activity—A controlled crossover trial,' *Metabolism* 49: 537–543.

Jenkins, D. J. A., Kendall, C. W. C., Vidgen, E., Agarwal, S., Rao, A. V., Rosenberg, R. S., Diamandis, E. P., Novokmet, R., Mehling, C. C., Perera, T., Griffin, L. C., & Cunnane, S. C. (1999) 'Health aspects of partially defatted flaxseed, including effects on serum lipids, oxidative measures, and ex vivo androgen and progestin activity: a controlled crossover trial,' *Am J Clin Nutr* 69: 395–402.

Knekt, P., Jarvinen, R., Reunanen, A., & Maatela, J. (1996) 'Flavonoid intake and coronary mortality in Finland: a cohort study,' *BMJ* 312: 478–481.

Lee, I.-M., Rexrode, K. M., Cook, N. R., Manson, J. E., & Buring, J. E. (2001) 'Physical activity and coronary heart disease in women,' *JAMA* 285: 1447–1454.

Marsh, J. D. (2000) 'Phytoestrogens and vascular therapy,' *J Am Coll Cardiol* 35: 1986–1987.

Merz-Demlow, B. E., Duncan, A. M., Wangen, K. E., Xu, X., Carr, T. P., Phipps, W. R., & Kurzer, M. S. (2000) 'Soy isoflavones improve plasma lipids in normocholesterolemic, premenopausal women,' *Am J Clin Nutr* 71: 1462–1469.

Nagata, C., Takatsuka, N., Kurisu, Y., & Shimizu, H. (1998) 'Decreased serum total cholesterol concentration is associated with high intake of soy products in Japanese men and women,' *J Nutr* 128: 209–213.

Nestel, P. J., Yamashita, T., Sasahara, T., Pomeroy, S., Dart, A., Komesaroff, P., Owen, A., & Abbey, M. (1997) 'Soy isoflavones improve systemic arterial compliance but not plasma lipids in menopausal and perimenopausal women,' *Arterioscler Thromb Vasc Biol* 17: 3392–3398.

The North American Menopause Society (NAMS). Report from the NAMS Advisory panel on postmenopausal hormone therapy. October 2002. Cited at [http://www.menopause.org] on 3 October 2002.

Olson, B. H., Anderson, S. M., Becker, M. P., Anderson, J. W., Hunninghake, D. B., Jenkins, D. J., LaRosa, J. C., Rippe, J. M., Roberts, D. C., Stoy, D. B., Summerbell, C. D., Truswell, A. S., Wolever, T. M., Morris, D. H., & Fulgoni, V. L., 3rd (1997) 'Psyllium-enriched cereals lower blood total cholesterol and LDL cholesterol, but not HDL cholesterol, in hypercholesterolemic adults: results of a meta-analysis,' *J Nutr* 127: 1973–1980.

Prasad, K. (1997) 'Dietary flax seed in prevention of hypercholesterolemic atherosclerosis,' *Atherosclerosis* 132: 69–76.

Ridges, L., Sunderland, R., Moerman, K., Meyer, B., Astheimer, L., & Howe, P. (2001) 'Cholesterol lowering benefits of soy and linseed enriched foods,' *Asia Pacific J Clin Nutr* 10: 204–211.

Rivas, M., Garay, R. P., Escanero, J. K., Cia Jr., P., & Alda, J. O. (2002) 'Soy milk lowers blood pressure in men and women with mild to moderate essential hypertension,' *J Nutr* 132: 1900–1902.

Sabate, J., Fraser, G. E., Burke, K., Knutsen, S. F., Bennett, H., & Lindsted, K. D. (1993) 'Effects of walnuts on serum lipid levels and blood pressure in normal men,' *N Engl J Med* 328: 603–607.

Scheiber, M. D., Liu, J. H., Subbiah, M. T., Rebar, R. W., & Setchell, K. D. R. (2001) 'Dietary inclusion of whole soy foods results in significant reductions in clinical risk factors for osteoporosis and cardiovascular disease in normal postmenopausal women,' *Menopause* 8: 384–392.

Sirtori, C. R., Pazzucconi, F., Colombo, L., Battistin, P., Bondioli, A., & Descheemaeker, K. (1999) 'Double-blind study of the addition of high-protein soya milk v. cows' milk to the diet of patients with severe hypercholesterolaemia and resistance to or intolerance of statins,' *Br J Nutr* 82: 91–96.

Teede, J. H., Dalais, F. S., Kotsopoulos, D., Liang, Y. L., David, S. R., & McGrath, B. P. (1999) 'Soy protein dietary supplementation improves lipid profiles and blood pressure: A double-blind, randomized, placebo-controlled study in men and postmenopausal women.' Third International Symposium on the Role of Soy in Preventing and Treating Chronic Disease, Washington, D.C., USA.

Tikkänen, M. J., Wähälä, K., Ojala, S., Vihma, V., & Adlercreutz, H. (1998) 'Effect of soybean phytoestrogen intake on low density lipoprotein oxidation resistance,' *Proc Natl Acad Sci* USA 95: 3106–3110.

Vanharanta, M., Voutilainen, S., Lakka, T. A., Van der Lee, M., Adlercreutz, H., & Salonen, J. T. (1999) 'Risk of actue coronary events according to serum concentrations of enterolactone: a prospective population-based case-control study,' *Lancet* 354: 2112–2115.

Wagner, J. D., Cefalu, W. T., Anthony, M. S., Litwak, K. N., Zhang, L., & Clarkson, T. B. (1997) 'Dietary soy protein and estrogen replacement therapy improve cardiovascular risk factors and decrease aortic cholesteryl ester content in ovariectomized cynomolgus monkeys,' *Metabolism* 46: 698–705.

Wangen, K. E., Duncan, A. M., Xu, X., & Kurzer, M. S. (2001) 'Soy isoflavones improve plasma lipids in normocholesterolemic and mildly hypercholesterolemic postmenopausal women,' *Am J Clin Nutr* 73: 225–231.

Washburn, S., Burke, G. L., Morgan, T., & Anthony, M. (1999) 'Effect of soy protein supplementation on serum lipoproteins, blood pressure, and menopausal symptoms in perimenopausal women,' *Menopause* 6: 7–13.

West, S. G., Stoney, C. M., Habash, D. L., Cook, K. M., & Nelligan, J. A. (2001) 'Soy supplements with phytoestrogens reduce blood pressure at rest and during stress in middle aged men.' 4th International Symposium on the Role of Soy in Preventing and Treating Chronic Disease, San Diego, USA.

WHO Expert Committee on Prevention of Coronary Heart Disease (1982) Prevention of coronary heart disease report of a WHO expert committee, Technical Report Series No 678. World Health Organisation, Geneva.

Wilcox, J. N., & Blumenthal, B. F. (1995) 'Thrombotic mechanisms in atherosclerosis: potential impact of soy proteins,' *J Nutr* 125: 631S-638S.

Writing Group for the Women's Health Initiative Investigators (2002) 'Risks and benefits of estrogen plus progestin in healthy postmenopausal women,' *JAMA* 288: 321–333.

Chapter 6

Alekel, D. L., Germain, A. S., Peterson, C. T., Hanson, K. B., Stewart, J. W., & Toda, T. (2000) 'Isoflavone-rich soy protein isolate attenuates bone loss in the lumbar spine of perimenopausal women,' *Am J Clin Nutr* 72: 844–852.

Alexandersen, P., Toussaint, A., Christiansen, C., Devogelaer, J. P., Roux, C., Fechtenbaum, J., Gennari, C., & Reginster, J. Y. (2001) 'Ipriflavone in the treatment of postmenopausal osteoporosis: a randomized controlled trial,' *Jama* 285: 1482–1488.

Anderson, J. J., Ambrose, W. W., & Garner, S. C. (1998) 'Biphasic effects of genistein on bone tissue in the ovariectomized, lactating rat model,' *Proc Soc Exp Biol Med* 217: 345–350.

Arjmandi, B. H., Alekel, L., Hollis, B. W., Amin, D., Stacewicz-Sapuntzakis, M., Guo, P., & Kukreja, S. C. (1996) 'Dietary soybean protein prevents bone loss in an ovariectomized rat model of osteoporosis,' *J Nutr* 126: 161–167.

Bachrach, L. K. (1993) 'Bone mineralization in childhood and adolescence,' *Curr Opin Pediatr* 5: 467–473.

Breslau, N. A., Brinkley, L., Hill, K. D., & Pak, C. Y. (1988) 'Relationship of animal protein-rich diet to kidney stone formation and calcium metabolism,' *J Clin Endocrinol Metab* 66: 140–146.

Col, N. F., Eckman, M. H., Karas, R. H., Pauker, S. G., Goldberg, R. J., Ross, E. M., Orr, R. K., & Wong, J. B. (1997) 'Patient-specific decisions about hormone replacement therapy in postmenopausal women,' *JAMA* 277: 1140–1147.

Dalais, F. S., Rice, G. E., & Wahlqvist, M. L., Grehan, M., Murkies, A. L., Medley, G., Ayton, R., & Strauss, B. J. G. (1998) 'Effects of dietary phytoestrogens in postmenopausal women,' *Climacteric* 1: 124–129.

Gallagher, J. C., Rafferty, K., Haynatzka, V., & Wilson, M. (2000) 'The effect of soy protein on bone metabolism,' *J Nutr* 130: 667S (abstr).

Harrison, E., Adjei, A., Ameho, C., Yamamoto, S., & Kono, S. (1998) 'The effect of soybean protein on bone loss in a rat model of postmenopausal osteoporosis,' *J Nutr Sci Vitaminol* (Tokyo) 44: 257–268.

Hegsted, D. M. (1986) 'Calcium and osteoporosis,' *J Nutr* 116: 2316–2319.

Horiuchi, T., Onouchi, T., Takahashi, M., Ito, H., & Orimo, H. (2000) 'Effect of soy protein on bone metabolism in postmenopausal Japanese women,' *Osteoporos Int* 11: 721–724.

Khalil, D. A., Lucas, E. A., Juma, S., Sinichi, N., Hodges, B., Hammond, L., Payton, M., Munson, M. E., & Arjmandi, B. H. (2001) 'Soy protein supplementation may exert benefical effects on bone in men.' FASEB: A727 (Abst).

Lacey, J. V., Mink, P. J., Lubin, J. H., Sherman, M. E., Troisi, R., Hartge, P., Schatzkin, A., & Schairer, C. (2002) 'Menopausal hormonal replacement therapy and risk of ovarian cancer,' *JAMA* 286: 334–341.

Lydeking-Olsen, E., Beck Jensen, J.-E., Setchell, K. D. R., Damhus, M., & Jensen, T. H. (2002) 'Isoflavone-rich soymilk prevents bone-loss in the lumbar spine of postmenopausal women. A two-year study,' *J. Nutr* 132: 581S (abs).

National Osteoporosis Foundation. (1999) Important Disease Facts.

Pansini, F., Bonaccorsi, G., Albertazzi, P., Costantino, D., Valerio, A., Negri, C., Ferrazzini, S., Bonocuore, I., De Aloysio, D., Fontana, A., Pansini, N., & Mollica, G. (1997) 'Soy phytoestrogens and bone.' Proceedings of the North American Menopause Society, *Abst* #97.061.

Pecis, M., de Azevedo, M. J., & Gross, J. L. (1994) 'Chicken and fish diet reduces glomerular hyperfiltration in IDDM patients,' *Diabetes Care* 17: 665–672.

Potter, S. M., Baum, J. A., Teng, H., Stillman, R. J., Shay, N. F., & Erdman, J. W., Jr. (1998) 'Soy protein and isoflavones: their effects on blood lipids and bone density in postmenopausal women,' *Am J Clin Nutr* 68: 1375S-1379S.

Scheiber, M. D., Liu, J. H., Subbiah, M. T., Rebar, R. W., & Setchell, K. D. R. (2001) 'Dietary inclusion of whole soy foods results in significant reductions in clinical risk factors for osteoporosis and cardiovascular disease in normal postmenopausal women,' *Menopause* 8: 384–392.

Setchell, K. D. R., Brown, N. M., & Lydeking-Olsen, E. (2002) 'The clinical importance of the metabolite equol – A clue to the effectiveness of soy and its isoflavones,' *J Nutr* 132: 3577–3584.

Setchell, K. D. R., Lydeking-Olsen, E. (2003) 'Dietary phytoestrogens and their impact on bone – Evidence from in vitro and in vivo, human observational and dietary intervention studies,' *Am J Clin Nutr* (in press).

Somekawa, Y., Chiguchi, M., Ishibashi, T., & Aso, T. (2001) 'Soy intake related to menopausal symptoms, serum lipids, and bone mineral density in post-menopausal Japanese women,' *Obstet Gynecol* 97: 109–115.

Spence, L. A., Lipscomb, E. R., Cadogan, J., Martin, B. R., Peacock, M., & Weaver, C. M. (2002) 'Effects of soy isoflavones on calcium metabolism in postmenopausal women,' *J Nutr* 132: 581S (abs).

Steinberg, K. K., Thacker, S. B., Smith, S. J., Stroup, D. F., Zack, M. M., Flanders, W. D., & Berkelman, R. L. (1991) 'A meta-analysis of the effect of estrogen replacement therapy on the risk of breast cancer,' *JAMA* 265: 1985–1990.

Chapter 7

Access Economics Pty Ltd. (Sept. 2001) 'The burden of brittle bones: Costing Osteoporosis in Australia,' Paper prepared for Osteoporosis Australia, Canberra ACT.

Adlercreutz, H., Hämäläinen, E., Gorbach, S., & Goldin, B. (1992) 'Dietary phyto-oestrogens and the menopause in Japan,' *Lancet* 339: 1233.

Albertazzi, P., Pansini, F., Bonaccorsi, G., Zanotti, L., Forini, E., & De Aloysio, D. (1998) 'The effect of dietary soy supplementation on hot flushes,' *Obstet Gynecol* 91: 6–11.

Alekel, D. L., Germain, A. S., Peterson, C. T., Hanson, K. B., Stewart, J. W., & Toda, T. (2000) 'Isoflavone-rich soy protein isolate attenuates bone loss in the lumbar spine of perimenopausal women,' *Am J Clin Nutr* 72: 844–852.

Baber, R., Templeman, C., Morton, T., Kelly, G., & West, L. (1999) 'Randomized placebo-controlled trial of an isoflavone supplement and menopausal symptoms in women,' *Climacteric* 2: 85–92.

Baird, D. D., Umbach, D. M., Lansdell, L., Hughes, C. L., Setchell, K. D. R., Weinberg, C. R., Haney, A. F., Wilcox, A. J., & McLachlan, J. A. (1995) 'Dietary intervention study to assess estrogenicity of dietary soy among postmenopausal women,' *J Clin Endocrinol Metab* 80: 1685–1690.

Brzezinski, A., Adlercreutz, H., Shaoul, R., Rösler, A., Shmueli, A., Tanos, V., & Schenker, J. G. (1997) 'Short-term effects of phytoestrogen-rich diet on postmenopausal women,' *Menopause* 4: 89–94.

Cassidy, A., Faughnan, M., Hughes, R., Fraser, C., Cathcart, A., Taylor, N., Setchell, K. D. R., & Bingham, S. A. (1998) 'Hormonal effects of phyto-etrogens in post-menopausal women and middle-aged men,' *Am J Clin Nutr* 68S: 1531S (abs.).

Dalais, F. S., Rice, G. E., & Wahlqvist, M. L., Grehan, M., Murkies, A. L., Medley, G., Ayton, R., & Strauss, B. J. G. (1998) 'Effects of dietary phyto-estrogens in postmenopausal women,' *Climacteric* 1: 124–129.

Eden, J. A. (2001) 'Herbal medicines for menopause: do they work and are they safe?' *Med J Aust* 174: 63–64.

Hope, S., Wager, E., & Rees, M. (1998) 'Survey of British women's views on the menopause and HRT,' *J Brit Meno Soc* 4: 33–36.

Jenkins, D. J. A., Kendall, C. W. C., Garsetti, M., Rosenberg-Zand, R. S., Jackson, C.-J., Agarwal, S., Rao, A. V., Diamandis, E. P., Parker, T., Faulkner, D., Vuksan, V., & Vidgen, E. (2000) 'Effect of soy protein foods on low-density lipoprotein oxidation and ex vivo sex hormone receptor activity—A controlled crossover trial,' *Metabolism* 49: 537–543.

Knight, D. C., Howes, J. B., & Eden, J. A. (1999) 'The effect of Promensil, an isoflavone extract, on menopausal symptoms,' *Climacteric* 2: 79–84.

Kronenberg, F. (1994) 'Triumph over menopause,' *Prevention* pp. 78–79 and 137–42.

Lock, M. (1986) 'Ambiguities of aging: Japanese experience and perceptions of menopause,' *Cult Med Psychiatry* 10: 23–46.

Lydeking-Olsen, E., Beck Jensen, J.-E., Setchell, K. D. R., Damhus, M., & Jensen, T. H. (2002) 'Isoflavone-rich soymilk prevents bone-loss in the lumbar spine of postmenopausal women. A two-year study,' *J Nutr* 132: 581S (abs).

MacLennan, A. H., Wilson, D. H., & Taylor, A. W. (1999) 'Hormone replacement therapies in women at risk of cardiovascular disease and osteoporosis in South Australia in 1997,' *Med J Aust* 170: 525–527.

Murkies, A. L., Lombard, C., Strauss, B. J., Wilcox, G., Burger, H. G., & Morton, M. S. (1995) 'Dietary flour supplementation decreases post-menopausal hot flushes: effect of soy and wheat,' *Maturitas* 21: 189–195.

Nachtigall, L. B., Fenichel, R., La Grega L., Lee, W. W., & Nachtigall, L. (1999) 'The effects of isoflavone derived from red clover on vasomotor symptoms, endometrial thickness, and reproductive hormone concentrations in menopausal women (abstract).' Presented at the 81st Annual Meeting of the Endocrine Society, San Diego, California.

Nagata, C., Takatsuka, N., Kawakami, N., & Shimizu, H. (2001) 'Soy product intake and hot flashes in Japanese women: results from a community-based prospective study,' *Am J Epidemiol* 153: 790–793.

Nagata, C., Takatsuka, N., Kurisu, Y., & Shimizu, H. (1998) 'Decreased serum total cholesterol concentration is associated with high intake of soy products in Japanese men and women,' *J Nutr* 128: 209–213.

North American Menopause Society (2000) 'The role of isoflavones in menopausal health: consensus opinion of The North American Menopause Society,' *Menopause* 7: 215–229.

Quella, S. K., Loprinzi, C. L., Barton, D. L., Knost, J. A., Sloan, J. A., LaVasseur, B. I., Swan, D., Krupp, K. R., Miller, K. D., & Novotny, P. J. (2000) 'Evaluation of soy phytoestrogens for the treatment of hot flashes in breast cancer survivors: A North Central Cancer Treatment Group Trial,' *J Clin Oncol* 18: 1068–1074.

Rowland, I. R., Wiseman, H., Sanders, T. A., Adlercreutz, H., & Bowey, E. A. (2000) 'Interindividual variation in metabolism of soy isoflavones and lignans: influence of habitual diet on equol production by the gut flora,' *J Nutr* 36: 27–32.

Scheiber, M. D., Liu, J. H., Subbiah, M. T., Rebar, R. W., & Setchell, K. D. R. (2001) 'Dietary inclusion of whole soy foods results in significant reductions in clinical risk factors for osteoporosis and cardiovascular disease in normal postmenopausal women,' *Menopause* 8: 384–392.

Seidl, M. M., & Stewart, D. E. (1998) 'Alternative treatments for menopausal symptoms. Systematic review of scientific and lay literature,' *Can Fam Physician* 44: 1299–1308.

Setchell, K. D. R., Borriello, S. P., Hulme, P., Kirk, D. N., & Axelson, M. (1984) 'Nonsteroidal estrogens of dietary origin: possible roles in hormone- dependent disease,' *Am J Clin Nutr* 40: 569–578.

Setchell, K. D. R., Brown, N. M., Desai, P., Zimmer-Nechemias, L., Wolfe, B. E., Brashear, W. T., Kirschner, A. S., Cassidy, A., & Heubi, J. E. (2001) 'Bioavailability of pure isoflavones in healthy humans and analysis of commercial soy isoflavone supplements,' *J Nutr* 131: 1362S-1375S.

Shaywitz, S. E., Shaywitz, B. A., Pugh, K. R., Fulbright, R. K., Skudlarski, P., Mencl, W. E., Constable, R. T., Naftolin, F., Palter, S. F., Marchione, K. E., Katz, L., Shankweiler, D. P., Fletcher, J. M., Lacadie, C., Keltz, M., & Gore, J. C. (1999) 'Effect of estrogen on brain activation patterns in postmenopausal women during working memory tasks,' *JAMA* 281: 1197–1202.

Thomas, K. J., Nicholl, J. P., & Coleman, P. (2001) 'Use and expenditure on complementary medicine in England: a population based survey,' *Complement Ther Med* 9: 2–11.

Tikkänen, M. J., Wähälä, K., Ojala, S., Vihma, V., & Adlercreutz, H. (1998) 'Effect of soybean phytoestrogen intake on low density lipoprotein oxidation resistance,' *Proc Natl Acad Sci* USA 95: 3106–3110.

Uchiyama, S., Ueno, T., & Shirota, T. (2001) 'The relationship between soy isoflavones and the menopausal symptoms in Japanese perimenopausal women,' *Ann Nutr Metab* 45: 113 (abstract).

Upmalis, D., Lobo, R., & Bradley, L. (1999) 'Evaluation of the safety and efficacy of an oral soy extract in the treatment of vasomotor symptoms in menopausal women.' Presented at 10th Annual North American Menopause Society Meeting, New York, New York.

Washburn, S., Burke, G. L., Morgan, T., & Anthony, M. (1999) 'Effect of soy protein supplementation on serum lipoproteins, blood pressure, and menopausal symptoms in perimenopausal women,' *Menopause* 6: 7–13.

Wilcox, G., Wahlqvist, M. L., Burger, H. G., & Medley, G. (1990) 'Oestrogenic effects of plant foods in postmenopausal women,' *BMJ* 301: 905–906.

Writing Group for the Women's Health Initiative Investigators (2002) 'Risks and benefits of estrogen plus progestin in healthy postmenopausal women,' *JAMA* 288: 321–333.

Chapter 8

Alzheimer's Society – Statistics about dementia, cited on website [www.alzheimers.org.uk/about/statistics.html] on 30 September 2002.

Baldereschi, M., Di Carlo, A., Lepore, V., Bracco, L., Maggi, S., Grigoletto, F., Scarlato, G., & Amaducci, L. (1998) 'Estrogen-replacement therapy and Alzheimer's disease in the Italian Longitudinal Study on Aging,' *Neurology* 50: 996–1002.

File, S. E., Jarrett, N., Fluck, E., Duffy, R., Casey, K., & Wiseman, H. (2001) 'Eating soya improves human memory,' *Psychopharmacology (Berl)* 157: 430–436.

Giem, P., Beeson, W. L., & Fraser, G. E. (1993) 'The incidence of dementia and intake of animal products: preliminary findings from the Adventist Health Study,' *Neuroepidemiology* 12: 28–36.

Graves, A. B., Larson, E. B., White, L. R., Teng, E. L., & Homma, A. (1994) 'Opportunities and challenges in international collaborative epidemiologic research of dementia and its subtypes: studies between Japan and the U.S.' *Int Psychogeriatr* 6: 209–223.

Henderson, V. W., Paganini-Hill, A., Emanuel, C. K., Dunn, M. E., & Buckwalter, J. G. (1994) 'Estrogen replacement therapy in older women. Comparisons between Alzheimer's disease cases and nondemented control subjects,' *Arch Neurol* 51: 896–900.

Jorm, A. F., & Jolley, D. (1998) 'The incidence of dementia: a meta-analysis,' *Neurology* 51: 728–733.

Kim, H., Xia, L. L., & Gewin, J. (1999) 'Modulation of neurodegeneration markers by dietary soy in a primate model of menopause.' 3rd International Symposium of the Role of Soy in Preventing and Treating Chronic Disease, Washington DC.

Pan, Y., Anthony, M., & Clarkson, T. B. (1999) 'Evidence for up-regulation of brain-derived neurotrophic factor mRNA by soy phytoestrogens in the frontal cortex of retired breeder female rats,' *Neurosci Lett* 261: 17–20.

Robertson, D., Amelsvoort, T., Daly, E., Whitehead, M., & Murphy, D. (1999) 'The effect of oestrogen on the aging of brain regions implicated in Alzheimers disease.' Presented at the 10th North American Menopause Society Annual Meeting, New York, New York.

Russell, C. G. (2000) 'Soy and wellbeing.' Honours Thesis, University of Adelaide.

Setchell, K. D. R. (1998) 'Phytoestrogens: the biochemistry, physiology, and implications for human health of soy isoflavones,' *Am J Clin Nutr* 68: 1333S–1346S.

Shaywitz, S. E., Shaywitz, B. A., Pugh, K. R., Fulbright, R. K., Skudlarski, P., Mencl, W. E., Constable, R. T., Naftolin, F., Palter, S. F., Marchione, K. E., Katz, L., Shankweiler, D. P., Fletcher, J. M., Lacadie, C., Keltz, M., & Gore, J. C. (1999) 'Effect of estrogen on brain activation patterns in postmenopausal women during working memory tasks,' *JAMA* 281: 1197–1202.

Tang, M. X., Jacobs, D., Stern, Y., Marder, K., Schofield, P., Gurland, B., Andrews, H., & Mayeux, R. (1996) 'Effect of oestrogen during menopause on risk and age at onset of Alzheimer's disease,' *Lancet* 348: 429–432.

White, L., Petrovitch, H., Ross, W., Masaki, K., Hardman, J., Nelson, J., Davis, D., & Markesbery, W. (2000) 'Brain aging and midlife tofu consumption,' *J. Am Coll Nutr* 19: 242–255.

Chapter 9

Adlercreutz, H., Bannwart, C., Wähälä, K., Mäkelä, T., Brunow, G., Hase, T., Arosemena, P. J., Kellis, J. T., Jr., & Vickery, L. E. (1993) 'Inhibition of human aromatase by mammalian lignans and isoflavonoid phytoestrogens,' *J Steroid Biochem Mol Biol* 44: 147–153.

Baber, R., Templeman, C., Morton, T., Kelly, G., & West, L. (1999) 'Randomized placebo-controlled trial of an isoflavone supplement and menopausal symptoms in women,' *Climacteric* 2: 85–92.

Bhathena, S. J., & Velasquez, M. T. (2002) 'Beneficial role of dietary phytoestrogens in obesity and diabetes,' *Am J Clin Nutr* 76: 1191–1201.

Cline, J. M., Paschold, J. C., Anthony, M. S., Obasanjo, I. O., & Adams, M. R. (1996) 'Effects of hormonal therapies and dietary soy phytoestrogens on vaginal cytology in surgically postmenopausal macaques,' *Fertil Steril* 65: 1031–1035.

Cramer, D. W., Wilson, E., Stillman, R. J., Berger, M. J., Belisle, S., Schiff, I., Albrecht, B., Gibson, M., Stadel, B. V., & Schoenbaum, S. C. (1986) 'The relation of endometriosis to menstrual characteristics, smoking, and exercise,' *JAMA* 255: 1904–1908.

Duncan, A. M., Merz, B. E., Xu, X., Nagel, T. C., Phipps, W. R., & Kurzer, M. S. (1999) 'Soy isoflavones exert modest hormonal effects in premenopausal women,' *J Clin Endocrinol Metab* 84: 192–197.

Fanti, P., Sawaya, B. P., & Stephenson, T. J. (2001) 'Effects of soy isoflavones on the immuno-inflammatory response of end-stage renal disease (ESRD) patients on chronic hemodialytic therapy (HD).' 4th International Symposium on the Role of Soy in Preventing and Treating Chronic Disease, San Diego, USA.

Foth, D., & Cline, J. M. (1998) 'Effects of mammalian and plant estrogens on mammary glands and uteri of macaques,' *Am J Clin Nutr* 68: 1413S–1417S.

Franke, A. A., Yu, M. C., Maskarinec, G., Fanti, P., Zheng, W., & Custer, L. J. (1999) 'Phytoestrogens in human biomatrices including breast milk,' *Biochem Soc Trans* 27: 308–318.

Ingram, A. J., Parbtani, A., Clark, W. F., Spanner, E., Huff, M. W., Philbrick, D. J., & Holub, B. J. (1995) 'Effects of flaxseed and flax oil diets in a rat-5/6 renal ablation model,' *Am J Kidney Dis* 25: 320–329.

Iwasaki, K., Gleiser, C. A., Masoro, E. J., McMahan, C. A., Seo, E. J., & Yu, B. P. (1988) 'The influence of dietary protein source on longevity and age-related disease processes of Fischer rats,' *J Gerontol* 43: B5–12.

Keung, W. M. (1993) 'Biochemical studies of a new class of alcohol dehydrogenase inhibitors from Radix puerariae,' *Alcohol Clin Exp Res* 17: 1254–1260.

Keung, W. M., Lazo, O., Kunze, L., & Vallee, B. L. (1995) 'Daidzin suppresses ethanol consumption by Syrian golden hamsters without blocking acetaldehyde metabolism,' *Proc Natl Acad Sci* USA 92: 8990–8993.

Keung, W. M., & Vallee, B. L. (1993) 'Daidzin: a potent, selective inhibitor of human mitochondrial aldehyde dehydrogenase,' *Proc Natl Acad Sci* USA 90: 1247–1251.

Kontessis, P., Jones, S., Dodds, R., Trevisan, R., Nosadini, R., Fioretto, P., Borsato, M., Sacerdoti, D., & Viberti, G. (1990) 'Renal, metabolic and hormonal responses to ingestion of animal and vegetable proteins,' *Kidney Int* 38: 136–144.

Korzenik, J., Barnes, S., & White, R. J. (1998) 'Possible efficacy of isolated soy protein in treatment of hereditary hemorrhagic telanigectasia associated epistaxis, gastrointestinal hemorrhage, and migraine: a pilot study,' *Am J Clin Nutr* 68: 1530S (abstract).

McArthur, J. W., & Ulfelder, H. (1965) 'The effect of pregnancy upon endometriosis,' *Obstet Gynecol Surv* 20: 709–733.

Sadowska-Krowicka, H., Mannick, E. E., Oliver, P. D., Sandoval, M., Zhang, X. J., Eloby-Childess, S., Clark, D. A., & Miller, M. J. (1998) 'Genistein and gut inflammation: role of nitric oxide,' *Proc Soc Exp Biol Med* 217: 351–357.

Salzman, A., Denenberg, A. G., Ueta, I., O'Connor, M., Linn, S. C., & Szabo, C. (1996) 'Induction and activity of nitric oxide synthase in cultured human intestinal epithelial monolayers,' *Am J Physiol* 270: G565–573.

Salzman, A. L., Preiser, J.-C., Setchell, K. D. R., & Szabo, C. (1999) 'Isoflavone-mediated inhibition of tyrosine kinase: a novel anti-inflammatory approach,' *J Medicinal Food* 2: 179–181.

Stephenson, T. J., Anderson, J. W., Jenkins, D. J., Kendall, C., & Fanti, P. (2001a) 'Beneficial effects of soy protein use on renal function in young type 1 diabetics with early diabetic nephropathy.' 4th International Symposium on the Role of Soy in Preventing and Treating Chronic Disease, San Diego, USA.

Stephenson, T. J., Sawaya, B. P., & Fanti, P. (2001b) 'Dietary intake of a soy protein isolate supplement improves nutritional status in malnourished hemodialysis patients.' 4th International Symposium on the Role of Soy in Preventing and Treating Chronic Disease, San Diego, USA.

Tabary, O., Escotte, S., Couetil, J. P., Hubert, D., Dusser, D., Puchelle, E., & Jacquot, J. (1999) 'Genistein inhibits constitutive and inducible NFkappaB activation and decreases IL-8 production by human cystic fibrosis bronchial gland cells,' *Am J Pathol* 155: 473–481.

Tomobe, K., Philbrick, D. J., Ogborn, M. R., Takahashi, H., & Holub, B. J. (1998) 'Effect of dietary soy protein and genistein on disease progression in mice with polycystic kidney disease,' *Am J Kidney Dis* 31: 55–61.

Upmalis, D., Lobo, R., & Bradley, L. (1999) 'Evaluation of the safety and efficacy of an oral soy extract in the treatment of vasomotor symptoms in menopausal women.' Presented at 10th Annual North American Menopause Society Meeting, New York, New York.

Wang, F., Zeltwanger, S., Yang, I. C., Nairn, A. C., & Hwang, T. C. (1998) 'Actions of genistein on cystic fibrosis transmembrane conductance regulator channel gating. Evidence for two binding sites with opposite effects,' *J Gen Physiol* 111: 477–490.

Wei, H., Bowen, R., Cai, Q., Barnes, S., & Wang, Y. (1995) 'Antioxidant and antipromotional effects of the soybean isoflavone genistein,' *Proc Soc Exp Biol Med* 208: 124–130.

Xie, C. I., Lin, R. C., Antony, V., Lumeng, L., Li, T. K., Mai, K., Liu, C., Wang, Q. D., Zhao, Z. H., & Wang, G. F. (1994) 'Daidzin, an antioxidant isoflavonoid, decreases blood alcohol levels and shortens sleep time induced by ethanol intoxication,' *Alcohol Clin Exp Res* 18: 1443–1447.

Chapter 10

Adlercreutz, H., Yamada, T., Wähälä, K., & Watanabe, S. (1999) Maternal and neonatal phytoestrogens in Japanese women during birth. *Am J Obstet Gynecol* 180: 737–743.

American Academy of Pediatrics Committee on Nutrition (1998) Soy protein-based formulas: recommendations for use in infant feeding. *Pediatrics* 101: 148–153.

Anthony, M. S., Clarkson, T. B., Bullock, B. C., & Wagner, J. D. (1997) Soy protein versus soy phytoestrogens in the prevention of diet-induced coronary artery atherosclerosis of male cynomolgus monkeys. *Arterioscler Thromb Vasc Biol* 17: 2524–2531.

Anthony, M. S., Clarkson, T. B., Hughes, C. L., Jr., Morgan, T. M., & Burke, G. L. (1996) Soybean isoflavones improve cardiovascular risk factors without affecting the reproductive system of peripubertal rhesus monkeys. *J Nutr* 126: 43–50.

Australia New Zealand Food Authority (1999) Phytoestrogens—an assessment of the potential risks to infants associated with exposure to soy-based infant formula.

Barnes, S., Grubbs, C., Setchell, K. D. R., & Carlson, J. (1990) Soybeans inhibit mammary tumors in models of breast cancer. *Prog Clin Biol Res* 347: 239–253.

Barrett, J. R. (2002) 'Soy and children's health: A formula for trouble?,' *Environ Health Perspect* 110: A294–A295.

Brown, N. M., & Lamartiniere, C. A. (1995) Xenoestrogens alter mammary gland differentiation and cell proliferation in the rat. Environ Health Perspect 103: 708–713.

Brown, N. M., & Setchell, K. D. R. (2001) Animal models impacted by phytoestrogens in commercial chow: implications for pathways influenced by hormones. *Lab Invest* 81: 735–747.

Businco, L., Bruno, G., Grandolfo, M., Novello, F., Fiore, L., & Amato, C. (1990) Response of poliovirus immunization and type of feeding in babies of atopic families. *Pediatr Allergy Immunol* 1: 60–63.

Chang, H. C., & Doerge, D. R. (2000) Dietary genistein inactivates rat thyroid peroxidase in vivo without an apparent hypothyroid effect. *Toxicol Appl Pharmacol* 168: 244–252.

Chen, Z., Zheng, W., Custer, L. J., Dai, Q., Shu, X. O., Jin, F., & Franke, A. A. (1999) 'Usual dietary consumption of soy foods and its correlation with the excretion rate of isoflavonoids in overnight urine samples among Chinese women in Shanghai,' *Nutr Cancer* 33: 82–87.

Cordle, C. T., Winship, T. R., Schaller, J. P., Thomas, D. J., Buck, R. H., Ostrom, K. M., Jacobs, J. R., Blatter, M. M., Cho, S., Gooch III, W. M., & Pickering, L. K. (2002) 'Immune status of infants fed soy-based formulas with or without added nucleotides for 1 year: Part 2: Immune cell populations.' *J. Pediatr Gastroenterol Nutr* 34: 145–153.

Dalais, F. S., Meliala, A., & Wahlqvist, M. L. (1999) 'Maternal and cord blood phytoestrogen levels in Indonesian women. Third International Symposium on the Role of Soy in Preventing and Treating Chronic Disease, Washington, DC USA.'

Divi, R. L., Chang, H. C., & Doerge, D. R. (1997) 'Anti-thyroid isoflavones from soybean: isolation, characterization, and mechanisms of action,' *Biochem Pharmacol* 54: 1087–1096.

Donath, S., & Amir, L. H. (2000) 'Rates of breastfeeding in Australia by State and socio-economic status: Evidence from the 1995 National Health Survey,' *Journal of Paediatric Child Health* 36: 164–168.

Essex, C., Smale, P., & Geddes, D. (1995) 'Breastfeeding rates in New Zealand in the first 6 months and the reasons for stopping,' *NZ Med J*: 355–357.

Food Standards Agency. Committee on Toxicology of Chemicals in Food, Consumer Products and the Environment (COT) Working Group on Phytoestrogens. [www.food.gov.uk]

Franke, A. A., Yu, M. C., Maskarinec, G., Fanti, P., Zheng, W., & Custer, L. J. (1999) 'Phytoestrogens in human biomatrices including breast milk,' *Biochem Soc Trans* 27: 308–318.

Fritz, W. A., Coward, L., Wang, J., & Lamartiniere, C. A. (1998) 'Dietary genistein: perinatal mammary cancer prevention, bioavailability and toxicity testing in the rat,' *Carcinogenesis* 19: 2151–2158.

Gaitan, E. (1990) 'Goitrogens in food and water,' *Annu Rev Nutr* 10: 21–39.

Guzman, R. C., Yang, J., Rajkumar, L., Thordarson, G., Chen, X., & Nandi, S. (1999) 'Hormonal prevention of breast cancer: mimicking the protective effect of pregnancy,' *Proc Natl Acad Sci* USA 96: 2520–2525.

Kurzer, M. S., & Xu, X. (1997) 'Dietary phytoestrogens,' *Annu Rev Nutr* 17: 353–381.

Lamartiniere, C. A., Moore, J., Holland, M., & Barnes, S. (1995) 'Neonatal genistein chemoprevents mammary cancer,' *Proc Soc Exp Biol Med* 208: 120–123.

Lasekan, J. B., Ostrom, K. M., Jacobs, J. R., Blatter, M. M., Ndife, L. I., Gooch, W. M., 3rd, & Cho, S. (1999) 'Growth of newborn, term infants fed soy formulas for 1 year,' *Clin Pediatr (Phila)* 38: 563–571.

Lund, T. D., Rhees, R. W., Setchell, K. D. R., & Lephart, E. D. (2001) 'Altered sexually dimorphic nucleus of the preoptic area (SDN-POA) volumes in adult Long-Evans rats by dietary soy phytoestrogens,' *Brain Research* 914: 92–99.

Mäkelä, S. (1994) 'Dietary soybean may be antiestrogeic in male mice,' *J Nutr* 125: 437–445.

Mäkelä, S., Santti, R., Salo, L., & McLachlan, J. A. (1995) 'Phytoestrogens are partial estrogen agonists in the adult male mouse,' *Environ Health Perspect* 103 Suppl 7: 123–127.

Miller, H. W., & Wen, C. H. (1936) 'Experimental nutrition studies of soymilk in human nutrition,' *Chinese Medical Journal* 50: 450–459.

Nagata, C., Takatsuka, N., Kurisu, Y., & Shimizu, H. (1998) 'Decreased serum total cholesterol concentration is associated with high intake of soy products in Japanese men and women,' *J Nutr* 128: 209–213.

Ostrom, K. M., Cordle, C. T., Schaller, J. P., Winship, T. R., Thomas, D. J., Jacobs, J. R., Blatter, M. M., Cho, S., Gooch III, W. M., Granoff, D. M., Faden, H., & Pickering, L. K. (2002) 'Immune status of infants fed soy-based formulas with or without added nucleotides for 1 year: Part 1: Vaccine responses, and morbidity.' *J. Pediatr Gastroenterol Nutr* 34: 137–144.

Phillips, H. (2002) 'Estimate of the number of Australian infants fed soy infant formula since its introduction onto the Australian market (personal communication).' Wyeth Australia.

Purba, M., Lukito, W., Wahlqvist, M. L., Kouris-Blazos, A., Hadisaputro, S., Lestiani, L., Wattanapenpaiboon, N., & Kamso, S. (1999) 'Food intake and eating patterns of Indonesian elderly before the 1998 economic crisis,' *Asia Pacific J Clin Nutr* 8: 200–206.

Quak, S. H., & Tan, S. P. (1998) 'Use of soy-protein formulas and soyfood for feeding infants and children in Asia,' *Am J Clin Nutr* 68: 1444S-1446S.

Setchell, K. D. R. (1998) 'Phytoestrogens: the biochemistry, physiology, and implications for human health of soy isoflavones,' *Am J Clin Nutr* 68: 1333S-1346S.

Setchell, K. D. R. (2001) 'Soy isoflavones – benefits and risks from nature's selective estrogen receptor modulators,' *J Am Coll Nutr* 20: 354S–362S.

Setchell, K. D. R., & Radd, S. (2002) 'Soy and other legumes: "Bean" around a long time but are they the "superfoods" of the millennium and what are the safety issues for their constituent phytoestrogens,' *Asia Pacific J Clin Nutr* 9: S13–S22.

Setchell, K. D. R., Welsh, M. B., & Lim, C. K. (1987) 'HPLC analysis of phytoestrogens in soy protein preparations with ultraviolet, electrochemical, and thermospray mass spectrometric detection,' *J Chromatography* 385: 267–274.

Setchell, K. D. R., Zimmer-Nechemias, L., Cai, J., & Heubi, J. E. (1997) 'Exposure of infants to phyto-oestrogens from soy-based infant formula,' *Lancet* 350: 23–27.

Setchell, K. D. R., Zimmer-Nechemias, L., Cai, J., & Heubi, J. E. (1998) 'Isoflavone content of infant formulas and the metabolic fate of these phytoestrogens in early life,' *Am J Clin Nutr* 68: 1453S-1461S.

Shepard, T., Pyne, G., Kirschvink, J., & McLean, M. (1960) 'Soybean goiter,' *NEJM* 22: 1099–1103.

Shu, X. O., Jin, F., Dai, Q., Wen, W., Potter, J. D., Kushi, L. H., Ruan, Z., Gao, Y. T., & Zheng, W. (2001) 'Soyfood intake during adolescence and subsequent risk of breast cancer among Chinese women,' *Cancer Epidemiol Biomarkers Prev* 10: 483–488.

Slavin, J. L. (1996) 'Phytoestrogens in breast milk—another advantage of breast-feeding?' *Clin Chem* 42: 841–842.

Strom, B. L., Schinnar, R., Ziegler, E. E., Barnhart, K. T., Sammel, M. D., Macones, G. A., Stallings, V. A., Drulis, J. M., Nelson, S. E., & Hanson, S. A. (2001) 'Exposure to soy-based formula in infancy and endocrinological and reproductive outcomes in young adulthood,' *JAMA* 286: 807–814.

Thigpen, J. E., Setchell, K. D. R., Ahlmark, K. B., Locklear, J., Spahr, T., Caviness, G. F., Goelz, M. F., Haseman, J. K., Newbold, R. R., & Forsythe, D. B. (1999) 'Phytoestrogen content of purified, open- and closed-formula laboratory animal diets,' *Lab Anim Sci* 49: 530–536.

Weber, K. S., Jacobson, N. A., Setchell, K. D. R., & Lephart, E. D. (1999) 'Brain aromatase and 5α-reductase, regulatory behaviors and testosterone levels in adult rats on phytoestrogen diets,' *Proc Soc Exp Biol Med* 221: 131–135.

Chapter 11

Adlercreutz, H., Mousavi, Y., Clark, J., Hockerstedt, K., Hämäläinen, E., Wähälä, K., Mäkelä, T., & Hase, T. (1992) 'Dietary phytoestrogens and cancer: in vitro and in vivo studies,' *J Steroid Biochem Mol Biol* 41: 331–337.

Adlercreutz, H., Yamada, T., Wähälä, K., & Watanabe, S. (1999) 'Maternal and neonatal phytoestrogens in Japanese women during birth,' *Am J Obstet Gynecol* 180: 737–743.

American Academy of Pediatrics Committee on Nutrition (1998) 'Soy protein-based formulas: recommendations for use in infant feeding,' *Pediatrics* 101: 148–153.

Australia New Zealand Food Authority (1999) 'Phytoestrogens—an assessment of the potential risks to infants associated with exposure to soy-based infant formula.'

Barnard, N. D., Scialli, A. R., Hurlock, D., & Bertron, P. (2000) 'Diet and sex-hormone binding globulin, dysmenorrhea, and premenstrual symptoms,' *Obstet Gynecol* 95: 245–250.

Bennetts, H. W., Underwood, E. J., & Shier, F. L. (1946) 'A specific breeding problem of sheep on subterranean clover pastures in Western Australia,' *Aust. J . Agric. Res.* 22: 131–138.

Biro, F. M., Lucky, A. W., Huster, G. A., & Morrison, J. A. (1995) 'Pubertal staging in boys,' *J Pediatr* 127: 100–102.

Chen, Z., Zheng, W., Custer, L. J., Dai, Q., Shu, X. O., Jin, F., & Franke, A. A. (1999) 'Usual dietary consumption of soy foods and its correlation with the excretion rate of isoflavonoids in overnight urine samples among Chinese women in Shanghai,' *Nutr Cancer* 33: 82–87.

Constantinou, A. I., Xu, H., Morgan Lucas, L., & Lantvit, D. (2001) 'Soy enhances tamoxifen's cancer chemopreventive effects in female rats. 4th International Symposium on the Role of Soy in Preventing and Treating Chronic Disease,' San Diego, USA.

Crouse, J. R., 3rd, Morgan, T., Terry, J. G., Ellis, J., Vitolins, M., & Burke, G. L. (1999) 'A randomized trial comparing the effect of casein with that of soy protein containing varying amounts of isoflavones on plasma concentrations of lipids and lipoproteins,' *Arch Intern Med* 159: 2070–2076.

Cruz, M. L., Wong, W. W., Mimouni, F., Hachey, D. L., Setchell, K. D., Klein, P. D., & Tsang, R. C. (1994) 'Effects of infant nutrition on cholesterol synthesis rates,' *Pediatr Res* 35: 135–140.

Cummings, S. R., Eckert, S., Krueger, K. A., Grady, D., Powles, T. J., Cauley, J. A., Norton, L., Nickelsen, T., Bjarnason, N. H., Morrow, M., Lippman, M. E., Black, D., Glusman, J. E., Costa, A., & Jordan, V. C. (1999) 'The effect of raloxifene on risk of breast cancer in postmenopausal women: results from the MORE randomized trial,' *Multiple Outcomes of Raloxifene Evaluation. JAMA* 281: 2189–2197.

Cunnane, S. C., Ganguli, S., Menard, C., Liede, A. C., Hamadeh, M. J., Chen, Z. Y., Wolever, T. M., & Jenkins, D. J. (1993) 'High alpha-linolenic acid flaxseed (Linum usitatissimum): some nutritional properties in humans,' *Br J Nutr* 69: 443–453.

Dalais, F. S., Meliala, A., & Wahlqvist, M. L. (1999) 'Maternal and cord blood phytoestrogen levels in Indonesian women. Third International

Symposium on the Role of Soy in Preventing and Treating Chronic Disease,' Washington, DC USA.

de Ridder, C. M., Thijssen, J. H., Van't Veer, P., van Duuren, R., Bruning, P. F., Zonderland, M. L., & Erich, W. B. (1991) 'Dietary habits, sexual maturation, and plasma hormones in pubertal girls: a longitudinal study,' *Am J Clin Nutr* 54: 805–813.

Divi, R. L., Chang, H. C., & Doerge, D. R. (1997) 'Anti-thyroid isoflavones from soybean: isolation, characterization, and mechanisms of action,' *Biochem Pharmacol* 54: 1087–1096.

Divi, R. L., & Doerge, D. R. (1996) 'Inhibition of thyroid peroxidase by dietary flavonoids,' *Chem Res Toxicol* 9: 16–23.

Eden, J. A., Mackey, R., & Ekangaki, A. (1999) 'The effects of soy protein on postmenopausal women and men with elevated plasma lipids. Third International Symposium on the Role of Soy in Preventing and Treating Chronic Disease,' Washington, DC USA.

Essex, C. (1996) 'Phytoestrogens and soy based infant formula,' *BMJ* 313: 507–508.

Franke, A. A., Yu, M. C., Maskarinec, G., Fanti, P., Zheng, W., & Custer, L. J. (1999) 'Phytoestrogens in human biomatrices including breast milk,' *Biochem Soc Trans* 27: 308–318.

Frisch, R. E. (1991) 'Body weight, body fat, and ovulation,' *Trends Endocrinol Metab* 2: 191–197.

Fritz, W. A., Coward, L., Wang, J., & Lamartiniere, C. A. (1998) 'Dietary genistein: perinatal mammary cancer prevention, bioavailability and toxicity testing in the rat,' *Carcinogenesis* 19: 2151–2158.

Garreau, B., Vallette, G., Adlercreutz, H., Wähälä, K., Mäkelä, T., Benassayag, C., & Nunez, E. A. (1991) 'Phytoestrogens: new ligands for rat and human alpha-fetoprotein [published erratum appears in Biochim Biophys Acta 1991 Dec 3;1133(1):113],' *Biochim Biophys Acta* 1094: 339–345.

Gotoh, T., Yamada, K., Yin, H., Ito, A., Kataoka, T., & Dohi, K. (1998) 'Chemoprevention of N-nitroso-N-methylurea-induced rat mammary carcinogenesis by soy foods or biochanin A,' *Jpn J Cancer Res* 89: 137–142.

Halpern, S. R., Sellars, W. A., Johnson, R. B., Anderson, D. W., Saperstein, S., & Reisch, J. S. (1973) 'Development of childhood allergy in infants fed breast, soy, or cow milk,' *J Allergy Clin Immunol* 51: 139–151.

Herman-Giddens, M. E., Slora, E. J., Wasserman, R. C., Bourdony, C. J., Bhapkar, M. V., Koch, G. G., & Hasemeier, C. M. (1997) 'Secondary sexual characteristics and menses in young girls seen in office practice: a study from the Pediatric Research in Office Settings network,' *Pediatrics* 99: 505–512.

Hodgson, J. M., Puddey, I. B., Beilin, L. J., Mori, T. A., & Croft, K. D. (1998) 'Supplementation with isoflavonoid phytoestrogens does not alter serum lipid concentrations: a randomized controlled trial in humans,' *J Nutr* 128: 728–732.

Hoel, D. G., Wakabayashi, T., & Pike, M. C. (1983) 'Secular trends in the distributions of the breast cancer risk factors— menarche, first birth, menopause, and weight—in Hiroshima and Nagasaki, Japan,' *Am J Epidemiol* 118: 78–89.

Jordan, V. C., & Morrow, M. (1999) 'Tamoxifen, raloxifene, and the prevention of breast cancer,' *Endocr Rev* 20: 253–278.

Key, T. J., Chen, J., Wang, D. Y., Pike, M. C., & Boreham, J. (1990) 'Sex hormones in women in rural China and in Britain,' *Br J Cancer* 62: 631–636.

Klein, K. O. (1998) 'Isoflavones, soy-based infant formulas, and relevance to endocrine function,' *Nutr Rev* 56: 193–204.

Lappe, M. A., Bailey, E. B., Childress, C., & Setchell, K. D. R. (1999) 'Alterations in clinically important phytoestrogens in genetically modified, herbicide-tolerant soybeans,' *J Medicinal Food* 1: 241–245.

Lu, L. J., Anderson, K. E., Grady, J. J., & Nagamani, M. (1996) 'Effects of soya consumption for one month on steroid hormones in premenopausal women: implications for breast cancer risk reduction,' *Cancer Epidemiol Biomarkers Prev* 5: 63–70.

Mackey, R., Ekangaki, A., & Eden, J. A. (2000) 'The effects of soy protein in women and men with elevated plasma lipids,' *BioFactors* 12: 251–257.

Martini, M. C., Dancisak, B. B., Haggans, C. J., Thomas, W., & Slavin, J. L. (1999) 'Effects of soy intake on sex hormone metabolism in premenopausal women,' *Nutr Cancer* 34: 133–139.

Merz-Demlow, B. E., Duncan, A. M., Wangen, K. E., Xu, X., Carr, T. P., Phipps, W. R., & Kurzer, M. S. (2000) 'Soy isoflavones improve plasma lipids in normocholesterolemic, premenopausal women,' *Am J Clin Nutr* 71: 1462–1469.

Messina, M. J., & Loprinzi, C. L. (2001) 'Soy for breast cancer survivors: A critical review of the literature,' *J Nutr* 131: 3095S–3108S.

Messina, M. J., Persky, V., Setchell, K. D. R., & Barnes, S. (1994) 'Soy intake and cancer risk: a review of the in vitro and in vivo data,' *Nutr Cancer* 21: 113–131.

Nestel, P. J., Pomeroy, S., Kay, S., Komesaroff, P., Behrsing, J., Cameron, J. D., & West, L. (1999) 'Isoflavones from red clover improve systemic arterial compliance but not plasma lipids in menopausal women,' *J Clin Endocrinol Metab* 84: 895–898.

Nestel, P. J., Yamashita, T., Sasahara, T., Pomeroy, S., Dart, A., Komesaroff, P., Owen, A., & Abbey, M. (1997) 'Soy isoflavones improve systemic arterial compliance but not plasma lipids in menopausal and perimenopausal women,' *Arterioscler Thromb Vasc Biol* 17: 3392–3398.

North, K., & Golding, J. (2000) 'A maternal vegetarian diet in pregnancy is associated with hypospadias,' *BJU Int* 85: 107–113.

Padgette, S. R., Taylor, N. B., Nida, D. L., Bailey, M. R., MacDonald, J., Holden, L. R., & Fuchs, R. L. (1996) 'The composition of glyphosate-tolerant soybean seeds is equivalent to that of conventional soybeans,' *J Nutr* 126: 702–716.

Paulozzi, L. J. (1999) 'International trends in rates of hypospadias and cryptorchidism,' *Environ Health Perspect* 107: 297–302.

Sahlberg, B. L., & Axelson, M. (1986) 'Identification and quantitation of free and conjugated steroids in milk from lactating women,' *J Steroid Biochem* 25: 379–391.

Sandermann, H., & Wellman, E. (1988) 'Bundesministerium fur Forschung und Technologie, (Hrsg),' *Biologische Sicherheit* 1: 285–292.

Setchell, K. D. R., Brown, N. M., Desai, P., Zimmer-Nechemias, L., Wolfe, B. E., Brashear, W. T., Kirschner, A. S., Cassidy, A., & Heubi, J. E. (2001) 'Bioavailability of pure isoflavones in healthy humans and analysis of commercial soy isoflavone supplements,' *J Nutr* 131: 1362S-1375S.

Setchell, K. D. R., Gosselin, S. J., Welsh, M. B., Johnston, J. O., Balistreri, W. F., Kramer, L. W., Dresser, B. L., & Tarr, M. J. (1987) 'Dietary estrogens—a probable cause of infertility and liver disease in captive cheetahs,' *Gastroenterology* 93: 225–233.

Setchell, K. D. R., Zimmer-Nechemias, L., Cai, J., & Heubi, J. E. (1998) 'Isoflavone content of infant formulas and the metabolic fate of these phytoestrogens in early life,' *Am J Clin Nutr* 68: 1453S-1461S.

Shultz, T., Bonorden, W., & Seaman, W. (1991) 'Effect of short-term flaxseed consumption on lignan and sex hormone metabolism in men,' *Nutr Res* 11: 1089–1100.

Stoll, B. A. (1998) 'Western diet, early puberty, and breast cancer risk,' *Breast Cancer Res Treat* 49: 187–193.

Strom, B. L., Schinnar, R., Ziegler, E. E., Barnhart, K. T., Sammel, M. D., Macones, G. A., Stallings, V. A., Drulis, J. M., Nelson, S. E., & Hanson, S. A. (2001) 'Exposure to soy-based formula in infancy and endocrinological and reproductive outcomes in young adulthood,' *JAMA* 286: 807–814.

Tansey, G., Hughes, C. L., Jr., Cline, J. M., Krummer, A., Walmer, D. K., & Schmoltzer, S. (1998) 'Effects of dietary soybean estrogens on the reproductive tract in female rats,' *Proc Soc Exp Biol Med* 217: 340–344.

Weber, K. S., Jacobson, N. A., Setchell, K. D. R., & Lephart, E. D. (1999) 'Brain aromatase and 5alpha-reductase, regulatory behaviors and testosterone levels in adult rats on phytoestrogen diets,' *Proc Soc Exp Biol Med* 221: 131–135.

Chapter 12

Adlercreutz, H., Markkanen, H., & Watanabe, S. (1993) 'Plasma concentrations of phyto-oestrogens in Japanese men,' *Lancet* 342: 1209–1210.

Arai, Y., Watanabe, S., Kimira, M., Shimoi, K., Mochizuki, R., & Kinae, N. (2000) 'Dietary intakes of flavonols, flavones and isoflavones by Japanese women and the inverse correlation between quercetin intake and plasma LDL cholesterol concentration,' *J Nutr* 130: 2243–2250.

Bloedon, L. T., Jeffcoat, A. R., Lapaczynski, W., Schell, M. J., Black, T. M., Dix, K. J., Thomas, B. F., Albright, C., Busby, M. G., Crowell, J. A., & Zeisel, S. (2002) 'Safety and pharmacokinetics of purified soy isoflavones: single-dose administration to postmenopausal women,' *Am J Clin Nutr* 76: 1126–1137.

Chen, Z., Zheng, W., Custer, L. J., Dai, Q., Shu, X. O., Jin, F., & Franke, A. A. (1999) 'Usual dietary consumption of soy foods and its correlation with the excretion rate of isoflavonoids in overnight urine samples among Chinese women in Shanghai,' *Nutr Cancer* 33: 82–87.

Coward, L., Smith, M., Kirk, M., & Barnes, S. (1998) 'Chemical modification of isoflavones in soyfoods during cooking and processing,' *Am J Clin Nutr* 68: 1486S-1491S.

Eldridge, A., & Kwolek, W. (1983) 'Soybean isoflavones: effects of environment and variety on composition,' *J Agri Food Chem* 31: 394–396.

Farnsworth, N., Bingel, A., Cordell, G., Crane, F., & Fong, H. (1975) 'Potential value of plants as sources of new antifertility agents II,' *J Pharm Sci* 64: 717–754.

Gibson, G. R., & Roberfroid, M. B. (1995) 'Dietary modulation of the human colonic microbiota: introducing the concept of prebiotics,' *J Nutr* 125: 1401–1412.

Golbitz, P. (1995) 'Traditional soyfoods: processing and products,' *J Nutr* 125: 570S-572S.

Hamilton, R. M., & Carroll, K. K. (1976) 'Plasma cholesterol levels in rabbits fed low fat, low cholesterol diets: effects of dietary proteins, carbohydrates and fibre from different sources,' *Atherosclerosis* 24: 47–62.

Horn-Ross, P. L., Barnes, S., Lee, M., Coward, L., Mandel, J. E., Koo, J., John, E.M., & Smith, M. (2000) 'Assessing phytoestrogen exposure in epidemiologic studies: development of a database (United States),' *Cancer Causes Control* 11: 289–298.

Insull, W., Oiso, T., & Tsuchiya, K. (1968) 'Diet and nutritional status of Japanese,' *Am J Clin Nutr* 21: 753–777.

Kwon, T. W., Song, Y. S., Kim, J. S., Moon, G. S., Kim, J. I., & Hong, J. H. (1998) 'Current research on the bioactive functions of soyfoods in Korea,' *Korea Soybean Digest* 15: 1–12.

Liggins, J., Bluck, L. J. C., Runswick, S., Atkinson, C., Coward, W. A., & Bingham, S. A. (2000) 'Daidzein and genistein contents of vegetables,' *Br J Nutr* 84: 717–725.

Owen, R. W., Mier, W., Giacosa, A., Hull, W. E., Spiegelhalder, B., & Bartsch, H. (2000) 'Phenolic compounds and squalene in olive oils: the concentration and antioxidant potential of total phenols, simple phenols, secoiridoids, lignans and squalene,' *Food Chem Toxicol* 38: 647–659.

Price, K. R., & Fenwick, G. R. (1985) 'Naturally occurring oestrogens in foods—A review,' *Food Addit Contam* 2: 73–106.

Purba, M., Lukito, W., Wahlqvist, M. L., Kouris-Blazos, A., Hadisaputro, S., Lestiani, L., Wattanapenpaiboon, N., & Kamso, S. (1999) 'Food intake and eating patterns of Indonesian elderly before the 1998 economic crisis,' *Asia Pacific J Clin Nutr* 8: 200–206.

Setchell, K. D. R., Brown, N. M., Desai, P., Zimmer-Nechemias, L., Wolfe, B. E., Brashear, W. T., Kirschner, A. S., Cassidy, A., & Heubi, J. E. (2001) 'Bioavailability of pure isoflavones in healthy humans and analysis of commercial soy isoflavone supplements,' *J Nutr* 131: 1362S-1375S.

Setchell, K. D. R., & Cassidy, A. (1999) 'Dietary isoflavones: biological effects and relevance to human health,' *J Nutr* 129: 758S-767S.

Setchell, K. D. R., & Cole, S. J. (2003) 'Variations in isoflavone levels in soy foods and soy protein isolates and issues of isoflavone fortification and labeling,' *J Agric Food Chem* (in press).

Simmone, A. H., Smith, M., Weaver, D. B., Vail, T., Barnes, S., & Wei, C. I. (2000) 'Retention and changes of soy isoflavones and carotenoids in immature soybean seeds (Edamame) during processing,' *J Agric Food Chem* 48: 6061–6069.

Singletary, K., Faller, J., Yuan Li, J., & Mahungu, S. (2000) 'Effect of extrusion on isoflavone content and antiproliferative bioactivity of soy/corn mixtures,' *J Agric Food Chem* 48: 3566–3571.

Wang, H. J., & Murphy, P. A. (1994) 'Isoflavone content in commercial soybean foods,' *J Agric Food Chem* 42: 1666–1673.

Weststrate, J. A., & Meijer, G. W. (1998) 'Plant sterol-enriched margarines and reduction of plasma total- and LDL-cholesterol concentrations in normocholesterolaemic and mildly hypercholesterolaemic subjects,' *Eur J Clin Nutr* 52: 334–343.

World Cancer Research Fund in Association with American Institute for Cancer Research. (1997) Food, Nutrition and the Prevention of Cancer: A Global Perspective.

Chapter 14

Adlercreutz, H. (1990) 'Western diet and Western diseases: some hormonal and biochemical mechanisms and associations,' *Scand J Clin Lab Invest Suppl* 201: 3–23.

Coward, L., Smith, M., Kirk, M., & Barnes, S. (1998) 'Chemical modification of isoflavones in soyfoods during cooking and processing,' *Am J Clin Nutr* 68: 1486S-1491S.

Cunnane, S. C., Hamadeh, M. J., Liede, A. C., Thompson, L. U., Wolever, T. M., & Jenkins, D. J. (1995) Nutritional attributes of traditional flaxseed in healthy young adults,' *Am J Clin Nutr* 61: 62–68.

Fraser, G. E. (2000) 'Nut consumption, lipids, and risk of a coronary event,' *Asia Pacific J Clin Nutr* 9 (suppl): S28-S32.

Milligan, S. R., Kalita, J. C., Heyerick, A., Rong, H., De Cooman, L., & De Keukeleire, D. (1999) 'Identification of a potent phytoestrogen in hops (Humulus lupulus L.) and beer,' *J Clin Endocrinol Metab* 84: 2249–2252.

Setchell, K. D. R., & Radd, S. (2000) 'Soy and other legumes: "Bean" around a long time but are they the "superfood" of the millennium and what are the safety issues for their constitutent phytoestrogens,' *Asia Pacific J Clin Nutr* 9: S13-S22.

Venter, C. S., & van Eyssen, E. (2001) 'More legumes for better overall health,' *SA J Clin Nutr* 14: S32-S38.

Index